The Politics of
Educational Reform in Alberta

The Politics of Educational Reform in Alberta presents a case study of educational restructuring in Alberta during the 'Klein revolution' – the period of dramatic political and economic change introduced by Premier Ralph Klein's Conservative government of the 1990s. The government's 1994 business plan introduced funding cuts in education, the amalgamation of school boards, the centralization of funding, charter school legislation, expanded provincial testing, and mandatory school councils. The buzzwords for education reform were efficiency, accountability, and choice.

Alison Taylor rigorously examines Klein's 'three-year plan' for school reform to unveil the ways in which the Alberta government has allied itself with corporate interests. She also examines what happens to the voices of teachers, parents, and labour groups who have a different idea what school should be.

The Politics of Educational Reform in Alberta is a timely and much-needed book. This multifaceted view of corporate involvement in schooling will be invaluable to policy makers, educators, academics, journalists, and concerned parents.

Alison Taylor is Assistant Professor in the Department of Educational Policy Studies at the University of Alberta.

The Politics of Educational Reform in Alberta

ALISON TAYLOR

UNIVERSITY OF TORONTO PRESS
Toronto Buffalo London

© University of Toronto Press Incorporated 2001
Toronto Buffalo London
Printed in Canada

ISBN 0-8020-4813-7 (cloth)
ISBN 0-8020-8352-8 (paper)

Printed on acid-free paper

Canadian Cataloguing in Publication Data

Taylor, Alison, 1959–
    The politics of educational reform in Alberta

    Includes bibliographical references and index.
    ISBN 0-8020-4813-7 (bound)   ISBN 0-8020-8352-8 (pbk.)

    1. Educational change – Alberta.   2. Education and state – Alberta.
    3. Education – Alberta – Aims and objectives.   4. Industry and
    education – Alberta.   I. Title.

    LC1085.4.C3T39 2000   379.7123   C00-932121-7

This book has been published with the help of a grant from the Humanities
and Social Sciences Federation of Canada, using funds provided by the Social
Sciences and Humanities Research Council of Canada.

The University of Toronto Press acknowledges the financial assistance to its
publishing program of the Canada Council for the Arts and the Ontario Arts
Council.

University of Toronto Press acknowledges the financial support for its
publishing activities of the Government of Canada through the Book Publishing Industry Development Program (BPIDP).

To my parents, Agnes and David

Contents

List of Tables viii

Preface ix

Abbreviations xiii

1 Introduction 3

2 The Crisis in Public Education 15

3 The Hegemonic Work of the Conference Board 34

4 The Hegemonic Work of Governments 52

5 Restructuring Education: 1993–1995 73

6 The Corporate Alliance 97

7 Partnerships as Sites of Struggle 132

8 The Fragmentation of Labour 167

9 The Diversity of 'Producers' 204

10 Students, Parents, and Community 242

11 Alberta and Beyond 285

Appendix A 313

Appendix B 315

Notes 321

References 337

Index 349

Tables

5.1 Selected Results of Angus Reid Education Polls, 1994 to 1999   82

6.1 Business Participants   99

8.1 Labour Participants   169

9.1 Public Education Participants   206

10.1 Students, Parents, and Community Participants   244

B:1 Total Labour Force by Industry Division   315

B:2 Calgary's Major Private Sector Employers   316

B:3 Calgary's Major Public Sector Employers   317

B:4 Occupation by Sex in Calgary, Alberta, and Canada   318

B:5 Employment Income by Sex and Work Activity   319

Preface

This book presents a case study of educational restructuring in Alberta, Canada, focusing on the period between 1993 and 1995. My interest in this topic arose from a growing awareness of the extent of involvement by business people in Canada's educational policy discussions at both national and provincial levels. In the spring of 1991 I heard about a conference on business-education conferences organized by the Conference Board of Canada. I attended this event, as well as others held in 1992 and 1993, and became interested in further exploring the discourses around educational reform that were promoted at such events. Moving to Alberta from Ontario in the fall of 1993 and being swept along in the New Right politics of the newly elected Progressive Conservative government of Ralph Klein enabled me to see parallels between these national level discourses and discussions around educational reform in Alberta. The three-year business plan for education released in 1994 reflected interests in tightening links between education and work, increasing efficiencies within the system while cutting costs, and increasing parental choice. It became clear that certain groups had influenced the policy process while others had resisted the vision for education that resulted. This study thus came to concentrate on hegemonic work in education as well as on the initial responses of other stakeholders to this work. The Alberta government uses the term *stakeholder* to refer to groups perceived to have a vested interest in education. The term also reflects the corporate language that has become pervasive in the province. While the focus here is the 1993 to 1995 period, updates based on what has happened in the province since the release of the three-year plan indicate that struggles continue.

Data for this book include interviews with forty participants, identified through news coverage, government and conference documents, and referrals from others. Interviews took place between June 1993 and September 1995, the majority conducted in the period immediately following the restructuring of Alberta Education in 1994. Participants include representatives from education groups identified as 'stakeholders' by the government: for example, school trustees, administrators, a teachers' association, and a mainstream parents' organization. I also interviewed a number of participants who were not a recognized part of the government's policy community: for example, representatives from organized labour, a nongovernmental organization, and an advocate for students studying English as a second language. In terms of organizational affiliation, there are eight business people, five from labour, fifteen from education, and twelve comprising students, parents, and other community members. There are twenty-four women, sixteen men, one person of colour, and one Native Canadian.

I was financially assisted during the research process by Social Sciences and Humanities Research Council doctoral and postdoctoral fellowships. Since this manuscript was adapted from a dissertation, I wish to thank supervisory committee members David Livingstone and Kari Dehli at the Ontario Institute for Studies in Education/University of Toronto for their supportive and constructive comments throughout that process. Thanks to David also for encouraging me to publish this work. At the time of writing the dissertation, I asked 'critical readers' with knowledge of the issues discussed in each of Chapters 6 to 10 to provide feedback, and I wish to acknowledge the contributions of these readers. I also appreciate the comments provided by anonymous reviewers. Thank you to David Flower for his assistance in the process of updating some of my information, and to Larry Booi for providing useful feedback on the manuscript. Georgie Kwan helped by typing some of my tables. Betty Mardiros from the Edmonton Raging Grannies kindly provided lyrics from some of their songs. My friend Ellen Murray, who teaches high school in Ontario kept me informed of changes there. Finally, the love and support of my partner, Dean, was as important in this endeavour as it has been in others. And thanks to Lilibeth for her help, and to my children, Robyn and Kieran, for their hugs and kisses.

Abbreviations

ACC	Alberta Chamber of Commerce
ACR	Alberta Chamber of Resources
AFL	Alberta Federation of Labour
AHS	Academic High School (pseudonym)
AHSCA	Alberta Home and School Councils' Association
AQE	Albertans for Quality Education
ASBA	Alberta School Boards Association
ASBOA	Association of School Business Officials of Alberta
ATA	Alberta Teachers' Association
AUPE	Alberta Union of Public Employees
BCNI	Business Council on National Issues
BHEF	Business–Higher Education Forum (U.S.)
BIAG	Business Involvement Advisory Group
CALM	Career and Life Management
CB	Conference Board of Canada
CBE	Calgary Board of Education
CCC	Calgary Chamber of Commerce
CCCS	Centre for Contemporary Cultural Studies
CCE	Corporate Council on Education (Conference Board)
CCHSA	Calgary Council of Home and Schools Association
CCPA	Canadian Centre for Policy Alternatives
CCSD	Calgary Catholic School District
CDLC	Calgary District Labour Council
CEQ	Centrale de l'Enseignement de Quebec
CFEE	Canadian Foundation for Economic Education

CFL	Canadian Forum on Learning
CH	*Calgary Herald*
CHEF	Corporate–Higher Education Forum (Canada)
CHRDC	Calgary Human Resources Development Centre
CLFDB	Canadian Labour Force Development Board
CMA	Canadian Manufacturers' Association
CMEC	Council of Ministers of Education, Canada
CNG	Careers: The Next Generation
CTF	Canadian Teachers' Federation
CTS	Career and Technology Studies
CUPE	Canadian Union of Public Employees
CWF	Canada West Foundation
ECC	Economic Council of Canada
ESL	English as a second language
ESP	employability skills profile
IB	International Baccalaureate program
IMF	International Monetary Fund
ITAC	Information Technology Association of Canada
JA	Junior Achievement
NBEC	National Business and Education Centre (Conference Board)
NCE	National Council on Education
NHS	Native High School (pseudonym)
OCT	Ontario College of Teachers
OECD	Organization for Economic Cooperation and Development
OFL	Ontario Federation of Labour
OQE	Organization for Quality Education
OSSTF	Ontario Secondary School Teachers' Federation
PAC	Parent Advisory Council
PACT	Parents Advocating for Children and Teachers
PEAC	Public Education Action Centre (ATA)
PSBAA	Public School Boards Association of Alberta
QEC	Quality Education Coalition
RAP	registered apprenticeship program
SAER	Society for Advancing Educational Research
SAIP	Student Achievement Indicators Program

SOS	Save Our Schools
SPE	Save Public Education
SPEAK	Save Public Education – Act for Kids
T2T	Toward 2000 Together
TIMSS	Third International Mathematics and Science Study
TQM	total quality management
TVEI	Technical and Vocational Education Initiative (Britain)
VAP	value assessment process

The Politics of
Educational Reform in Alberta

CHAPTER ONE

Introduction

Shortly after the Progressive Conservative government in Alberta was re-elected with a new leader in 1993, Premier Ralph Klein introduced a budget that introduced significant cutbacks and restructuring of the public sector. Journalist Mark Lisac (1995) refers to this period as the 'Klein revolution,' since changes involved aggressive deficit and debt reduction, downsizing of the role of government in the economy, and a shift in the way government approached the management of remaining functions. The 'Alberta model,' as it has been called, has gained national and international attention as evidenced by articles in the *Globe and Mail* (Feschuk and Cernetig, 21 February 1995) and the *Wall Street Journal* (Fund, 23 February 1995), although critics note that the government appeared to be following in the footsteps of previous governments in New Zealand, Britain, and the United States.

This book focuses on educational restructuring during the early part of Klein's term as premier. Reforms announced in the 1994 three-year business plan for education included funding cutbacks, centralized provincial control over the collection and allocation of funds, amalgamation of school boards, stronger school council legislation, site-based management, charter school legislation, expanded standardized testing, and increased focus on preparing students to meet the needs of business and industry. Restructuring was driven by the perceived need to improve the efficiency of the public sector while cutting costs, and the need to increase educational standards, improve outcomes, and ensure accountability. While some of these changes in roles and responsibilities reflect national trends (Dunning 1997), Alberta has been a leader in the country in the introduction of other reforms, such as charter schools. Alberta also stands out in terms of the number of significant changes introduced at the same time. Given that Alberta has been at the forefront of the reinvention of the public sector in Canada, it warrants attention.

Key Concepts

The thesis of this book is that the Klein government's three-year business plan represents an 'educational settlement.' Drawing on Gramsci's theory of hegemony, writers from the Centre for Contemporary Cultural Studies (CCCS 1981) use the term to refer to the outcomes of hegemonic work in and around schooling. Hegemony describes a 'contested and shifting set of ideas by means of which dominant groups strive to secure the consent of subordinate groups to their leadership' (Strinati 1995: 170). Hegemonic work thus involves the negotiated construction of a political and ideological consensus that incorporates both dominant and dominated groups. As a result, the securing of hegemony by a dominant group may involve concessions to the ideas and values of subordinate groups. However, because hegemony involves social and class struggles, it is neither fixed nor guaranteed.

The concept of hegemony helps to explain why subordinated groups consent to agendas that do not seem to reflect their objective interests. At the same time, it moves away from structural-Marxist interpretations that ignore the agency of individual subjects by emphasizing the subjective sense-making of individuals and the fragility of hegemonic settlement. Cultural-studies writers have moved beyond class domination to explore social divisions based on gender and race (cf., Hall 1996a). This broader view informs this work as well.

I have borrowed the term *educational settlement* to refer to the accomplishment of hegemony or consensual control within the sphere of education. Such settlements entail 'some more or less enduring set of solutions to capitals' educational needs, the putting together of a dominant alliance of forces, and a more widespread recruitment of popular support or inducement of popular indifference' (CCCS 1996a: 32). Because they reflect the balance of social forces at a particular time, settlements are said to be unstable and contradictory arrangements that pass easily into crisis.

CCCS authors (1981) trace the history of educational policy as a series of crises and settlements between 1944 and 1979 in Britain. Authors argued that, in the 1960s and 70s, declining faith in the existing social-democratic settlement permitted spokespersons from the New Right to propose an alternative vision of social reality. By questioning the benefits of previous educational reforms, the vision appealed to parents who were concerned about their children's futures and/or progressive methods of teaching. The panic about schools that developed was assisted by economic crisis, government and research reports, the activities of New Right propagandists, and various branches of the media that all claimed popular support.

This study's focus is the three-year business plan in Alberta particularly as a moment of educational settlement. It explores the balance of social forces and conditions that resulted in this settlement, by asking who the key players were, what alliances were formed, how problems and solutions in schooling were defined, and how the message of restructuring proponents was disseminated and consent won. A reading of policy documents suggests that business representatives were influential in hegemonic work at provincial and federal levels, which in turn influenced the restructuring of education in Alberta. The agenda of corporate spokespersons was similar to that identified by Livingstone (1983) in his discussion of class-based ideologies. This agenda called for making education a service industry for business, increasing control over the labour market, equating school discipline with labour discipline, emphasizing work-related skills, rationalizing education processes, and increasing the use of technology. Through the Conference Board of Canada and other groups, corporate spokespersons in the 1990s articulated an *organic ideology*, defined by Hall (1988: 166) as one which 'articulates into a configuration different subjects, different identities, different projects, different aspirations,' and 'constructs a "unity" out of difference.' As a result, unhappy parents joined with dissatisfied employers in calls for increased standards and accountability.

As noted, hegemony involves struggle. This study thus had to move beyond the ideological work of elites to examine how other individuals and groups positioned themselves in relation to the dominant discourses of the time. An analysis of the relationships among groups and their responses to restructuring discourses has indicated resistance as well as new prospects for counter-hegemonic work. The latter in fact represents the primary purpose of this work: to explore both the conditions under which hegemonic work was accomplished and settlement reached, and the conditions under which 'individual and collective subjects become mobilized as part of counter-hegemonic resistance' (Morrow and Torres 1995: 38). An analysis of 1993 to 1995 – that is, the period leading up to the three-year business plan to the period immediately following its release – provides fertile ground for this study.

This work might be described as a micro-political analysis of macro-level change, since it presents interviews with participants at the local level after reviewing policy documents at federal and provincial levels. This approach reflects the view that an analysis of educational change must address the social, political, and economic context that informs those changes. Chapters 2 to 5 articulate this context with a focus on the hegemonic work of *dissatisfied employers* and *unhappy parents* in the area of education. The work of these groups was facilitated at the state level by the discourse of *fiscal crisis of the state* and culminated in the three-year business plan. Chapters 6 to 10 are based on transcript data from interviews with the forty participants listed in Appendix A.

In most cases, participants were selected as *representatives* of particular groups. It is assumed, therefore, that ideas may have come from and thus reflect the material conditions in which each social group and class finds itself (Hall 1996b). At the same time, the analysis reflects a sensitivity to the idea that groups are usually not homogeneous and that identities are multi-faceted and complex.

It is noteworthy that most interview participants were located in Calgary. This focus is justified because, as Lisac (1995: 43) writes, 'This was the city where business organizations had been learning the practice of "downsizing" and the Thatcher-Reagan theory of political economy. Calgary was the place where people like Madsen Pirie, a theorist of Margaret Thatcher's privatization movement had been brought in for speaking engagements. People all over were reading a surge of economic and management theories from the like of Peter Drucker, Tom Peters, Kenichi Ohmae, Ted Gaebler and David Osborne, and others. But this was the one city in Alberta with the strongest white-collar milieu in which those ideas could thrive and strike off new ones. Calgary could support a new political movement because Calgary had the intellectual theories to justify it. The Klein revolution started in Calgary.'

Calgary has more head offices than Montreal and Vancouver combined. It is also the city where Ralph Klein had been a popular mayor for three terms in the 1980s, and where seventeen of twenty MLAs were Progressive Conservative in the 1990s. In terms of politics, Newman (1998) adds, 'The Klein Gang was a cadre of the most powerful and wealthy in the Calgary establishment. Almost without exception, they were men in high positions in business, and they had a great deal to gain in personal wealth from the success of fiscal reform' (440). Newman adds also that Reform leader Preston Manning's inner circle also consisted almost entirely of local business leaders in the city. Therefore, while the main focus here is not on ties between individual politicians and business people, these ties do form part of the terrain on which the politics of educational restructuring in Alberta arose.

Context of Educational Reform

The similarity of educational 'reforms'[2] across industrialized countries in recent decades has been noted by several writers (Whitty, Power, and Halpin 1998; Levin 1997; Dale and Ozga

1993). Although they are careful to address differences as well as similarities, Whitty, Power, and Halpin point to common themes based on their study of five countries. These include the devolution of financial and managerial control to more local levels, promotion of parental choice, increasing diversity of provision, and a change in the role of governments. Regarding the last trend, they suggest that neoliberal political alternatives – for example, the development of quasi-markets in education – dominate in the countries they examined. At the same time, states continue to regulate education through increased control over standards, accountability measures, and funding. The trend is therefore towards a strong state that steers at a distance, and an increasingly market-oriented civil society.

The three-year business plan introduced in Alberta is consistent with these trends for the most part. The tension between centralizing and decentralizing trends is evident in the removal of taxing authority from school boards while encouraging school-based management. Parental choice and participation were promoted by charter school legislation and stronger school council legislation. In addition to charter schools, the government also encouraged diversity of provision through steadily increasing funding to private schools and showcasing 'magnet' schools (e.g., those specializing in science and technology). The introduction of charter schools has further encouraged the proliferation of specialized alternative programs within the public system.

At the time of the reforms, the Alberta Teachers' Association (ATA) and other groups pointed to England and New Zealand as countries where similar reform programs had been introduced. In England, changes between 1980 and 1993 moved education in the direction of devolution to local bodies along with increased state control. The Assisted Places Scheme, introduced as part of the 1980 Education Act, provided public funding to allow children from low-income families to attend private schools. The 1986 Education Act required the governing bodies of schools to increase representation by parents and business people. Diversity of provision was increased by the introduction of City Technology Colleges, which were to be run by 'independent trusts with business sponsors and with a curriculum emphasis on science and technology' (Whitty, Power, and Halpin 1998: 18). The 1988 Education Reform Act accelerated restructuring by allowing schools to opt out of their Local Education Authority and run as grant-maintained schools. By the late 1990s, grant-maintained schools were educating about 10 per cent of the school-age population (19). Open enrolments also helped create a quasi-market for schools. The national curriculum introduced in the 1988 Education Reform Act specified programs of study and accountability measures, permitting greater state control over outcomes. Finally, the 1992 Education Act was said to have increased public accountability by introducing private inspection teams to evaluate schools.

In 1989 New Zealand's Labour government introduced reforms that shifted educational responsibility in several areas from the central government and regional boards to individual schools. In a sense, every school became a charter school, with a board of trustees composed of parents and business people. The conservative National Party increased the financial devolution to schools in 1990. It also announced the equivalent of England's Assisted Places Scheme, which amounts to a voucher program for students from low-income families. Also like England, it adopted an outcomes-based approach to national assessment.[3]

Similarities between Australia and Canada suggest that reforms there may also be relevant to discussion. As in Canada, education is the responsibility of the states and territory in Australia. Whitty, Power, and Halpin (1998) write that in Victoria nearly all schools had almost full control over budget and personnel. At the same time, funding cutbacks meant cuts and contracting out of programs and services, school closures, and an increase in teacher workloads. Mackay and Flower (1999) suggest that the restructuring process in Australia has involved an attack on teachers and their unions. As in other jurisdictions, the state also increased its control over curriculum and set standards for assessment.

The free trade of ideas from the United States also has resulted in policy-borrowing from Canada's neighbour to the

south. Popular reforms in the United States have included parental choice through charter schools and voucher programs,
school-based management, and performance measures. By 1996,
twenty-five states had charter school programs and over 200
schools had been granted charters (Whitty, Power, and Halpin
1998). Publicly funded voucher programs had been introduced
in Milwaukee, Cleveland, and Florida by 1999. The number of
publicly funded schools run by for-profit companies had also
become a trend. One of the most prominent companies, Edison
Schools Inc., was running seventy-nine schools in sixteen different states by the year 2000.[4] Whitty, Power, and Halpin cite a
study suggesting that three-quarters of America's school districts had introduced school-based management (26). Finally,
President Clinton's educational bill, Goals 2000, continued the
push for national standards and methods of assessment throughout public education. Shapiro (1998: 48) writes that 'during the
1980s and 90s the number of standardized tests administered to
students during their pre-college years has increased by almost
400 percent.' As evidence of concerns about performance, at
least forty-five states were planning, developing, or implementing new curriculum standards. Shapiro and others (Noble 1997;
Aronowitz 1997) note also that Clinton's education agenda assumes that the primary purpose of education is to prepare students for the job market.

There are clear parallels between the articulation of reforms
in Alberta and those in England, New Zealand, Australia, and
the United States. The shift in the role of the state governments,
development of quasi-markets, attacks on the teaching profession, and preoccupation with outcomes and accountability can
be seen across several jurisdictions. Comparisons lead us to ask
why there is such similarity, and if there are differences when
we look more closely. This study of Alberta contributes to the
discussion, as Whitty, Power, and Halpin (1998: 6) suggest, by
attempting to connect the 'empirical detail and the theoretical
bigger picture.' It purports, in fact, to link analysis of change in
Alberta to those in other sites while keeping sight of the
province's unique historical social, political, and economic features. Therefore, while this study focuses on understanding one

particular case, it provides insight into issues and theoretical understanding of other sites as well.

Chapters 2 to 5 go on to highlight key aspects of the federal and provincial context of educational reforms in Alberta. Chapter 2 begins this process with an analysis of three prominent discourses that have shaped educational reforms in Alberta and more broadly: *the fiscal crisis of the state, the unhappy parent,* and *the dissatisfied employer.* An analysis of the ideological roots of these discourses, their proponents, and critics indicates how and by whom positions have developed historically as well as in areas where dominant discourses have been challenged. For example, the discourse of the fiscal crisis of the state was adopted by business groups and policy-makers at federal and provincial levels in Canada in the 1990s. However, critics challenge its neoliberal assumptions about the role of the state and its emphasis on spending as opposed to revenues. Similarly, discourses of the unhappy parent and dissatisfied employer contain assumptions that are open to debate. This analysis informs later chapters, where stakeholders' views of educational reforms are presented.

It also informs the discussion in Chapter 3 concerning the role of the Conference Board of Canada in promoting the discourse of *education for economic prosperity* at the behest of its mostly corporate members. Chapter 3 examines the hegemonic work of this group in putting together a dominant alliance of forces around educational reform, constructing solutions to perceived educational problems, and recruiting popular support for these solutions. Examples of such perceived problems are high illiteracy and dropout rates and a lack of science and technology graduates, while solutions include developing a national vision for education and promoting the close link between education and the economy through business-education partnerships. This look at the Conference Board of Canada as seen through documents and conferences reveals its dual role as a national strategist and a catalyst for educational reform.

Chapter 4 extends this analysis by examining the hegemonic work of governments that was illustrated in three visioning processes. The first was the Prosperity Initiative undertaken by the

federal government in the early 1990s. The second was the Toward 2000 Together project undertaken by the Alberta government around the same time. Both initiatives aimed to develop a
direction for future policy through consultations with citizens.
The third was undertaken by Alberta Education as part of
Toward 2000 Together. An examination of these processes indicates the alliance between political and business elites that
facilitated consensus-building, as well as the discourses that
underlie this consensus. It also reveals quite clearly the place of
education within broader economic policy. The overlap between
events at the federal and provincial levels as well as the unique
aspects of the Alberta vision are also discussed.

Chapter 5 turns to the restructuring undertaken by the Conservative government in Alberta between 1993 and 1995. In the
midst of the 'Klein revolution,' news reports, public opinion
polls, and reports from government and stakeholder groups tell
the story of educational restructuring from the time of the government-sponsored roundtable talks in the fall of 1993, to the
release of the three-year business plan for education in 1994,
and the early stages of implementation in 1995. The latter plan
can be seen to represent the culmination of the hegemonic work
described in Chapters 3 and 4. Key themes were accountability,
standards, devolution of power, and choice – echoing reforms
in Britain, New Zealand, Australia, and the United States. The
influence of international policy shifts, as well as local conditions and forces, were undoubtedly important to the development of educational settlement.

Chapters 6 to 9 shift the focus from the period leading up to
the three-year business plan to that immediately following it,
including the responses of various 'stakeholder' groups. Chapter 6 presents an analysis of interviews with seven participants
in Calgary's business-in-education network. Themes from these
interviews include the interconnections and tensions within the
network, educational problems and solutions envisioned by
participants, and their roles in achieving and maintaining educational settlement. Comments made by these participants
suggest a high level of cohesion within the network, general

support for the government's restructuring agenda, and involvement in promoting this agenda in various ways.

Chapter 7 focuses on partnerships between schools and businesses. Partnerships have been described by the Organization for Economic Cooperation and Development (OECD), the federal government, business groups, and Alberta Education as a way of ensuring that schools are more responsive to employers' labour force needs. Following the cutbacks to education funding introduced in the three-year business plan, they are also seen by schools as a way of accessing needed resources such as computer equipment and expertise. This chapter introduces the partnership programs that have been in place in Calgary public schools since the mid-1980s, and in separate schools since the early 1990s, followed by two case studies of school-business initiatives that provide a sense of business involvement in practice. The latter studies indicate both the growing pressure on schools from government and school districts to form partnerships and to uncritically accept business offerings, and the process of struggle, compromise, and resistance that results when business partners attempt to put their visions into practice at the level of the school.

Chapter 8 describes the response of labour to government restructuring. Interviews with representatives from unions representing teachers and other educational workers, as well as coalitions of labour groups, suggest that the fragmentation of labour opposition in the period immediately following the release of government business plans was related to employees' differing relationships to the labour process, gender divisions, lack of resources, and lack of established networks. However, this does not mean that groups passively accepted restructuring plans. On the contrary, participants expressed opposition to the discourses of fiscal crisis, the unhappy parent, and the dissatisfied employer. They were beginning to recognize that counter-hegemonic work required the education of members, formation of coalitions across labour and social justice groups, and, ultimately, the development of a broadly based alternative vision.

In Chapter 9, the diversity within and across education stake-holders is explored through interviews with board- and school-level participants: administrators, trustees, and teachers. Partici-pants' comments suggest that five elements have contributed to the maintenance of educational settlement: the work of Calgary school board administrators, the distinction made between gov-ernment restructuring and the work of business partners, ac-ceptance of the fiscal crisis discourse, the 'little bit of truth' within discourses, and the lack of communication channels among teachers who were most likely to engage in counter-hegemonic work.

Interviews with parents and students in Chapter 10 provide an opportunity to further explore the discourse of the unhappy parent and its relationship to that of dissatisfied employers. Find-ings suggest that aside from the group Albertans for Quality Education (AQE), parents and students felt powerless in the face of government restructuring. Like organized labour, they tended to lack resources and established coalitions across par-ent groups. In contrast, the AQE had developed a conservative alliance united around a notion of choice that included parents concerned about morals and pedagogy, and also representa-tives of the private sector. At the time of the three-year business plan, this group was acknowledged to be influential, although there were tensions within the coalition.

Chapter 11 synthesizes the key findings of this case study, focusing on both the work leading up to educational settlement and the responses of other stakeholders. The chapter also ex-plores reasons for the achievement of settlement and the lack of effective resistance in the 1993 to 1995 period. However, recog-nizing that settlements are not unchanging, some attention is given to events since 1995, as well as shifts in the balance of forces. A comparison with educational reforms in Ontario, the United States, England, and New Zealand provides further in-sights into restructuring in Alberta in relation to these other sites. Finally, the chapter offers several implications of the study for further counter-hegemonic work.

CHAPTER TWO

The Crisis in Public Education

While educational reforms introduced in a number of industrialized countries in recent years have followed a similar
direction, struggles over policy also have been shaped by local
histories and conditions. The popularity of policies of the Klein
government in Alberta may therefore owe as much to the right-
wing populist tradition of the province as to earlier policies
introduced by Margaret Thatcher in Britain and by Ronald
Reagan in the United States. Discussion leading up to Alberta
Education's three-year business plan for education also draws
on discourses that appear to be partly borrowed, partly new. As
noted, three such discourses are the fiscal crisis of the state, the
unhappy parent, and the dissatisfied employer.

Discourses of the unhappy parent and the dissatisfied employer can be tied to broader questions around the role of the
state in providing education. For example, a 1992 report of the
OECD, entitled *Schools and Business: A New Partnership*, states,
'Until relatively recently, it was tacitly accepted in many countries that the State was a satisfactory vehicle for transmitting
society's priorities to the education system. Now, that consensus has disappeared. There is instead a broad movement to
widen the range of organisations and individuals who influence
and get involved with education (fashionably referred to as
'stockholders'). This movement is very new in some countries;
in others it dates from the 1970s. It has been motivated by a
number of perceptions, mainly relating to supposed failures of

education systems financed and government almost entirely by the State. A central concern is that schools have become increasingly out of touch with the knowledge and skills that pupils will require when they start work' (9).

In Alberta, prominent educational reformers have included advocates for parents who are unhappy with their children's schools and corporate executives who are concerned about the skills of youth entrants into the workplace. These groups' shared belief that schools must be more responsive to their concerns, as well as agreement over the general direction of desired school reform, provided the basis for alliance in the early 1990s. The focus of the discourse of fiscal crisis on the government's ability to pay for a variety of public services also legitimized the demands of parents and employers.

This chapter examines these discourses – their ideological roots, proponents, and critics. Exploring the historical roots of discourses reveals how the new 'common sense' around education has developed, while a closer look at proponents and critics suggests differences in the ways social groups and classes make sense of society. Since references to these three discourses recur in discussion of interviews in later chapters, such analysis here is essential.

The Fiscal Crisis of the State

A preoccupation with government debt and deficits developed in the 1990s in Alberta, as it did in many other sites. Concerns about government spending were related partly to the crisis experienced in the world capitalist economy since the 1970s, which was characterized by stagnation in industrial production and high levels of unemployment and inflation (Veltmeyer 1987). Globalization also impacted Canada through the flight of capital and jobs to low-wage, newly industrialized countries and the liberalization of international trade. As a result of these trends, governments in several industrialized countries faced a crisis concerning the legitimacy of the capitalist welfare state. The challenge to what is perceived to have been a Keynesian approach to the economy,[1] coupled with increasingly intense international competition, led to a widespread view among neoliberal and neoconservative critics that social welfare policies were an unaffordable luxury (Pannu, Schugurensky, and Plumb 1994). The tension between the state's role in providing the conditions for capitalist accumulation while providing programs designed to redress some of the 'externalities' created by the capitalist system became more acute.

The discourse of the fiscal crisis of the state was adopted by both federal and provincial governments in Canada in the 1990s. The Klein Conservatives in Alberta promised to balance the budget in four years while also creating a more competitive tax environment in a 1993 pre-election report entitled *Seizing Opportunities* (Klein 1993). This had implications for education, which represented 21 per cent of social spending (Alberta 1995). Across Canada, a 1995 poll found that '86 per cent of respondents, regardless of income or education, believed that controlling taxes and spending to fight public debt were either "important" or "very important"' (Laird 1998: 88). The dominance of this view prompts us to ask who promoted it and how it became so influential.

Two groups that played important roles in this work were the Reform Party and the Fraser Institute. The Reform Party worked with independent think-tanks and business lobbyists to convince middle-class Canadians that the country was hitting the 'debt wall,' while the Vancouver-based Fraser Institute awarded Premier Ralph Klein the annual prize for 'the best fiscal performance' of any North American government in 1994 (Laird 1998). Within Alberta, the Calgary-based Canada West Foundation (CWF) – a conservative think-tank formed in 1971 to provide a voice for western Canada in public policy debate – also played a key role. Former CWF president Stan Roberts ran against Preston Manning for the leadership of the Reform Party in 1987. The group apparently became less overtly political and more moderate under Roberts's successor, David Elton, a political scientist at the University of Lethbridge. Although the CWF describes itself as independent, its executive and governing council largely include business leaders from the western provinces. According to promotional materials, the group is sponsored by 'hundreds of individual and corporate members.' In the fall of 1993, it released a report entitled *The Red Ink: Alberta's Deficit, Debt and Economic Future.*

The Red Ink (CWF 1993) suggests that federal and provincial deficits and debt pose a significant problem for governments because of debt-servicing costs and the potential actions of domestic and foreign investors. According to its authors, weak economic growth after 1975 made it difficult to keep pace with the rising expenditures associated with federal social programs that were implemented in the more prosperous 1960s. The primary cause of fiscal crisis thus was tied to the ever-expanding expectations of certain groups in society. At the provincial level, the Alberta government's debt was attributed to a 1986 drop in energy prices as well as to the growth in government expenditures.

The CWF has been influential at both provincial and federal levels in public policy debate; CWF president David Elton was a prominent contributor during the Alberta government's economic visioning consultations in the early 1990s. These consultations culminated in the Klein government's pre-election strategy (Klein 1993). At the federal level, the CWF was one of a number of organizations that supported the 1988 Free Trade Agreement. It produced four task-force reports between June and September of 1987 that articulated the positions on free trade of industry associations and management spokespersons in western Canada. The parallels between the position espoused by this group and that later adopted by governments is noted by Kachur (1994).

While less politically influential in this period, the Canadian Centre for Policy Alternatives (CCPA) and a handful of academics in Alberta challenged the prevailing arguments around debt and deficits. At the federal level, in the preface to *Bleeding the Patient*, the CCPA suggested that the actual causes of rising federal debt were the 'inflated interest rates maintained by the Bank of Canada, the failure to make wealthy individuals and corporations pay their fair share of taxes, and the drain on government revenues caused by inexcusably high unemployment' (CCPA 1993). The problem was thus seen as a monetary issue tied to the relationship between the Bank of Canada and the federal government, and a revenue problem resulting from changes to the tax structure that benefit the wealthy. Therefore, while the CWF focused on the increasing costs of social programs, the CCPA highlighted the decline in revenues.

The suggestion that changes in the tax structure over time have benefited corporations is reinforced by a number of writers. Deaton (1973) argues that the corporate share of federal income tax revenues fell by approximately 38 per cent between 1962 and 1970 while the share contributed by individuals increased by more than 23 per cent. Studying the period between 1951 and 1988 in Canada, Vermaeten, Gillespie, and Vermaeten (1995) similarly note a decrease in the importance of the corporate share of income tax revenues. At the same time, Deaton suggests that the expansion of the public sector in the 1960s effectively socialized the costs of providing a technical infrastructure that disproportionately benefited the corporate sector. This discussion informs our understanding of the Alberta case, where low corporate tax rates have prevailed for decades and where the promise of even lower rates in the pursuit of the 'Alberta Advantage'[2] has been promoted by Conservative governments.

Writers who challenge the CWF emphasis on the 'expense' side of government tried to shift attention to the government's revenue problem, which was reportedly exacerbated by government reductions in gas royalty rates and tax holidays and incentives provided to oil producers in Alberta since 1980 (Cooper and Neu 1995). Taft (1997) adds that the government's financial troubles could be attributed largely to massive subsidies to the private sector beginning in the mid-1970s, when private sector subsidies cost taxpayers billions more than was collected in corporate income taxes in the province. Thus, the attack on social spending was seen as inappropriate.

Despite disagreement over the causes of debt and deficits, the vision of bloated, inefficient governments seems to have captured the public imagination. A key part of the solution to fiscal crisis, as outlined in *The Red Ink* and other CWF publications, was the idea of *reinventing government*, borrowing from the book by Americans Osborne and Gaebler (1993).[3] CWF authors in fact borrow several of these authors' recommended approaches to providing government services, including contracting out, encouraging public sector employees to create private companies, shifting delivery of services to local community groups and existing institutions, financing services through user fees, selling assets, and establishing greater interprovincial cooperation. The Klein government subsequently adopted several of these ideas: for example, it deinsured certain health-care services and cut funding for kindergarten programs (which became subject to user fees); privatized liquor stores, registries, and child welfare services; and contracted out highway maintenance and provincial parks management. The effect of cuts to school board funding also resulted in increased user fees and the contracting out of janitorial and other services.

In contrast to the CWF emphasis on reinventing government, CCPA writers (1992, 1993) suggested that controlling the deficit and lowering the federal debt could be accomplished by making the tax system more progressive and by stimulating economic growth through job creation. In the Alberta context, economists have argued that provincial deficits should be tackled by a combination of expenditure reductions and revenue increases (McMillan and Warrack 1993; Drugge 1995). However, the fact that much of this oppositional discourse occurred after the actions of the Klein government, suggests that the forces promoting the discourse of fiscal crisis had already coalesced and become dominant.

This discourse was embraced by politicians in Alberta in the early 1990s. Economic visioning reports produced through the Alberta government's Toward 2000 Together consultations supported the view that spending on programs such as education should be made more efficient. The pre-election report *Seizing Opportunities* announced the Klein government's plans to balance the budget in four years, and to change the role of government from 'manager' of the economy to 'partner and facilitator' (Klein 1993). The Liberal opposition also focused on the problem of debt and deficits (and the fiscal mismanagement of the Getty Conservatives) during the 1993 election campaign. Largely because of the endorsement of this discourse by government and the media, it became part of the common sense revolution in Alberta in the 1990s and posed a formidable challenge to those concerned about declining education funding.

The legitimacy of the state as provider of educational services has been challenged in more than one jurisdiction. Schools are seen to lack flexibility and adaptability because of their bureaucratic structures. Promoters of the discourse of *educational crisis* in Alberta include unhappy parents who raise concerns based on their experiences with their children's schools, and dissatisfied employers who raise concerns based on their views of youth entrants into the workplace. In the Alberta context, the shared belief that schools must improve provided a basis for alliance in the early 1990s.

The Unhappy Parent

The discourse of the unhappy parent can be placed within the context of debates over pedagogical approaches that have caused swings in Alberta's policy-making pendulum for decades. In 1935 the Social Credit government introduced progressive education ideas in response to the movement begun by the United Farm Women of Alberta who hoped to improve education in rural areas (Wilson 1992; Kach 1992). Just over twenty years later, the Cameron Report (Alberta 1959) provided a plan that was described as the 'antithesis of the educational policy and practices of progressive education,' in response to an alliance of conservative critics (Kach and Mazurek 1992: 148). However, changes introduced into Alberta schools in the 1960s and early 70s returned to progressive practices such as nongraded classrooms, individualized progress, and integrated programs of study espoused later in the Worth Report (Alberta 1972). But in the mid 1970s this was countered by a back-to-basics movement and the Harder Report (Alberta Education 1977), which returned education to the straight and narrow.

A similar shift occurred in Britain in the 1960s and 70s as progressive ideas and methods were linked to problems with student achievement and discipline by conservative critics. Authors describe how the concept of 'the parent' was used in policy discussions: 'In a classic "populist" manoeuvre, a version of "ordinary parents" and of parental interests was set against the forces by whom they were scorned. ... As a reference point, "the parent" was classless, without gender, and seeking a better life for the child – a generalizing focus for worries about "the nation" and its children' (CCCS 1981: 202).

The concept of 'the parent' also became something of a political slogan in policy discussions in Alberta in the 1990s. Andrew Nikiforuk, the Calgary-based former education columnist for the *Globe and Mail*, Dr Joe Freedman, a radiologist from Red Deer, and the group Albertans for Quality Education (AQE) emerged as representatives for unhappy parents in the province and beyond. In a 1993 position paper, the AQE describes itself as 'a decentralized organization consisting of parents, business people, educators and students in many communities throughout Alberta' (AQE 1993: 2), and in the *Calgary Herald* it was reported to represent approximately 325 members in Alberta in 1994 (Dempster 11 February 1994).

The AQE juxtaposes 'populist' and 'progressive' educational approaches in its position paper. The former (which might also be described as a *traditional* approach) is associated with the development of knowledge, skills, and decision-making capabilities of children along with values of honesty, integrity, hard work, diligence, commitment, and cooperation. The teacher commands respect and there is usually a 'zero tolerance discipline' policy. The progressive approach, on the other hand, is described as being more child-directed in terms of the pace of learning and the ability for children to choose attitudes and values for themselves (AQE 1993). Representatives of the AQE are clearly aligned with the traditional view. One prominent member, Dr Joe Freedman, describes himself as representing other unhappy parents across the country who are 'seriously concerned about the degree to which their children are acquiring adequate levels of knowledge and skills as well as solid traditional values' (Freedman 1993: 6).[4] Nikiforuk (1993: xii) also described his book, entitled *School's Out: The Catastrophe in Public Education and What We Can Do about It*, as a 'populist manifesto' claiming to represent people interested in clarity, relevance, and common sense. While Nikiforuk was based in Calgary, he was writing for a national audience, and, like Freedman, claimed to articulate concerns of other parents across the country.

Reasons for Nikiforuk and Freedman's dissatisfaction with schools include the alleged decline in literacy levels, students' lack of preparation for life, and the superior performance of Japanese and German students on international achievement tests. According to its first newsletter, the AQE was formed to address concerns that the quality of education in Alberta had 'declined to unacceptably low levels.' In support of the idea of literacy crisis, Nikiforuk notes that children no longer learn how to read very well in school. Freedman adds that student achievement on the Canadian Test of Basic Skills dropped 6.3 per cent between 1966 and 1991, despite the fact that pupil-teacher ratios went down by one-third and costs per student more than doubled.

Class Warfare authors Barlow and Robertson (1994) challenge the discourse of educational crisis presented by Nikiforuk and Freedman, suggesting that it was largely manufactured. They counter that literacy statistics such as those presented by Freedman are distorted, and suggest the need to look more closely at data comparing student achievement and costs per student to see what is included and what is obscured. In opposition to Nikiforuk's (1993: 100) emphasis on moving back to a core curriculum that 'builds on 3,000 years of tradition,' Barlow and Robertson emphasize the politics of curriculum and ask, 'whose interests are being served and at what price?' (112).

Representatives for unhappy parents suggest that a primary reason for the decline in literacy is the predominant progressive educational philosophy in North America. Freedman critiques child-centred approaches as being concerned with process over outcomes and emphasizing discovery, exploration, and experimentation instead of the skills and disciplines of knowledge. Nikiforuk (1993: 93) adds that 'the progressive experiment' has robbed children of a proper education, arguing that progressive ideas encourage undisciplined thought and unrealistic expectations of schools. According to the AQE, 'attempts in B.C. and Ontario to force a progressive philosophy on school systems seem to be backfiring for these two governments' (1993: 5). In short, Nikiforuk, Freedman, and the AQE believe that schools should be transmitters of traditional social values.

The backlash against 'progressive' educational ideas can be related to the growing contradiction within capitalist society between 'production' values such as discipline and restraint, and 'consumption' values such as pleasure and gratification. Shapiro (1990: 38), quoting Bell, writes: 'On the one hand, the business corporation wants an individual to work hard, pursue a career, accept delayed gratification – to be, in the crude sense, an organization man [sic]. And yet, in its products and its advertisements, the corporation promotes pleasure, instant joy, relaxing and letting go. One is to be "straight" by day and a "swinger" by night.' Thus, while unhappy parents tend to link the erosion of discipline within schools and the promotion of self-indulgence to progressive educational practices, it may just as easily be seen as rooted in the contradictory demands of the capitalist system. A decline in 'production values' may also be tied to students' perceptions that they will face unemployment/underemployment and economic uncertainty regardless of their educational attainments (Ray and Mickelson 1993).

Other causes of educational decline from the perspectives of dissatisfied parents include bureaucracy, union contracts, and 'bibles of political correctness' (Nikiforuk 1993: 58). The solution to these problems, as well as to struggles over pedagogical approaches, involves promoting choice in schools through charter schools or other market model reforms. As the AQE position paper recommends, 'Effective schools can only be implemented by relatively autonomous schools which: a) are primarily accountable to parents; b) meet required but not excessively bureaucratic standards set by Alberta Education; c) are free to develop "customer satisfying" programs, styles and cultures; d) free parents and students to choose among programs and schools, and e) are allocated financial resources according to the popularity of each choice' (1993: 3). Nikiforuk and Freedman agree that charter schools may allow schools to break free of school board constraints and bureaucracy and become more effective.

In this scenario, all schools (including private schools) which meet government standards and agree to serve students living in their catchment areas would receive government funding. Schools would be accountable to their customers through the performance of students on standardized tests and would be rewarded for their responsiveness to changing consumer preferences. The intention is to break the monopoly of public schools. Proponents argue that reforms in this direction benefit all parents and students by allowing greater input into processes previously guarded by bureaucrats and professional educators. Essentially, the AQE position supports a market model and increased private delivery of education.

The discourse of unhappy parents in Alberta is motivated by a view of educational bureaucracies as sprawling, irrational, and wasteful. However, in endorsing a market model for education, there is an implicit privileging of the state's role in accumulation over its role in addressing the inequities that result from the economic system. The elitist effect of this discourse is addressed by oppositional writers who comment that 'For some, public education of any kind is inconsistent with "parents' rights," for others it is inconsistent with reaping the rewards of privilege; for a few it is inconsistent with the unbridled right to profit from children's futures' (Robertson and Barlow 1995: 205). From this perspective, the 'market model' promoted by charter schools promotes 'winners,' 'losers,' and self-interested behaviour. Authors argue that disadvantaged children will be further disadvantaged by a free market scenario.

The concept of choice within a market model of education is also critiqued by Ball (1993: 3), who argues that the ideology of the market and choice is 'underpinned by dangerous idealisations about the working of markets, the effects of parental choice and of profit incentives in education.' Proponents of market ideology characterize markets as efficient and responsive to the needs of customers and downplay the fact that they ignore power differences and undermine educational values. Schools tend to recruit more able students and concentrate resources on those with the highest ability and/or the most vocal and influential parents, leading to a more stratified educational system. Working-class families are systematically disadvantaged because choice in the market presumes certain skills and material possibilities such as access to time, transportation, and childcare facilities. Differences are then blamed on parental choices rather than systemic inequities.

Despite challenges to the discourse of the unhappy parent, it has been politically influential in Alberta as in other jurisdictions. Joe Freedman emerged as a prominent parent reformer and media spokesperson in the early 1990s. AQE representatives were included in government consultations on educational reform in the fall of 1993. And, most importantly, reforms introduced by Alberta Education in 1994 accommodated reformers' demands to include increased parental control, expanded standardized testing, and charter schools. Correspondingly, the role of government shifted away from ensuring equitable delivery towards the role of standard-setter and provider of information to parent 'clients.'

The Dissatisfied Employer

Employers have in turn influenced educational reform through their promotion of the discourse of *education for economic prosperity*, rooted in human capital theory and a vision of the knowledge economy. Articulated by Becker (1964) and others in the 1960s, human capital theory is generally the view that a society with more formally educated workers will be a more productive society. There is an assumed relationship between more education and increased earnings at both an individual and societal level. Knowledge economy advocates predict that the emerging economy will require large numbers of highly educated workers (Bell 1973). Together, human capital/knowledge-economy assumptions have fuelled employers' claims about the poor quality of educational 'outputs.'

A look at the way human capital theory has adapted since the 1960s is instructive. In the early 1960s, Alberta writer John Cheal (1963: 143) noted the growing interest in human capital ideas and connected it to questions about whether the education system could meet 'today's space age challenge' – referring no doubt to the 1957 launching of Sputnik as well as the shift from primary goods to manufacturing. Based on surveys of manufacturers in the province, an Alberta Royal Commission in the late 1950s concluded that 'the day of the unskilled, uneducated worker is gone' (7). Concerns were raised about school dropout rates and the waste of human resources potential. Cheal recommended greater investment in education as a form of human capital that would 'raise the standard of living qualitatively and quantitatively, promote economic growth through greater productivity, and enable the nation to maintain its place in an increasingly technological and competitive world' (13).

Human capital discourse continues to be related to economic change – more recently, to the shift to a 'knowledge economy' and globalization. But given the emphasis on government restraint, while writers like John Cheal called for greater public investment in education in the 1960s, more recent proponents of human capital ideas call for individuals to invest in themselves, or for governments to share the costs of education and training with private sector partners. However, increasing rates of unemployment and underemployment during a period when school attainment levels and funding have increased challenge assertions about the societal return on investment from education. In response, some contemporary human capital advocates suggest that improving the quality of schooling and encouraging 'lifelong learning' will revitalize economic growth. Others point out that those with higher levels of formal education continue to do better economically than those with low levels. As Livingstone (1999: 166) notes, human capital theory has been 'retooled' for the 1990s.

This is evident in the reports of groups like the Conference Board of Canada and the Alberta Chamber of Resources (ACR). The ACR in cooperation with Alberta Education produced a study in 1991 entitled *International Comparisons in Education*, which presents the findings of how Alberta schools compare with those in Japan, Germany, and Hungary. The presumed link between education and economic competitiveness is evident in a message from Eric Newell, ACR Education Committee chairman and president of Syncrude, in a preface to the report: 'In Canada, we must recognize the forces of global competition and the role of science and technology in reducing cost, improving reliability and quality. Our economic prosperity and standard of living depend on our ability to compete in the world and to that extent we must be open to lessons from the international community.'

The fact that the study was undertaken at the urging of Joe Freedman, who approached the ACR for support in 1990, indicates an alliance between unhappy parents and dissatisfied employers. As the report notes, '"Although Alberta has one of the strongest education systems in the country, the competitive world is leaving us behind" [Freedman] insisted ... *Why not prove the case* [my emphasis] by simply making a direct comparison of what is taught in Alberta versus other countries through an examination of textbooks? Dr Freedman's words fell on receptive ears. The Chamber had already established an Education Committee out of its concern for provincial education and had recently considered the proposed revisions to the Alberta high school science curriculum' (ACR and Alberta Education 1991: 1). According to Freedman, 'what parents want and what a country needs are the same: a strong curriculum, effective methods and a system that works' (ii).

The report presents the problem and its causes followed by major findings and recommendations. Employers see the problem as the 'low level of interest in science and technology and skilled trade careers among Alberta youth,' and particularly the lack of preparation of non-college-bound students (i). This is traced to the poor quality of math and science education in Alberta, and, ultimately, to misguided educational values: 'In Alberta, societal values have drifted towards individualism, self-discovery and self-indulgence, and resistance appears to have built up against the operation of a more demanding, outcome focused education system' (2). In contrast, comparison counties are said to be characterized by 'a dominance of economic values, a strong work ethic, self-discipline, co-operation, and acquisition of specific skills' (4). Again, the decline in production values within schools is cause for concern.

Critics of the discourse of education for economic prosperity challenge several of the assumptions of knowledge economy/ human capital proponents. In response to the claim that the 'post-industrial' economy requires large number of highly skilled people, Livingstone (1999: 162) presents evidence which indicates that 'Trends in the workplace are much more modest than the visions of a knowledge-based economy initially expressed by post-industrial theorists in the 1960s projected, and especially modest in comparison with the massive expansion of advanced schooling and adult education.'

The claim that the *supply* of skilled labour is not the problem is reinforced by Barlow and Robertson (1994: 48), who note that 'each year Canada produces nearly three times as many science and engineering graduates per capita as does Germany and 50 per cent more than Japan.' Further, the decline in real wages that has accompanied the increase in educational investment and attainment since the 1970s challenges the 'learning-earning' link at the societal level promoted by human capital proponents (Livingstone 1999). From this view, the problem resides more in the growing gap between people's learning efforts/knowledge and the number of commensurate jobs where they can be applied, than in a lack of highly skilled workers. The discourse of education for economic prosperity obscures this general situation with talk of particular skills shortages, claims about the poor quality of job entrants, and credential inflation. Two effects of accepting this discourse are increased efforts by students to pursue further education when faced with a tight job market and the legitimacy granted to business involvement in educational reform.

For example, the ACR-sponsored report recommends that business become more involved by communicating its expectations to the education system and promoting greater public awareness of the link between education and economic prosperity. Other recommendations include increasing the emphasis on achievement and outcomes, implementing national standards, improving the efficiency and effectiveness of classroom practices, developing strategies to encourage excellence in science and mathematics through the recruitment and training of teachers in these subjects, and establishing partnerships between educators, industry, the public, and other education stakeholders to improve education. The restoration of *production values* is a clear priority in proposed reforms.

Acknowledging that these education improvements may not be possible to implement in the face of a large and established system, the report goes on to suggest that 'it may be necessary to introduce more fundamental changes to the education system itself' (8). Authors favour introducing the element of choice into schooling, whereby schools would compete for students on the basis of school performance. Schools would have more local authority and accountability for strategy, budgets, staffing, scheduling, curriculum, and procedures. Again, we see the priority given to the state's role in accumulation over its other roles.

Concluding Comments

Chapter 1 suggested that hegemonic work involves the formation of alliances, the development of solutions to perceived problems, and the recruitment of popular support for these solutions. Analysis of the discourses of fiscal crisis, the unhappy parent, and the dissatisfied employer suggests that these discourses were complementary and that business people were involved in promoting or supporting all three. The fiscal crisis of the state was promoted by business leaders and business-sponsored groups such as the Fraser Institute and CWF. The discourse of the unhappy parent was promoted by Albertans for Quality Education – a group representing private school operators and other business people as well as 'ordinary' parents interested in their children's schooling. A prominent member of this group, Joe Freedman demonstrated a knack for securing corporate support for his endeavours. Financial backers for his video *Failing Grades* included the Royal Bank, the Bank of Nova Scotia, Syncrude, and Kodak. Freedman was also supported by the ACR and Alberta Education in the *International Comparisons* study.

Shared interests were the basis for this alliance. Unhappy parents' concerns about progressive educational ideas were echoed in the employers' view that societal values have drifted towards 'self-discovery and self-indulgence.' Both groups lament a decline in 'production values' within schools. Solutions promoted by both dissatisfied parents and employers have included setting higher standards, focusing more on outcomes, introducing greater parental choice/market-directed reforms, and making educators more accountable. In sum, the concerns of certain parents with the lack of discipline in schools fits neatly with concerns of certain employers about the lack of work discipline exhibited by students entering the labour force. The solution of greater choice allows both groups to potentially achieve what they want from public schools.

But there was also tension within the parent-employer alliance. For example, Nikiforuk (1993: 131) challenges the discourse of education for economic prosperity when he says '[T]he attempt to tie schools to purely economic goals, or to make them institutions designed to serve purely economic needs, will be just as disastrous as the "progressive" plan to have schools deliver one failed social agenda after another.' The neoconservative emphasis on morality and tradition does not necessarily fit well with a neoliberal focus on adjusting to the economic norms of the new global economy, suggesting that this alliance is built on fragile compromises. Further, parents may be just as concerned about the corporate promotion of *consumer* values through schools as they are about the decline in *production* values. The parent-employer alliance thus may be jeopardized by increasing commercial involvement of business in schools. The fact that unhappy parents embrace a model of consumer choice is somewhat ironic in this respect.

The discourse of fiscal crisis of the state effectively sets the parameters for solutions to the 'crisis' in education constructed by unhappy parents and dissatisfied employers. Solutions that highlight less bureaucracy and greater efficiency, more local accountability, and alternative delivery systems have been consistent with ideas around reinventing government. In this construction, economic prosperity depends on improving workplace productivity through education *within the context of continued government restraint*. The privileging of the role of the state in fostering conditions for accumulation is the common thread.

Strategies used by advocates of the three discourses to promote discourses also display common elements. The first involves the claiming of popular support. Unhappy parents Joe Freedman and Andrew Nikiforuk and the group AQE claimed to speak for the majority of other parents, while the CWF has purported to represent 'concerned western Canadians.' Critics counter that these groups actually represent very narrow interests and threaten collectivist and democratic values.

A second strategy centres on gaining political and media acceptability and public recognition. Between the mid-1970s and mid-1990s the CWF produced over forty reports on issues related to western Canada's economy, trade, labour markets, and public debt. Joe Freedman gained national attention with the release of his video and later became a recognized spokesperson for charter schools in Alberta. Soon after its inception, the AQE began to produce local newsletters and organize annual conferences to attract members and disseminate its message. Members presented a position paper during government consultations on education in 1993. In addition to sponsoring the *International Comparisons* report in 1991, the ACR spearheaded an initiative in 1994 called Careers: The Next Generation (CNG), aimed at increasing the number of youth in skilled trades in

Alberta through cooperative education and apprenticeships. This initiative was strongly supported by Alberta Education, and in 1998 a CNG foundation was established by business, education, and government partners. The strategies of identifying allies and potential partners, providing solutions to government, and informing the public/through reports and the media are important aspects of hegemonic work. As Chapter 3 will demonstrate, the Conference Board of Canada (CB) has also been a key player.

CHAPTER THREE

The Hegemonic Work
of the Conference Board

> [W]hatever the 'needs' of the capitalist mode of production, a vast amount of ideological work remains to be done before coherent policy can be formulated, consent won and real change initiated. (CCCS, *Unpopular Education*)

The Conference Board's influence on educational policy-makers in Alberta is evident from a reading of provincial documents which reference the CB's employability skills profile, local partnerships that have won CB awards, and ethical guidelines for school-business partnerships. The CB's ethical guidelines for partnerships and ESP were used in developing the *Framework for Enhancing Business Involvement in Education*, a document produced as part of the implementation of the 1994 business plan for education (Alberta Education 1996a). The influence of the CB may be explained in part by the fact that between 1992 and 1994 the deputy minister of education and an administrator from the Calgary Board of Education were members of the CB's National Council on Education (NCE). In addition, approximately one-third of the members of the Corporate Council on Education (CCE) were located in Calgary. Therefore, Alberta was well represented within CB education groups. This chapter looks at the CB's role as a coordinating agency in putting together a dominant alliance of forces around educational reform, constructing solutions to perceived educational problems, and recruiting broader support for these solutions. The analysis suggests a close relationship between the hegemonic work of the Alberta government in achieving consent for educational reforms and the work of the CB in promoting its vision for education.

Allies in the Vision

> Every social group ... creates together with itself, organically, one or more strata of intellectuals which give it homogeneity and an awareness of its own function not only in the economic but also in the social and political fields.   (Antonio Gramsci, *Selections from the Prison Notebooks*)

A key function of the CB is to act in the interests of its corporate members in assembling 'stakeholders' who can bring about change. The group has held annual conferences on business-education collaboration across Canada since 1990, and in his introduction to the 1994 conference, the CB president acknowledged that it was 'designed to bring together the stakeholders in a forum for building consensus that cuts across geographical boundaries and unites individual perceptions.'[1] The CB researcher responsible for organizing these conferences describes how he identifies potential participants, stating, 'the ultimate determinant of whether they are important stakeholders is whether they manage to develop a relationship with those who have the central role in the education system, and that means whether they have resources and energy to move forward, and the staying power' (Interview 3).[2] In fact, several leaders from government, education, and business who have been keynote speakers at these conferences can be described as 'organic intellectuals' in the promotion of a corporate-driven vision for educational reform. This section explores alliances within the corporate community as well as those between corporations and education, government, and teacher-training institutions. But first, a brief look at the history of CB involvement in education.

The fact that the U.S. Conference Board began holding business-education conferences in 1983 no doubt encouraged its Canadian affiliate to consider how business could be more involved in education in Canada. Involvement by American businesses at the local level in 'adopt-a-school programs' and at federal and state levels in policy-making arguably provided a model for Canadian business. An American presence was particularly noticeable at the 1991 conference where speakers from U.S. corporations and institutes were invited to speak about reform trends there. However, the Canadian organization's relationship with education is described as being more collaborative than that in the United States.

According to a CB researcher, the Canadian group began to focus on education at the request of its mostly corporate associates in 1989. A year later it established a National Business and Education Centre (NBEC) to 'assist business in developing strategies to work with the education system to ensure that Canada's youth is prepared to meet workplace needs.' The NCE, comprising leaders primarily from business and education, and the Corporate Council on Education, comprising twenty-five corporate members, were formed soon afterward. It is noteworthy that while the NCE included representation (although minimal) from organized labour, a labour perspective was noticeably lacking at business-education conferences and in CB publications.

Business representatives on the NCE and CCE were generally from successful blue chip corporations. CCE members represent telephone/utilities, technology, natural resources, banking and business services, and transportation industries. Several members of the NCE and CCE were aligned with other business-sponsored organizations. For example, the president of the Conference Board was an ex officio member of the Corporate–Higher Education Forum (CHEF) and approximately one-third of the companies belonging to the NBEC also belonged to CHEF. A spokesperson from the Business Council on National Issues (BCNI) acknowledged that a number of BCNI members were key funders of the CB. Over a dozen member companies of the NBEC were also on the board for Junior Achievement (JA) in 1991/2, and a number were on the board of the Canadian Foundation for Economic Education (CFEE). These connections help to explain ideological similarities between groups and the seemingly common corporate front that developed around education.

In addition to alliances within the corporate community, the CB played an important role in developing alliances with representatives from government, parent groups, post-secondary institutions, and schools. This is evident from the list of speakers included in conferences on business-education collaboration that the CB began organizing in 1990. These conferences were held across the country and generally included federal and provincial officials as keynote speakers. For example, Education Minister Jim Dinning spoke at the 1993 conference held in Calgary. At the same conference, Dr Joe Freedman was invited to represent parents in a panel in which participants were asked to respond to the CB vision for education. An alliance with education leaders was institutionalized through the NCE, whose members included both corporate CEOs and education leaders.[3] A similar format is found in the Corporate-Higher Education Forum (CHEF) in Canada and the Business-Higher Education Forum (BHEF) in the United States. Slaughter's (1990) analysis of the latter group suggests that although it formed to address issues of mutual concern to business and education leaders, the interests of business leaders tended to prevail in reports. She concludes that the BHEF represents an effort by the corporate community to draw educators into its hegemonic vision. This raises the question of whether the NCE plays a similar role. To answer this question, it is useful to look at the vision promoted by business groups and the extent to which it is likely to be shared by educators and others.

Educational Crises and Solutions

In the early 1990s the CB began to identify concerns about education and to develop recommendations. By 1994 the NCE had developed a national vision for education in response to concerns about student illiteracy, dropout rates, and poor performance on international tests. Evidence of these problems was drawn from sources that included the *International Comparisons* study sponsored by the ACR and Alberta Education (see Chapter 2), the federal government's *Learning Well ... Living Well* report (described in more detail in Chapter 3), the Economic Council of Canada report *A Lot to Learn* (1992), and CB research (e.g., Lafleur 1992).

Annual conferences provided opportunities to share information and develop common perspectives across groups. For example, at the first conference in 1990, speakers from corporations, government, and educational institutions shared concerns about high illiteracy and dropout rates, poor student performance compared to other countries, and a lack of science and technology graduates. Four of the corporate participants were on the CB board of directors. At the second conference, a more geographically diverse group of speakers described examples of structural reform in the United States, Britain, and Europe, as well as within Canada. For example, Union Carbide established a Corporate Task Force in Education that led to a report entitled *Undereducated, Uncompetitive U.S.A.* (Bloom 1991: 9–10). As a result of the leading role taken by this company in the United States, Chairman and CEO Robert Kennedy was invited to share his views. Kennedy spoke of the need for business to become involved in local community programs but also to support reforms at state and national levels and to help shape the public debate. He outlined nine characteristics of a successful school system (adopted by the Business Roundtable in the United States), which emphasized standards, outcomes, rewards, and accountability.[4] Another American, John Chubb of the Brookings Institute, also spoke at this conference. Chubb had co-written a book called *Politics, Markets, and America's Schools*, which argued that educational reforms must challenge the political and bureaucratic control of schools (Chubb and Moe 1990). He recommended '[a] market system that gives educational choices to those most immediately involved. Schools compete for the support of parents and students who are free to choose among schools. The system is built on decentralization, competition and choice ... In the long run, schools that deliver a good educational product would prosper while those that do not would disappear' (Bloom 1991: 24).

Chubb went on to outline elements of President Bush's 1991 National Education Strategy that supported his recommendations such as the adoption of choice throughout the United States, national achievement tests in grades four, eight, and twelve based on a national curriculum, and the acceptance of alternative providers such as businesses and universities into the system. Parental choice, standards, testing, and competition among schools were key ingredients of the message provided to delegates at the session.

This message was reinforced by the presentation given by John Woolhouse of the University of Warwick, former chair of Britain's Manpower Services Commission. Woolhouse spoke approvingly of changes emanating from the Education Reform Act introduced in 1988 in Britain, changes such as the shift in school governance away from control by local education authorities, greater parental choice, more standardized assessment of students, the introduction of a national curriculum, greater emphasis on science/technology and vocational education, and government support for business-education partnerships (Bloom 1991).

While these suggestions sounded radical at the time, a number of ideas were reiterated in subsequent conferences and reports. For example, at the 1992 conference, the chair of the Economic Council, Judith Maxwell, discussed the report *A Lot to Learn* (Economic Council 1992) and its recommendations around increased school-business partnerships, greater support for parents' choice, core curricula, greater emphasis on testing, balancing academic and vocational curricula, and responding more to the needs of employers. The NCE subsequently undertook consultations to develop a national vision for education and a report based on this process recommended increasing autonomy and accountability for schools (decentralized decision-making), rewarding initiative and performance, eliminating bureaucracy and duplication, supporting partnerships with business, and implementing national standards (Souque 1994).

The theme of testing was explored in greater detail during the 1993 conference at a session on the Third International Mathematics and Science Study (TIMSS) and the Student Achievement Indicators Program (SAIP). At this time, four provinces in Canada (including Alberta) and fifty other countries were participating in the ten-year TIMSS for the reported purpose of learning how to improve educational practice by reducing dropout rates and increasing participation rates in mathematics and science. SAIP had been launched by the Council of Ministers of Education, Canada (CMEC) to assess student performance in math, reading, and writing across provinces. Also at the 1993 conference, past president and CEO of Xerox Canada, David McCamus discussed the work of the Prosperity Initiative, a federally sponsored process aimed at consulting Canadians and developing an economic vision for the future.

CB Discourses

The key discourse that predominated in work undertaken by the CB was not surprisingly that of education for economic prosperity promoted by the dissatisfied employer. Chapter 2 suggests that this discourse is rooted in human capital theory and a vision of the knowledge economy. In Alberta, employers' concerns about a perceived decline in students' work ethic, self-discipline, and outcomes compared to 'competitor countries' were presented in the *International Comparisons* report (ACR and Alberta Education 1991). Recommendations included increasing business involvement in education, greater emphasis on achievement and outcomes, and increasing choice within schooling.

The CB also presented employers' concerns about various aspects of education. In an effort to raise public awareness of the link between education and a successful economy, it sponsored a study of the economic consequences to individuals and society of dropping out of school. Authors of this 'dropout report' describe the problem and its implications as follows: 'Problems facing the educational system threaten to reduce the national standard of living, heighten demands on social safety nets, and increase the economic burden on individual and corporate taxpayers. One of the most important of these problems is a high school dropout rate that stands at 34 percent – meaning that one in three Canadian high school students fails to graduate' (Lafleur 1992: 1). The high level of dropouts is thus constructed as a drain on the Canadian society. The obvious solution is to reduce the number of dropouts by reforming education.

The NCE also emphasized 'matching education to the needs of society' in its consultations with selected stakeholders across the country concerning a vision for schools. A report that summarized these consultations identified specific impediments to change in education that included 'The lack of support for innovation, the absence of national standards, the poor system of teacher training and professional development, the outdated labour relations framework, the fragmentation and inflexibilities of the education system, and the great number of school boards (Souque 1994: 5).

Developing a vision for education followed up on previous work by the CCE which identified the employability skills required of students by Canadian employers. A one-page profile (ESP) was developed and disseminated broadly. Here again, the link between education and the economy *and* a focus on the education side of the equation was emphasized. The connection between the CCE process of telling educators what employers want in a student and the NCE process of developing a vision based on 'matching education to the needs of society' is evident once we understand that the *needs of society equal the needs of certain employers* in this work.

The 1992 report by the Economic Council of Canada (ECC) reinforced the vocational role of schools. After documenting a crisis in education in terms of illiteracy statistics based on data from Statistics Canada, and student performance on the test of basic skills over time, authors suggested that Canada was lacking in terms of the importance placed on education's role in preparing students for work as compared with Germany and Japan. The report concluded that Canada's education and training systems must change if Canadians were to maintain their standard of living. The theme of crisis in education and a need to focus on reform was thus promoted by a number of sources through the CB as it attempted to 'build consensus that cuts across geographical boundaries and unites individual perceptions.'

The discourse of the unhappy parent, while not central to the CB, was promoted as it aligned with the discourse of dissatisfied employers. For example, Joe Freedman represented parents on a panel that was asked to respond to the NCE vision statement at the 1993 conference, and his Society for Advancing Educational Research (SAER) had a booth at this conference. Further, the presentation by American John Chubb drew attention to the potential alliance between dissatisfied employers and unhappy parents through the mechanism of increased educational choice. The concept of choice, when accompanied by increased standardized testing, heightens the market aspect of education and is presumed to pressure providers of educational services to increase their efficiency and productivity. Chubb's presentation lent legitimacy to recommendations around increasing choice in reports of the Economic Council of Canada (1992) and the Alberta Chamber of Resources and Alberta Education (1991).

Finally, the discourse of fiscal crisis of the state, while not central in the identification of educational problems, also influenced the type of solutions that were promoted. The CB's key idea of business-education partnerships provides a good example. The concept is based on the assumption that schools and businesses must share the task of preparing students for the twenty-first century. The role of business in working with local schools and taking on a larger role in educational reform is legitimated in this way. However, the CB supports the view that local school-business partnerships should involve the exchange of human resources rather than money. Partnerships are framed as a means of 'strengthen[ing] the culture of change' within schools and providing teachers as well as students with opportunities to expand their range of experiences (Souque 1994: 7–8). They are said to provide 'children with a window on the reality of life' (5). They also bring an awareness of the required link between investment and outcomes to education. For example, the CCE developed a 'value assessment process' (VAP) to be used by school and business partners in setting objectives and measuring outcomes. Bloom (1993: 2) provides a rationale for VAP as follows: 'The corporate economic imperative in difficult times further increases the need for help [provided by VAP]: companies cannot afford to invest in programs solely for a "warm fuzzy feeling." If it ever was, businesses' collaborative involvement with education cannot be regarded solely as a philanthropic or charitable activity.' This statement suggests that schools can learn from business how to become more effective through partnerships. Furthermore, this mechanism for change does not involve increased financial commitment by the state.

Other recommendations also emphasize increasing value for money in education rather than increasing government funding. For example, the CCE's employability skills profile (ESP) identifies the skills, qualities, and competencies that all elementary and secondary school students need to develop to meet employers' needs for productive employees (McLaughlin 1992). The marketing of this profile by the CB to schools provides a clear message of desired outcomes.[5] Similarly, recommendations around increased parental choice and an increase in market aspects of education encourage the state to shift its focus from ensuring equity in provision to ensuring that minimum standards are met and that competition is fair. The market, not the state, decides winners and losers in this construction. Discussion of the Third International Mathematics and Science Study at the 1993 conference repeats the message that the challenge for nations is to provide the most effective education system possible while containing expenditures. The focus on mathematics and science suggests a particular valuing of literacy in these subject areas. CB work overall signals that schools should focus on achieving outcomes that are related to workplace productivity as defined through partnerships with business. The predicted result is a more efficient and effective system.

The similarity between the discourses adopted by the CB and those adopted by different groups in Alberta (including some CB members) suggests that a unity of perspective has indeed developed. But it is useful to ask, as in Chapter 2, what is missing from this perspective and why? Quite simply, it appears that the voices of 'ordinary' teachers and students are muffled and those of organized labour and 'ordinary' workers are largely absent. As Slaughter (1990) suggests about the BHEF, the work of the CB draws educators into the hegemonic vision of the corporate community. The result is an exaggeration of educational crisis as perceived by employers and a lack of attention to the economic side of the education-economy equation.

The exaggeration of educational crisis is noted by several authors. Barlow and Robertson (1994) challenge the illiteracy figures presented in the 1992 Economic Council report, while the Canadian Teachers' Federation challenges the 34 per cent dropout statistic presented in the CB study (Lafleur 1992). More generally, Livingstone (1999: 167–8) writes: 'The claim that declining school quality is serving to depreciate human capital is typically made in terms of young people's falling performance on standardized tests. Such historical comparisons are often fraught with fallacy of composition errors of logic. That is, either average scores of entire current youth cohorts are compared with those of more restricted earlier enrolments, or specific bits of knowledge are used to argue an increasing general ignorance thesis. While most of these claims have now been systematically refuted ... they continue to be recycled in evermore selective forms ... In sum, the evidence does not show any cumulative general decline in the quality of education.' In contrast to the managerialist focus on what is wrong with schools, Livingstone argues that the more significant problem is the waste of human resources in the workplace as evidenced by the numbers of unemployed, overqualified, and underutilized workers.[6]

From a critical perspective, the solutions promoted by the CB and its allies represent attempts by large employers to reduce uncertainty during a period of rapid economic change by ensuring a supply of appropriately skilled labour that comes with guaranteed skills and attitudes. Solutions that emphasize students' employability skills, closer ties between business and education, and making education more efficient and flexible reflect these needs. However, if solutions also emphasize technocratic rationality, individualism, and economic values at the expense of broader societal goals around citizenship, social justice, and the common good, they may be problematic. The next section explores how the idea that 'what is good for corporate Canada is good for everyone else' has been promoted.

Mobilizing Support

> [T]hese employers as a group are only a small part of the whole. But they have enough profile that they can interest people and get some attention, and build up that broader support ... [W]e're trying to move towards change, we're trying to move each year, and ... move in a manner that's perceptible, by our members and by other people.   (Lawrence Grant, Conference Board of Canada)

In this candid statement, CB researcher Grant describes the role of the CCE in business-education conferences. 'Building broader support' and 'moving forward' in a perceptible way are evident in several CB initiatives around education. For example, initiatives that focus on building broad-based support include annual business-education conferences, consultations with 'stakeholders,' the presentation of annual awards for business-education partnerships, and the organization of summer institutes for teachers. With regard to moving forward, conference themes between 1990 and 1993 suggest a logical progression over this period from the construction of crisis to action.

The function of annual conferences, as acknowledged by the president of the CB, was to bring stakeholders together in order to develop consensus. The following comments by Mandy Thompson, a partnership coordinator from a school board in Ontario during a conference panel presentation on VAP at the April 1993 conference, indicate the success of this approach: 'The call for measuring outcomes has typically been cast as being part of the business agenda in this country. However that is changing. Bottom line considerations and the identification of learning outcomes are important goals in education. (Witness

that every provincial Ministry of Education is involved in assessing how to measure the outcomes of their education systems.) I believe that the dialogue between sectors that has resulted from partnerships has had an impact on this change. As
an example, I'm reminded of the power and potential impact of
the Employability Skills List developed by the CB. This mile-
stone in evaluation [VAP] represents an agreement on outcomes
by education, public sector, labour and business and it came
about as a result of partnering.' The construction of common
interests and goals among stakeholders is clearly a key part of
developing consensus.

A second strategy for broadening support involved the na-
tionwide consultations with selected participants organized by
the NCE (on a national vision) and CCE (on employability skills).
Participants in NCE-sponsored vision consultations were reportedly chosen 'for their leadership roles as practitioners and stakeholders in education' (Souque 1994: 1). However, the fact that
they were asked to comment on the vision developed by the
NCE as opposed to creating their own vision suggests that the
purpose of consultations was to 'test-market' the document rather
than to invite substantive change. As Grant comments: '[T]hey
have to sell it to the country. Otherwise, God, my room is full of
documents issued by groups that are well meaning and may
have good material in them, but they're just in my room, and in
everybody else's room but they're not being used. So, our little
"employability skills profile" was useful because it has been
used; it's all over the place and it's now getting used in making
changes. This "national vision" will have to be the same' (Interview 3). The 'selling' of the national vision is clearly the responsibility not only of NCE members, but also of the various stakeholders that they enlist through consultations.

The presentation of national awards for business-education
partnership represents a third strategy for developing broad-
based support. Awards sponsored by Stentor Canadian Network Management – an amalgamation of major telecommunications companies – have been presented at conferences since
1991. Describing winning partnerships, Florence Campbell, vice-

president and director of the NBEC, stated that the CB and sponsors expect the awards program to 'provide a year-round incentive for creating business-education collaboration and [to] become a key instrument for national leadership in educational reform.'[7]

Lawrence Grant spoke enthusiastically about the increase in entries over time and the spin-off effects of the awards, as follows: '[The judges] learn a lot about partnerships in doing it, and some of them have taken that and involved their own organizations. So there are several ways you can have ... spins from a program: the winners, yes, the press coverage of the winners; the judges themselves who are leading people, get them on side; and then build up support in the education system. And now we're finding that some of our winners, it's helping them get grants ... from granting bodies, or foundations or whatever' (Interview 3). The Canadian Chamber of Commerce distributed the 'call for entries' to its members Canada-wide, and more than 15,000 copies of the brochure were mailed to public education institutions in the country.

Grant's comments suggest that the reward structure for partnership awards has four effects: first, it raises public awareness of partnerships and corporate sponsors, and enlists supporters as judges; second, it promotes the development of a particular model of partnerships through the criteria that are developed (see Notes, Ch. 3, n 7); third, it promotes competition among educational institutions; and, finally, it calls for the transfer of the reward structure to other government and charitable funding institutions.

A final strategy for building broader support for CB ideas around education has involved developing 'strategic alliances' with teacher-training institutions. In 1993 such an alliance was developed between the CB and the faculty of education at Queen's University. The NBEC director's report for the second half of 1992 stated that the university was working with ministries of education in different provinces to identify 'exceptionally talented and motivated elementary and secondary school teachers,' who would explore ways of operationalizing the CB's

ESP within schools at a summer institute. Bloom (1994) notes that the Queen's model was modified by Laval University in the fall of 1993, and was to be used by the Toronto Learning Consortium in 1994. Lawrence Grant was hopeful that this model would be replicated by every faculty of education across the country, since, as he acknowledges, 'teachers are crucial' to change.

The faculty of education at Queen's University was involved in two other activities in 1993: a preservice course dealing with employability skills; and a new academic journal which was to include articles focusing on innovative business-education partnerships, curricular materials, and interviews with prominent educators and business and labour leaders (only one issue was published). Grant described these activities as consistent with the efforts of the CB, as follows:

> It's acceptable I think to set up a course [on employability skills] ... Right, so that's pre-service; then you have the summer institute, in-service, and then if you can find ways of keeping it going once [teachers] get back into service, you have a nice tri-partite, pre-, in-, and implementation. Which, if you took forty institutes with forty teachers, you're suddenly starting to see *significant changes of people* ... So this was a prototype. [The CB] doesn't usually get involved in things like this, but we really feel that it's important. And I also think another strategy, I've agreed to be [involved] in the new journal ... And the reason I did that was because I think you have to connect these things into a *strategic plan*, and to me, the plan has to be: you have an institute, you have a follow-up, you connect it to your conference, you support research that's tied into it, so that you're doing a lot of things that tie together to move towards a consistent objective' (Interview 3) [my emphasis].

The idea of tying things together and moving towards a consistent objective is evident also in the progression of conferences between 1990 and 1994. The first conference in 1990 set the frame for discussion by involving mostly Canadian speakers from business, education, and government, who told the audience what was wrong with education and provided a vision based on knowledge economy/human capital theory. The theme of the first conference could be described therefore as 'Sharing the Vision of Organic Intellectuals.' The second conference moved discussion from education in Canada to models of reform introduced in Britain, the United States, and other industrialized countries. Fundamental educational reform thus began to appear inevitable and models from elsewhere made Canadian proposals appear moderate.

The conference in 1992 was described by Lawrence Grant as follows: 'In the third year we were in Calgary and we focused on "creating advantage with people." It was trying to bring a little bit more attention to the notion that there was really a very strong serious economic aspect to this for this group of stakeholders to be aware of, and we were looking at what that meant for educational activities' (Interview 3). The focus on the economic was partly achieved through the CB report on the cost of dropping out and the Economic Council report. It was also achieved by a speaker who addressed the economic advantages of promoting diversity in the workplace. Roosevelt Thomas from the American Institute for Managing Diversity rationalized giving primacy to managerial goals by suggesting that discrimination made bad business sense and that affirmation action programs were ineffective. Therefore, while the conference theme was 'Creating Advantage with People,' it might have been subtitled 'Justifying Economic Rationality' as the basis for reforms.

The focus of the fourth conference in 1993 was 'Creating Strategic Commitment,' which moved participants from analysis of problems towards action. The director of the NBEC noted that while Phase 1 of business-education collaboration involved partners learning about one another, by Phase 2 the partners were more concerned about assessing results. The VAP was presented as a way of facilitating this process. The 'vision panel' reinforced the impression that consensus had been reached regarding the direction for change. The panel included a parent, a student, a teacher, and an employer; but it was clear that these participants were not chosen at random. The parent was Joe Freedman, the high school student was an articulate young woman from an upper-middle-class neighbourhood in Toronto, the teacher was involved in a winning partnership, and the employer was from the company that sponsored the partnership awards (Stentor). When asked how the panel was chosen, Lawrence Grant admitted they were atypical, suggesting that they were like a 'platonic ideal' of those stakeholders. His subsequent comments about the process of selecting conference participants are revealing: 'We set up a grid when we're doing this, and ... it's the usual Canadian problem. On the one hand, you have to balance the stakeholder groups, proportionally, according to how significant they are in this area. So education and business, then government, then the others. Then you have to say, where are the people from in the country? Then you have to say, what level are they in the system [elementary/secondary, post-secondary]? Then you have to say, what kind of rank are they?' (Interview 3). These comments indicate the care taken by organizers to develop a program that is strategic in furthering the goals of CB members.

Concluding Comments

Much has happened since the CB was asked by its members to focus on education in 1989. The organization has served as co-ordinator and a catalyst for educational change at the national level. It has engaged in the important hegemonic work of putting together an alliance of forces around a particular vision for educational reform, and recruiting popular support for that vision. This vision draws primarily on the discourse of education for economic prosperity (the dissatisfied employer), although discursive elements of the unhappy parent and fiscal crisis of the state are also present. It is a vision that fits well with the interests of corporations that wish to secure skilled, motivated workers and improve productivity without increasing their tax burden.

Ideologically, the main challenge has been to convince key stakeholders and the broader public that these interests are consistent with the needs of society as a whole. The extent to which discourses around employability skills and partnerships with business have been taken up within schools is one measure of success. Another is the extent to which governments have promoted – and the broader public appears to have accepted, however pragmatically – the view that increasing business-education collaboration produces a 'win-win' situation. Part of this acceptance is prompted no doubt by the neediness of schools that results from cuts to public education funding. What is striking about this ideological work is that it shifts our focus from the economic and social performance of corporations to that of schools without presenting a particularly convincing empirical argument that education is in crisis or that economic problems are tied to education. Nevertheless, a number of governments across Canada have jumped on the reform bandwagon.

Alberta has been and continues to be influenced by CB work – no doubt due to the relatively high level of CB involvement by corporations and government there. Discussion in Chapter 5 of the educational reforms introduced by the province in 1994 suggests parallels with the CB vision. One of five MLA implementation teams explored ways of increasing business involvement in education. In 2000 the NCE was co-chaired by Syncrude CEO Eric Newell. Alberta Learning, the super-department that resulted from the amalgamation of Alberta Education and Advanced Education and Career Development, in 1999, was a member of the NBEC, and several groups that have been active in bringing about business-education collaboration in Alberta were members of the CB's Employability Skills Forum.[8] For these players, the CB arguably plays a coordinating role; it legitimates and offers opportunities to build broader support for a corporate-driven vision of reform. The next chapter examines the economic and educational visions developed by the federal and Alberta governments and their connections with that of the CB.

CHAPTER FOUR

The Hegemonic Work of Governments

> As documents authorized by the government, based on 'objective' knowledge and representing consensus among important 'stakeholders,' policy reports produce powerful truths about the world in which we live, work and learn. (Kari Dehli, 'Subject to the New Global Economy')

A look at consultation processes and reports at federal and provincial levels in the early 1990s indicates that they are ideological and have potentially powerful effects. For example, talk about 'ordinary' Canadians and Albertans obscures the prominence of business stakeholders and the emphasis on the needs of capitals within reports. The active involvement of governments in achieving hegemonic settlement in the 1990s is therefore noteworthy. But we may ask why governments in so many Western industrialized countries have embraced neoliberal solutions in recent years. In England, the rise of Thatcherism has been linked to the breakdown of the postwar settlement and the need for the state to regain legitimacy in the midst of economic crisis. The move away from an interventionist welfare state and towards market forces stemmed from the need to address the crisis of accumulation and profitability (Larrain 1996). In North America, declining faith in public institutions in the 1970s and 80s has led to various types of 'reinvention' activities on the part of governments. In education, as in other areas of state provision, solutions that increase efficiency, competition, and accountability have been favoured.

Acknowledging these broader trends, there is a need for concrete analysis of political shifts in Canada. Two examples of consultation processes in the early 1990s provide the focus for the discussion that follows. The first is the economic visioning process undertaken by the federal government through its Prosperity Initiative. While education is a provincial responsibility in Canada, the role of education in the knowledge economy was a key theme in national discussions. The second set of consultations was initiated by the Getty government in Alberta around the same time and was called Toward 2000 Together (T2T). It too focused on economic visioning and involved consultations in various areas, including education. When policy documents produced through these two sets of consultations are read beside those produced by the Conference Board and other key stakeholders, the alliances among elites become apparent.

The Federal Prosperity Initiative

A number of other organizations and provincial governments have undertaken similar consultations, and results indicate that a consensus is building. In fact, many people have been struck by the similarity of most of the conclusions. This outcome should not be a surprise, given that in most cases an emphasis was placed on giving a voice to individual Canadians.   (Canada, *The Prosperity Action Plan*)

In October of 1991 Brian Mulroney's Progressive Conservative federal government established a Steering Group on Prosperity, composed of twenty task force members who were to give 'a voice to individual Canadians' and make recommendations about how to ensure Canada's future economic and social prosperity. The group was co-chaired by David McCamus and Marie-Josee Drouin. McCamus was past president and CEO of Xerox

Canada and a member of the CB's National Council on Education, and Drouin was executive director of the Hudson Institute of Canada. While the Steering Group described itself as a group of volunteers 'from a wide range of backgrounds' (Canada 1993), critics suggested it was 'stacked with business leaders and economists' (McQuaig 1995: 12). And while the Steering Group claimed that its action plan reflected the views expressed by thousands of Canadians, a Calgary labour representative had this to say:

[This discussion paper] comes out in September 1991. And all of a sudden, governments who would never return our calls and never invite us to the time of day – Brian Mulroney's cohorts, Michael Wilson and Bernard Valcourt, and our infamous Trade Minister – aren't their offices phoning me on a daily and hourly basis all of a sudden to convince us to come and take part in this Prosperity Initiative. And one has to attend these meetings here in Calgary at the Palliser [Hotel]. And two days before the meeting, you get a hundred page document that you're supposed to review, be very knowledgeable on, and establish your views at this. So reluctantly, with the wishes of my executive, I attended these meetings with Valcourt and Wilson. And right from the start we were misled. I was told there would be approximately eighty people at these meetings, of whom ten to fifteen would be from labour. When I show up, there's a grand total of ten people there and I am the token labour person at these meetings. The other people are there from the Alberta Chamber of Commerce, the Petroleum Club, the Alberta Chamber of Resources. You basically name it, all the old friends of Brian Mulroney and Michael Wilson. And it was a real sham ... All they wanted was you to attend the meetings so they can say 'we had consultations with labour.' But that Prosperity Initiative was nothing more than the corporate agenda, the free trade agenda, all wrapped up in a real glossy brochure from the government. (Interview 24)

These comments confirm the suggestion by Bowe, Ball, and Gold (1992: 10), that 'Who becomes involved in the policy process and *how* they become involved is a matter of a combination of administratively based procedures, historical precedence and political manoeuvring, implicating the State, the State bureaucracy and continual political struggles over access to the political process ...'

Though the above-mentioned labour representative suggests that his group was not well represented in consultations, business leaders and politicians appeared to be 'regulars' on each other's guest lists. At the 1993 business-education conference, Steering Group Co-chair McCamus discussed the work of the Prosperity Initiative, and Employment and Immigration Minister Valcourt gave a speech entitled 'Towards a Competitive and Self-Reliant Society,' which supported this work. The action plan lists several corporate members of CB education councils who submitted briefs during the Prosperity Initiative (Steering Group 1992: 70).[1] In a speech to the Canadian Learning Forum Feasibility Group on 26 May 1993, the Minister of Industry, Science and Technology (Michael Wilson) thanked the president of the CB for his work in 'ensuring that the vision of the Prosperity Action Plan gets put into effect.' For example, NCE consultations on a vision statement for education were undertaken in response to recommendations made by the Steering Group, and reports on the 'costs of dropping out' and 'assessing business-education partnerships' (using VAP) both acknowledge federal support. Given these overlaps, it is not surprising that reports shared common assumptions, visions, and recommendations regarding educational reform.

Three documents reflect key stages of the 'prosperity' process: the discussion paper *Learning Well ... Living Well* (Canada 1991); the action plan *Inventing Our Future* (Steering Group 1992); and the government's response to action plan recommendations (Canada 1993). The predominant vision emerging from reports is that of a competitive economy based on high-skill, high-wage jobs. The image of education in crisis evidenced by high dropout and illiteracy rates, poor student performance, and the lack of science and technology graduates recalls discussion of the CB in Chapter 3. Similarly, recommendations focus on results, clearer goals, standards, and accountability, and closer coordination between schools and the workplace.

The purpose of the discussion paper was to initiate a 'national, consensus-building discussion on targets and priorities for learning in Canada,' based on the view that 'Canada's learning performance is simply not good enough' (Canada 1991, S-1, S-3). Statements about foreign competitors who are 'outsmarting us' (S-2) in the drive to achieve an 'innovative competitive economy based on high skill, high-pay jobs' (V-2) suggest that assumptions of human capital/knowledge economy theory frame the discussion. This focus on education as a means to an economic end is rationalized as follows: 'It is also important to remember that, while competitiveness may be the force that is driving the pace of international reforms of learning systems, all forms of learning – whether directed to social, environmental, economic, cultural or intellectual goals – will benefit from those reforms' (Canada 1991: I-3). Giving priority to economic goals is thus assumed to have a trickle-down effect.

But despite the adoption of a discourse that links investment in education with outcomes, it is implied that current levels of government spending on education and training are sufficient. According to the discussion paper, a number of changes 'do not require increased expenditures at all, but greater awareness and a change in attitude on the part of users' (I-3). This presumption guides recommendations in the action plan, which emphasizes that since Canadians already spend more per capita on education than most industrialized countries, we need to take 'greater advantage of existing facilities and community resources' (Steering Group 1992: 52). This framing of problems and their causes within a vision of 'education for economic prosperity' that accepts the need for fiscal restraint, clearly limits the range of possible solutions.

The action plan presents a four-part strategy for building a strong learning culture in the country that has much in common with the Economic Council's (1992) *A Lot to Learn* report.[2]

Both recommended focusing more on results and strengthening linkages between schools and the world of work – ideas that appeal to both unhappy parents and dissatisfied employers. For example, the action plan wrote: 'Canadians believe that we have been putting too much emphasis on the manner of teaching and learning rather than on the acquisition of knowledge and skills' (Steering Group 1992: 36). The Steering Group recommends defining learning expectations nationally, developing indicators of performance based on Canadian and international standards, and adopting a competence-based approach to primary and secondary education. The federal government responded by providing funding: to establish a Canadian Forum on Learning,[3] to help coordinate the Third International Mathematics and Science Study (TIMSS) in 1994, and to support the development of indicators (SAIP) by CMEC (Canada 1993: 30). These initiatives, along with the Economic Council report, were highlighted at the CB's 1993 business-education conference.

The second element of the learning strategy aims to strengthen linkages between 'schools, other learning institutions and the world of work' (Steering Group 1992: 40). The action plan recommends greater use of cooperative education; job shadowing and school-business partnerships; increasing students' practical knowledge in the areas of mathematics, science, and technology; and giving teachers opportunities to spend time in other work sites as part of their professional development. The federal government responded by increasing funding to cooperative education programs and to school-business partnerships via the Stay-In-School initiative, increasing post-secondary scholarships for science, math, and technology areas, and promoting the Innovators in the Schools initiative.[4]

The third part of the learning strategy highlights technology as a means of improving learning, consistent with the 'knowledge economy' vision presented throughout. The Steering Group recommends expanding the number of computers in schools; training teachers to use computers effectively, making it easier for those with strong backgrounds in math, science, and technical subjects to become teachers; and incorporating technology into the design and delivery of education. Specific government actions involved distributing surplus computer software and equipment to schools across Canada, and providing awards for teaching excellence in science, technology, and mathematics.

The final strategic element concerned getting Canadians involved. The proposed Canadian Forum on Learning was charged with the task of leading an 'effective Canada-wide communications campaign' that would stress the importance of learning and its connection to collective economic success (Steering Group: 51). The discourse of education for economic prosperity must be sold to ordinary Canadians.

Elements of the action plan flow logically from the discussion paper frame, and were consistent with ideas expressed in the work of the Economic Council, and the CB, and other groups in Alberta. But while the discussion paper attributed this consistency to the emphasis of groups on 'giving voice to individual Canadians,' a more convincing argument is that the construction of policy discourses occurred in private arenas through social networks as well as in the more visible public arena of consultations and conferences. The people positioned as 'knowers' within reports tend to be elites (business leaders, politicians, and consultants); they had a hand in constructing the frame for discussion and consensus around it, while those positioned as 'social problems' had little access to this realm (cf., Dehli 1993). A look at the work of the Alberta government around the same time extends our understanding of how a particular vision for prosperity became dominant.

Toward 2000 Together

[Toward 2000 Together] was a huge exercise in bringing together the people of Alberta to write a new economic policy for the province. It took months. It gathered ideas from thousands of people. It included public meetings with a broad invitation list, and private meetings for a leadership elite. (Mark Lisac, *The Klein Revolution*)

In 1991 the Progressive Conservative government under Premier Getty launched Toward 2000 Together (T2T) with a discussion paper followed by a plethora of reports in 1992 and 1993. A thirty-one member Advisory Committee (similar to the Prosperity Steering Group) acted as coordinator – reviewing reports, presentations, and submissions and drafting an economic strategy. It was chaired by Hal Wyatt, a developer who held positions in almost a dozen corporations and foundations, and co-chaired by Don Simpson,[5] the director of the Banff Centre for Management. Kachur (1994: 274) writes that the Canada West Foundation also played a key role in T2T, for example, helping to prepare background information for the report of the advisory committee. Premier Ralph Klein released a pre-election economic strategy in response to recommendations from the advisory committee in the fall of the same year.

The Getty discussion paper claimed that the purpose of the process was to 'stimulate dialogue and to elicit valuable insights and opinions from all Albertans' (Alberta 1991: 1). However, journalist Mark Lisac (1995: 49) describes the process more cynically: 'Ideas suddenly seemed important in Alberta. The views of unelected people suddenly seemed to count. Cooperation and consensus seemed to be possible. It did not take long for the image to fray ... The department coordinating the gathering of ideas was already writing policy. It had apparently started sometime in late 1991, before the first public meetings for Toward 2000 Together were held. No one knew that until a leaked copy of the draft manufacturing strategy reached New Democrat members of the legislature that spring. In mid-March another signal arrived. The Education Department had collaborated with the Alberta Chamber of Resources on a study called "International Comparisons in Education."' Lisac's comments imply that the main function of T2T consultations was to manufacture consent for a particular vision rather than to stimulate dialogue. His mention of the ACR study suggests that this group influenced subsequent educational policy development,[6] just as the Economic Council and Conference Board played key roles in the federal initiative.

In addition to the similar organizational structures of the Prosperity Initiative and T2T, there were other overlaps. The moderator at the T2T Calgary conference referred to the work of the Prosperity Initiative. Steering Group co-chair David McCamus gave a presentation at this conference and stated, 'I was delighted with [Don Simpson's] report this morning because you would think that we were reading from each other's notes along the way' (Kachur 1994: 266). A representative from the Economic Council also spoke at the Calgary conference, while several delegates represented corporations that were affiliated with the CB. There were overlaps both in actual participants and in the types of people who participated. Most prominent were government and business leaders, intellectual experts, political insiders, and others who could afford the time and expense required to participate in the process.

The T2T process involved articulating the different components of a future vision and communicating that vision to Albertans. Like the Prosperity Initiative, priority was given to economic goals over other societal goals. A member of the advisory committee talked in an interview about the 'consensus-building' process that was followed within the group: '[Y]ou've also got to appreciate that there are many employers who were on that committee, and very successful entrepreneurs. And it became a dichotomy of approach between some of us and some of them, kind of thing. And often there's a compromise, and often because we got our point, they had to give up something. They got their point; we had to give something. So we tried to arrive at consensus. And to a certain extent, look at it from a strictly economic perspective, not a societal perspective' (Interview 37). This member's final comment suggests that the building of consensus occurred within a frame that had already constructed economic concerns as paramount. The difficulty in challenging this frame is exemplified by the actions of the executive director of the Alberta Association of Social Workers, who resigned from the advisory committee because she thought the 'report formalized and legitimized a business-dominated province where the poor and the damaged were expected to keep quiet and go away' (Lisac 1995: 55).

The assumption that economic growth is a precondition for achieving social goals is reinforced in T2T, just as in the Prosperity Initiative. The Getty discussion paper states: 'A strong economy will provide Alberta with the financial resources to take action in areas considered important, and to fund the programs and services that will enhance our quality of life' (Alberta 1991: 6). Since the private sector is seen as the engine of economic growth, a key role for government is to develop an infrastructure that is conducive to business. The role of government in capital accumulation is thus underscored and issues around social equity are subordinated.

Ralph Klein's pre-election strategy (Klein 1993) outlines ways of developing the 'Alberta Advantage' that include creating a competitive tax environment and simplifying the regulatory environment for business, examining ways of privatizing services that could be operated in the private sector more economically, fostering positive attitudes to entrepreneurialism, and supporting the development of a highly educated and trained workforce for jobs created by the science and technology expansion. The education system was seen as partly responsible for realizing the last two elements. However, developing highly educated workers was not to be accomplished through an influx of government funds, given concerns about spending.[7] The Getty discussion paper had warned that it would be necessary to 'make even more effective use of the limited resources in years ahead' (Alberta 1991: 9). In this context, reinventing government became key to the vision for prosperity.

The advisory committee recommended that health care, education, and social services deliver services more efficiently and cost-effectively through rationalization and restructuring rather than increasing public funding. Under 'what Albertans can do' to make the T2T vision a reality, two recommendations stand out: individual Albertans must reduce their expectations of what services government can and should provide, and they must become more self-reliant. A member of this committee elaborates this line of thinking: 'How do you prepare people within the educational system to fit into the changing world of economics, the world economy and so on? And underneath that is how you get people off social services into becoming people with a vision, with a sense of purpose. Giving them that motivation to make that decision that "I will be self-reliant." ... But I believe that if you create the environment and people have a sense of comfort that they can become self-reliant in that new environment, that they can help themselves away from social services into becoming a person who contributes to the overall economic prosperity or economic future of Alberta' (I-37: 4–5). These comments assume that jobs for all Albertans are either available or can be created, and that people simply need to become motivated to work.

There are ideological parallels between the Prosperity Initiative and T2T. Both visioning processes focus on the problem of economic competitiveness. Visions are based on an innovative competitive economy based on high-skill jobs, particularly in science and technology areas. To achieve this vision, individuals and the education system must take seriously the connection between education and economic prosperity and act accordingly. Ideally, this involves developing appropriate work skills, values, and attitudes, foremost of which are self-reliance and entrepreneurialism. The discourses, as David McCamus implies, are almost interchangeable at federal and provincial levels. At the same time, a comparison of Alberta and other provinces suggests some unique challenges.

The Alberta Economy

The economic base in Alberta developed historically around agriculture and petroleum. Boom and bust have characterized the economy since capital-intensive production processes typify these industries, a high degree of risk, and externally determined and highly variable prices and policies. Between 1961 and 1993 Alberta had one of the least stable regional economies in Canada (Mansell 1997). This was partly related to the fact that between 1946 and 1956 the petroleum industry became a key industry that impacted most sectors and regions in Alberta. The growth in this industry hastened urbanization and provided the basis for an increased managerial/entrepreneurial class. It also led to an economy characterized by 'a large primary sector that exports most of its output, an underdeveloped manufacturing sector, and an industrial sector based on providing inputs for the extractive sector or processing raw materials prior to export' (20).

In the 1970s, under Premier Lougheed, the province recognized the need for diversification and industrial development to break the cycle of boom and bust. But the question of how to diversify became critical. While the Lougheed government believed that the key to diversification lay in the private sector, governments in Alberta have been 'rhetorically laissez-faire but interventionist in practice' (20). For example, Dickerson and Flanagan (1995) note that expenditures on 'Industrial Development and Resource Conservation' between 1985 and 1993 under Premier Getty were three to five times larger per capita than in other provinces in Canada. Expenditures in this category included grants, loans, and various types of government support made to industries and individuals as incentives for expanding in the province. However, while some diversification has taken place in Alberta with the growth of forestry and manufacturing, the petroleum sector remained a key element of Alberta's economy in 1990, accounting for almost 20 per cent of GDP, about 30 per cent of total investment, 60 per cent of Alberta's exports, and 30 per cent of provincial government revenues (Mansell, 33).[8]

In terms of the labour force, Statistics Canada data from the 1991 census indicate that in Alberta approximately 12.8 per cent of the total labour force for all industries was employed in primary industries compared to 6.1 per cent for Canada overall. In juxtaposition, approximately 14.6 per cent of the Canadian labour force was employed in manufacturing compared to 7.6 per cent in Alberta (see Appendix B, Table 1). The Alberta Economic Development Authority reports that the province has the highest number of engineers per capita, almost two for every hundred Albertans in the labour force. Analyses of employment data published in 1992 'found Alberta to be the most volatile provincial economy, and indeed perhaps the most volatile in North America' (Chambers 1998). These data confirm the distinctiveness of the Alberta economy.

What implications does this have for the economic visioning process that took place in Alberta through Toward 2000 Together? First, it allows us to better understand the province's attempts to accommodate the interests of representatives of traditional primary industries (agriculture, forestry, resources) while also encouraging diversification through the development of high-technology industries. Like Thatcher in Britain, the Klein government presented a vision of the future that was rooted in the past – a vision described by Hall (1988) as 'regressive modernism.' Second, the traditional dependence of the Alberta economy on agriculture and petroleum industries potentially explains the government's emphasis on the distinctive Alberta values of *self-reliance* and *entrepreneurialism* throughout the visioning process. Mansell (1997: 22) suggests that the development of the petroleum sector 'simply enhanced the basically rural conservative values of rugged individualism, risk-taking, entrepreneurship, and a unique mix of self-reliance and co-operation.' While this probably overstates the values held in common by Albertans, the government adopts this construction of the mythic Albertan in justifying its course of action.[9] Third, the tendency of Alberta governments to be *laissez-faire* rhetorically but interventionist in practice highlights a tension in Advisory Committee recommendations where Albertans who are dependent on social programs are asked to reduce their expectations of government while certain industrial sectors continue to benefit from public spending on industrial development. The historical disjuncture between policy and practice and the differential treatment of different groups is noteworthy. Similar tensions are evident when we examine Alberta Education's vision for education.

The Vision of Alberta Education

In the early 1970s, the commissioners who recorded their vision for education in *A Future of Choices, a Choice of Futures* (the Worth report), identified two choices for Alberta society.[10] The first involved the transition from a 'first-phase industrial society' to a 'second-phase industrial society' and the second involved the transition to what they describe as a 'person-centred society' (Alberta 1972). The authors argued for the latter choice as follows:

> The central question involved in a choice between our alternative futures is this: will the traditional values and beliefs that have brought us to the present point of technological and economic development continue to work in the decades ahead? The evidence is mounting that these traditional values are not serving us well. Economic disparities, inequality of opportunity, unemployment, crime, serious threats to the environment, social unrest, alienation, powerlessness of the individual and loss of a sense of community are already facts of life. These and other problems forecast earlier ... will become more severe in the future, and there is good reason to assume that they will not be solved within the context of present values. Along with other social ills they can, in large part, be attributed to traditional values, which emphasize economic goals and technological advance without regard for their costs and consequences to the individual, society and the environment. (33)

Related to more recent discussion in education, the report contrasts the *traditional* view that schooling should produce the skills that are needed by the economy with a more *person-centred* view that schooling should provide students with skills that help them develop their own sense of personal worth and competence (182). Consistent with the latter, the Worth Report recommends the abolition of grade twelve departmental examinations since such standardized tests 'inhibit learners, restrict teachers, perpetuate corrosive and artificial subject and program distinctions, and subvert the meaningful goals of education' (206). Authors also recommend action to ensure that all students have educational opportunities, including those who have been disadvantaged because of their socioeconomic status, gender, age, race, and physical ability.

Twenty years later, the 'second-phase industrial paradigm' better describes government policy. In 1991 Education Minister Jim Dinning produced a plan of action as part of T2T entitled *Vision for the Nineties*. Progress reports were released by Dinning in 1992, and his successor Halvar Jonson followed in 1993 by outlining the steps taken by the department towards achieving this vision. *Vision for the Nineties* was based on the view that Alberta's education system was 'good, but not as good as it could be or must be' (Alberta Education 1991: 1). The familiar refrain of 'education for economic prosperity' was heard again: 'Education is key to our young people being full partners in shaping a global future – in shaping our province's and our nation's future. Business and community leaders, parents and people from all walks of life are saying that if we want to be able to compete in the world of the future, we need to lay that groundwork now. And that groundwork comes from an education system that is second to none' (1).

The vision assumes that the economic changes brought about by globalization, technological innovation, and an expanding knowledge base necessitate educational reform, that changes must focus on 'goals, results and accountability' and require the efforts and energies of new partners – business, industry, media, and the professions – as well as traditional partners (2). More specifically, Dinning envisioned Alberta students as being 'at the top on national and international test results,' the dropout rate decreasing by 10 per cent, a 'three-fold increase' in students choosing careers in science, all schools having 'dynamic partnerships with businesses and other community groups,' greater financial equity across schools, and improved success for Native, immigrant, and disabled children (4–5).

The government's shift in priorities away from the early 1970s vision of a 'person-centred society' is striking. Despite mention in the vision of improving the chances of success for Native, immigrant, and disabled children, equity issues appear to be lower on the priority list than other issues. First, goals related to increasing equity for disadvantaged groups receive less space – in the thirty-nine-page report released in 1992, two pages each are devoted to success for Native and immigrant children compared to four pages that discuss ways of promoting 'excellence in science' and three devoted to 'challenging our most capable students.' More importantly, pages devoted to improving science achievement and challenging 'gifted' students tend to be more specific, to state targets and timelines, and to commit resources compared to those dealing with Native, immigrant, and disabled students.

For example, in the section entitled Success for Native students, the phrase 'continuing to' in five of six of the actions listed suggests that it is business as usual in this area.[11] To better meet the needs of immigrant and disabled students, recommendations focus on better coordination and integration of programs across government and community organizations. In contrast, science facilities in Alberta schools are to be upgraded to support programs: '[F]rom 1991 to 1994, school facility capital projects will upgrade 43 schools in 27 jurisdictions and build two new high tech senior high schools to improve delivery of science courses' (Alberta Education 1992: 33). The department also promises to support school boards that wish to establish 'magnet' science schools for their jurisdictions. In 'challenging our most capable students' Alberta Education promises to work with business, professional, communities and school boards to 'establish public and private specialized schools in Alberta that provide more opportunities for students to develop their strengths and talents in a variety of areas of study' (29). The lower priority given to the needs of historically disadvantaged groups of students is clear.

This discrepancy between 'priority areas' continues in the subsequent report (Alberta Education 1993a). Adopting a new format, the report presents feedback from stakeholders to help measure the progress made on different initiatives. Surveys with graduates, parents, teachers, trustees, superintendents, and post-secondary instructors are a key source of data. But while the purpose is ostensibly to communicate more and better information, certain initiatives continue to take precedence over others. For example, when asked about the 'preparation of Native students for citizenship, the workplace, and post-secondary education,' close to half of the survey respondents in each group could not respond to this question. The same groups had a 30 to 40 per cent non-response rate when asked the same question about immigrant students, and between 25 and 33 per cent did not respond when asked about disabled students.

However, there was no mention of non-response for other items where information was clearly sought with more rigour. In the 'excellence in science' section, the results of six focus groups that explored students' perceptions and attitudes towards science and technology are provided (59). Progress reports also indicate the department's interest in the views of employers. The report released in 1992 refers to *Senior Executives' Views on Education*, a survey commissioned by Alberta Education (Meanwell and Barrington 1991). The 1993 report refers to *International Comparisons in Education*, co-produced by Alberta Education and the Alberta Chamber of Resources. These examples suggest greater involvement by some partners than by others.

The government's rating of its progress in priority areas provided in reports released in 1992 and 1993 confirms this sense of differential treatment. Policy areas receiving a 'fair' rating in the report released in 1992 were Native children achieving success in school, immigrant children achieving success in school, fiscal equity across school boards, and students staying in school. A year later, the rating for students staying in school had improved to 'good,' but other areas continued to be rated 'fair.' The issue of fiscal equity was directly addressed in the three-year business plan in 1994, unlike issues concerning Native and immigrant children. In contrast, both progress reports rated 'excellence in science' and 'challenging our most capable students' as 'very good.'

Consistent with the priority given to economic goals, Alberta Education reports echo the Prosperity Steering Group's action plan in several ways. First, there was increased interest in results. *Vision for the Nineties* devoted six pages to student performance on standardized provincial achievement tests, diploma exams, and international tests. A year later, the department promised to update provincial assessment programs, continue to support national assessment instruments (e.g., SAIP), and implement a province-wide information system to track student participation and progress in school (Alberta Education 1991).

Second, both Prosperity and Alberta Education visions recommend strengthening links between school and work. Following the CB, Alberta reports promote the importance of partnerships. The 1992 progress report refers to companies that are helping implement technology in Alberta classrooms, while the 1993 report highlights models of business-education partnership. Alberta Education also sees a more active role for business and industry in curriculum decisions and standard-setting in order to prepare students to 'compete in a global economy' (1992: 11). A specific initiative is the development of a Career and Technology Studies (CTS) curriculum designed to keep students in school while preparing them for careers in 'highly skilled and technical fields' (12). Business was to be a key player in the development and delivery of different CTS strands. These ideas were later expanded and formalized in Alberta Education's *Framework for Enhancing Business Involvement in Education* (1996a).

Concluding Comments

Both federal and provincial policy reports from the early 1990s frame political initiatives in terms of changing economic requirements. But does the similarity of conclusions suggest that a democratic consensus developed across sites? McQuaig (1995) suggests that business leaders and economists were overrepresented in the Steering Group on Prosperity, while Lisac (1995: 53) observes that the cross-section of Alberta society represented at Toward 2000 Together's Calgary conference 'seemed to favour close-cropped hair and blue suits.' The conference moderator noted with regret that the conference 'had not included enough women, minorities, environmental groups, or people "from the less privileged sectors of society"' (55). The example of the Advisory Committee member who resigned suggests that there was little tolerance for those who held dissenting views even when they were present. These perspectives suggest that rather than promoting consensus through a democratic process, governments manufactured consent through selective consultations with economic and political elites.

Prosperity and T2T consultations and reports reflect hegemonic alliance between political and business leaders, formed around the assumed link between education and economic prosperity. The tactics of putting together a dominant alliance of forces, forming solutions to capitals' educational needs, and recruiting public support for these solutions are evident in vision reports, just as they are in the reports and activities of the Conference Board, discussed in Chapter 3. The consultations and reports orchestrated by governments legitimized the hegemonic work of such groups by producing 'truths' based on the discourses of educational and fiscal crisis and neoliberal solutions. The effect was the shifting role of government from regulation and redistribution towards developing the conditions for capital accumulation. Interviews with participants in later chapters indicate the extent to which these political visions had entered everyday discourse and became common sense.

But while parallels between federal and provincial processes and themes are apparent, Alberta's vision is also shaped by its unique economic, political, and social context. In attempting to lower public expectations while cutting funding, the government appealed to values of self-reliance and hard work that characterize the mythical Albertan. The vision of a high-tech future had to be balanced against the traditional interests of agriculture and resource sectors. The interests of the latter were particularly well-represented in the political sphere. As Frank Dabbs notes in his biography, *Ralph Klein: A Maverick Life*, the coalition of Klein supporters included land developers and oil explorers, and, more generally, 'men in high positions in business [who] had a great deal to gain in personal wealth from the success of fiscal reform' (see Newman 1998: 440; Dabbs 1995). The cause of restructuring was aided by the fact that the opposition Liberals also adopted the discourse of fiscal crisis in the 1993 election campaign.

The fact that Jim Dinning was Education Minister in the early 1990s is also of political note since he later became treasurer in the Klein government.[12] More than one education representative suggested in interviews that Dinning was critical of education groups and frustrated by what he was able to accomplish during his tenure as minister. This is relevant because of the key role played in 1994 by Treasury in setting the budget agenda and establishing three-year business plans for departments. Senior officials in Alberta Education indicated in interviews that they 'had the basic elements of a reform package in place for some time, but were frustrated by their inability to move forward with the changes' (Kneebone and McKenzie 1997: 203). These comments suggest that Dinning had a great deal of influence on educational reforms both during his term as minister and during his subsequent term as Alberta treasurer.

So what were the main components of the government restructuring and restraint foreshadowed by T2T and announced by the Klein government in 1994? These were outlined in a response from Klein to the Canadian Manufacturers Association during his leadership bid in 1992, as follows: reduce the number and size of government departments; decrease overlap and regulation; privatize some government operations; maintain low taxes and perhaps even lower corporate tax rates; reduce the deficit by cutting expenditures; and encourage economic development by supporting key business projects, attracting international investment, linking education more directly to employers needs, and upgrading resources in traditional industries (Lisac 1995).

Education reforms were part of this broader agenda. As in other departments, there were calls for fundamental change in the roles and responsibilities of government and other stakeholders. Special priority was given to increasing the roles of industry and of parents. Alberta Education became more involved in setting standards, allocating resources, coordinating partnerships, and disseminating results. Greater efficiency and flexibility were to be achieved by amalgamating school boards and introducing charter schools. Funding cuts resulted in job losses within the department and in local jurisdictions. Chapter 5 examines in greater depth the response of education stakeholders and the introduction of reforms.

CHAPTER FIVE

Restructuring Education, 1993–1995

> [E]ducation minister Gary Mar is doing it [building] in the new education system, not the old one. It is an education system that demands high standards, and is monitored through detailed performance measurement: a system that gives more say to the teacher and the parent, and less to the administrator; a system that ensures equitable funding for a student regardless of where he or she lives in Alberta; and an education that guarantees a student an equal opportunity, not an equal outcome. In short, we are building an education system that will make our kids better prepared, to be more competitive, in a world that demands excellence.   (Ralph Klein, in Mackay and Flower, *Public Education*)

In this way, Premier Klein summed up the educational restructuring of the previous three years at a breakfast meeting of the Calgary-Elbow Progressive Conservative Association in 1996. A similar speech could have been given by other political leaders – Prime Minister John Major in Britain, Minister Roger Douglas in New Zealand, or, later, by Premier Mike Harris in Ontario. The sharing of information across jurisdictions and the similarity in the types of individuals and groups involved is part of travelling policy tales (cf. Dehli 1996). But how these tales are taken up in different contexts differs.

This chapter focuses on the period between 1993 and 1995 in Alberta – from just before government restructuring announcements and the release of the three-year business plan for education to the implementation phase. The key argument is that the 1994 business plan represents the culmination of the hegemonic work of dissatisfied employers and unhappy parents. However, even as educational settlement was achieved, it became clear that it would be contested. News reports provide evidence of struggles among and between educational stakeholders and the government. Discussion in this chapter thus moves from the features of educational settlement based on the work of allies discussed in earlier chapters, to the initial responses of other stakeholders and possibilities for counter-hegemonic work, explored further in subsequent chapters.

Reporting of Events in Alberta, and Public Opinion

The writing's on the wall. And following next week's provincial roundtables, the face of education in Alberta will be changed forever.   (Lisa Dempster, *Calgary Herald*, 10 October 1993)

[T]he contents [of the government's seventeen business plans] ... will take weeks to digest, years to implement, and perhaps a decade to prove beneficial or damaging as Alberta is pushed into the post-deficit era.   (Don Martin, *Calgary Herald*, 25 February 1994)

These newspaper excerpts announce significant political changes beginning with the government roundtables in the fall of 1993 and continuing with the release of three-year business plans by departments in the spring of 1994. The increased media interest in education is evidenced by the fact that a database search yielded 101 education articles in the *Calgary Herald (CH)* in 1994 compared with fifty in 1993 and twenty-four in 1992. Since newspapers are a major source of information for the public, this section begins with the story that emerged from 170 *CH* articles collected between the fall of 1993 and the spring of 1995.

Education became increasingly politicized during this period as journalists relied on what Winter (1992) calls 'authorized knowers' to frame and support their stories. Since a variety of groups also tried to use media sources to influence and mobilize public opinion, journalists and reporters played a key role in the public relations wars that were waged as government policy unfolded. This role involved highlighting conflict, identifying and/or constructing protagonists and antagonists, and making sense of events for the lay reader.

The week before the government-sponsored education roundtables in Calgary, *CH* reporter Lisa Dempster wrote, 'Hot lunches. Kindergarten. French immersion. Health and gym classes. The amalgamation of hundreds of school boards into regional superboards. Every possible facet of education is up for discussion, on the table for change ... But not everybody is convinced the quality of education is uppermost in the minds of their elected officials, who have vowed to wring $369 million out of the provincial education budget over the next three years' (10 October 1993: B2).

Basic Education Roundtables were organized by Alberta Education to 'consult' with Albertans. The department issued invitations to 240 educational stakeholders to attend meetings held in Calgary and Edmonton in mid-October. The roundtable workbook suggested that a key issue for discussion involved how to cut 20 per cent ($369 million) from the education budget (Alberta Education 1993c).

The Alberta Teachers' Association and the Alberta Home and School Councils Association (AHSCA) objected to the exclusivity of the government roundtables and to the fiscal mandate, and organized their own consultations across the province. Approximately 1,500 people were involved in alternative roundtables held in Calgary on 27 October 1993. On the same day, a student rally to protest potential cuts to programs was staged in front of the provincial MacDougall Centre, involving 3,000 students from across Calgary. Other student protests across the provinces followed. The premier responded by suggesting that teachers had rallied students against the government and threatened to invoke the Truancy Act to enforce attendance.

On the Saturday following the alternative roundtables in Calgary, the ATA and the AHSCA organized a public forum attended by approximately 2,000 people. As public concerns began to be voiced, contradictions in the messages from politicians became evident. The premier and education minister continued to publicly confirm the planned 20 per cent cut to educational funding outlined in the workbook, while Treasurer Jim Dinning suggested that the cuts would unlikely be that high. The public would have to wait until the release of the budget in the new year to find out what the actual figure would be.

On 17 January 1994 Premier Klein outlined his budget-balancing plans in a televised address. The next day a government release described in greater detail the restructuring of education that was to take place. Planned changes included a budget cut of 12.4 per cent, the province assuming full responsibility for education funding (previously shared with municipalities), reducing the number of school boards from about 140 to 60, appointing superintendents at the ministry level, cutting kindergarten funding in half, and introducing charter school legislation.

The media response was immediate, as this 19 January *CH* article by Don Martin indicates: 'The powerful school board of today will become merely the caretaker, bus driver and middle money manager of the near future ... [Fiscal equity measures are] designed to scoop money from wealthier urban boards and share it with struggling rural districts. The rural Tory powerhouse is a happy camper tonight ... [Charter schools]: Don't like your local school? Want only academic topics or tougher discipline? Well, find enough like-minded parents and teachers, petition for a charter and the province's per-student funding is yours ... A system of powerless trustees, partisan senior officials and part-time or user-pay kindergarten was not the future envisioned by the public.'

The response of educational stakeholders soon followed. On 24 January 4,000 people attended a meeting organized by Calgary Catholic school trustees to protest the government's decision to administer all education funding. Public school trustees in Calgary soon joined in the fight against the government and held their own public meetings. Over the next few months, this struggle would escalate with members of the educational establishment and the government exchanging criticisms and threats. A notable media event, reported by Alberts and Johnson of the *Calgary Herald*, on 21 May 1994, was the resignation from the Conservative party of David King, director of the Public School Boards Association of Alberta (PSBAA). King had been minister of education in the Lougheed government between 1979 and 1986, and quit the party in 1994 over amendments to the School Act along with other concerns over the government's 'style of politics.'

January 1994 saw the launching of the ATA's $500,000 public awareness program against cuts to education.[1] According to Dave Pommer, writing in the *Calgary Herald* on 11 February, the newspaper and television campaign was designed to 'educate Albertans about public education so they recognize the value of the system and will speak up to defend it,' according to the ATA president. The association was also reacting to proposals from the Tory caucus designed to erode the union's control, which included splitting the ATA into professional and bargaining organizations and introducing province-wide bargaining.[2] The premier had already announced that he would be reducing provincial grants to school boards by 5.6 per cent and expected teachers to accept a wage rollback. However, when the ATA attempted to strike a deal with the government by offering to encourage teachers to accept the rollback in exchange for a 300-day moratorium on further cutbacks, it was rejected. The battle between the ATA and the government was a popular theme in media reporting during this period.

In March of 1994 Alberta Education's three-year business plan detailed the restructuring plans for education. Five MLA teams were established to assist in the local implementation of different parts of the plan. By this point, media focus had shifted to the local level with the release of school board budgets for the 1994/5 school year. According to Ron Collins of the *Calgary Herald* on 9 March, the Calgary public board's proposed budget estimated that it would have $33.7 million less in government grants for this period. It called for $48 million in spending cuts and estimated a loss of 525 jobs, assuming that employees agreed to a 5 per cent rollback.

In April of 1994, 800 Albertans were polled about proposed changes to public education (Angus Reid 1994). Of those polled, 68 per cent indicated they were aware of changes to the education system and 67 per cent of these felt that changes would have a 'somewhat' or 'very' negative effect. When asked about the amount of change and the speed of change to public education, 55 per cent felt there was too much change and 63 per cent felt that changes were being introduced too fast. Sixty-eight per cent felt that there was not enough input into education changes. The public was clearly becoming concerned about government actions in this area.

The Amended School Act (Bill 19) was tabled in the legislature at the end of March and provoked renewed discussion over the control of education. As reported by Lisa Dempster of the *Calgary Herald*, supporters of Catholic schools organized a rally in Calgary that was attended by more than 7,000 people, with thousands of others participating via satellite linkups with Edmonton, Lethbridge, Medicine Hat, and Red Deer. The purpose was to 'pass around a collection plate to help fund their looming [court] battle with the government' over its right to collect and distribute all school funding. After a number of failed attempts, a deal between Catholic board members and Tory caucus members was reached which allowed Catholic boards to opt out of the centralized provincial education fund without financial loss. However, as reported by Dempster and Jeffs of the *Calgary Herald* on 27 May, when Bill 19 received royal assent on 25 May 1994, the Alberta School Boards Association (ASBA) announced its intention to launch a court challenge over 'unfair and discriminatory amendments to the school act.' In subsequent court challenges, public school boards questioned the special treatment given to Catholic boards and to all boards opposed to the reduction in municipal autonomy represented by the provincial government's decision to collect education tax funds. A decision on the PSBAA case in November 1995 (later appealed) stated that the amended School Act violated the guarantee of treating public and Catholic school boards in the same way, and therefore public boards must also be allowed to opt out of the centralized fund without financial penalty. The matter was still before the courts in early 2000.

While trustee organizations were launching their fight to regain control of education funding, teachers across the province were fighting to limit wage rollbacks. In negotiations between the Calgary Board of Education (CBE) and the ATA, the trade-off between wages and job security was reported by Dempster on 12 April 1994: 'Contract talks begin today to hammer out a new deal for Calgary's 6,200 public school teachers – just two days after their Edmonton colleagues joined the stampede of Alberta locals accepting wage rollbacks ... Edmonton's 4,200 public school teachers agreed Sunday to take a five percent pay cut to save threatened teaching jobs.'

This managerial way of framing the issue continued when teachers rejected a two-year deal with the CBE on 12 May. According to Dempster (13 May), 'Defiant Calgary public school teachers have rejected a wage rollback proposal that would have saved almost 300 teaching jobs ... The vote makes Calgary public teachers one of the last major holdouts in Alberta to refuse a wage cut ... New collective agreements are already in place for the board's 800 workers represented by the Canadian Union of Public Employees and 2,000 staff association workers. Both groups have agreed to five percent rollbacks.' It was later reported that the teachers had been asked to take more than a 5 per cent pay cut. However, the teachers' 'holdout' was short-lived. On 14 June Calgary teachers narrowly voted to accept a deal that would see a 4.5 per cent reduction in wages and a reduction in benefits over two years. It was reported that despite the deal, 180 probationary first year teachers would not be rehired by the board in the fall.

News reporting between the fall of 1994 and spring of 1995 focused mainly on the work of MLA implementation teams in consulting and reporting recommendations in the various areas of the three-year business plan for education. Coverage again highlighted conflicts between stakeholder groups and the government. For example, on 11 April 1995, Lisa Dempster writes: 'Meanwhile, a fractious battle between public school trustees and Calgary MLAs over education issues may finally be coming to a head. Trustees have asked for a meeting "to discuss our respective roles as they relate to schools" ... MLAs have complained that the two school boards are trying to block them from getting the government's message across to local schools.' Parent groups and the ATA had also been involved in conflicts with MLAs over the implementation of the three-year plan.[3]

At the beginning of the school year in 1994, the links between provincial cutbacks and impacts on Calgary classrooms began to be reported. There were stories about families unable to qualify for kindergarten waivers, parents' frustrations over increased user fees, and increasing pupil-teacher ratios. By September the number of school boards stood at seventy-one, through voluntary amalgamation, and the number of trustees had been cut from 1,000 to 435. Charter school proponent Joe Freedman also hit the news, in a report by Lisa Dempster, with his proposal to use a public school for a three-year research experiment featuring teacher-directed instruction, in an environment 'free from control by the local school board and the ATA.' To make the offer more attractive, Freedman had secured more than $465,000 in funding from the federal government and corporations such as the Royal Bank, the Bank of Montreal, and Syncrude. But although he approached the Calgary Board of Education, among others, with his plans, they were unable to reach agreement.[4]

After much delay, regulations for charter schools were released in April 1995. A charter school was defined as a public school operating within or outside a school board under a specific set of rules or guidelines drawn up by an interested group. Education Minister Halvar Jonson predicted that four charter schools would open in September. As it turned out, five schools opened in 1995 and another three in 1996. Four of the eight schools were in Edmonton, three in Calgary, and one in Medicine Hat. By January 1998 eleven charter schools had been approved in the province, but two of the eleven were closed in the spring of that year by the minister of education because they failed to meet legislated conditions (Mackay and Flower 1999).

Clearly, education reporting in the *Calgary Herald* between 1993 and 1995 focused on struggles between stakeholder groups, especially between the governments and the educational establishment. While it is difficult to determine the effect of this reporting on public opinion, the *Calgary Herald* reported the results of an Angus Reid poll conducted in Calgary in September 1995 which indicated concerns about the impact of changes in education. Sixty-seven per cent of respondents saw the impact of changes on the quality of education as negative while only 26 per cent saw these changes as positive. Forty-one per cent said the quality of education in city classrooms was worse compared to the previous year while 36 per cent said they were the same, and only 7 per cent said they were better (16 per cent did not know).

A more general opinion survey of approximately 1,000 adult Albertans had been conducted a few months earlier by Archer and Gibbins (1997). They found that while 80.8 per cent of respondents supported the government's goal of eliminating the deficit, 54.3 per cent felt that the government's pace of deficit elimination was too fast. In addition, 56.6 per cent felt that the cuts to primary and secondary education were too big. Interestingly, when asked to pick 'winners' and 'losers' resulting from the budget-cutting exercise, the only clear winner chosen was 'big business.' Approximately 60 per cent saw children and teachers as 'losers.' Therefore, despite the high approval rating for the Klein government overall, education continued to represent an area of public concern over reform policies.

Table 5.1, below – borrowed from Mackay and Flower (1999: 73) and updated for 1998 and 1999 – presents findings from Angus Reid polls between 1994 and 1999. We see that while the number of respondents who thought the government was spending too little on education was only 31 per cent in 1994, it had grown to 70 per cent by 1999. These figures suggest that opposition to this aspect of educational settlement has steadily increased.

TABLE 5.1
Selected Results of Angus Reid Education Polls, 1994 to 1999

Education Spending	1994 (%)	1995 (%)	1996 (%)(%)	1997 (%)	1998 (%)	1999 (%)
Spending too much	19.0	5.0	3.0	3.0	3.0	3.0
Spending right amount	41.0	35.0	26.0	27.0	29.0	22.0
Spending too little	31.0	52.0	62.0	65.0	60.0	70.0
Unsure	9.0	8.0	9.0	5.0	2.0	5.0

Source: Mackay, Bauni, and David Flower 1999. *Public Education: The Passion and the Politics*. Edmonton: Authors.
Note: Updates for 1998 and 1999 were provided by David Flower (personal communication, February 2000).

The Roundtables and Alternative Roundtables

Media representations tell a story of controversy and struggle that informs this analysis of government restructuring. But it is also important to explore some of the key educational events within the context of other reforms. The consultations held in the fall of 1993 and the business plan for education released in the spring of 1994 provide the focus for such an analysis.

The first of the government roundtables was a Budget Roundtable held in March 1993 to determine how to address the deficit. Journalist Mark Lisac (1995) describes it as a refinement of Toward 2000 Together, and asks whether the purpose was to find out the views of the mostly corporate and professional leaders in Alberta who participated or to enlist support for a government agenda that had already been set. Mansell (1997: 51) implies that it was probably a little of both, in his comment that the outcome of the Budget Roundtable confirmed the popularity of an 'aggressive approach to the deficit much as was suggested by the growth in support for the Reform Party and the Canadian Taxpayers Association.' This first roundtable set the stage for those that followed.

Subsequent roundtables were held to determine how to cut budgets in the areas of education and health. Bruce, Kneebone, and McKenzie (1997) suggest that these meetings were held both to reaffirm to the government that the public was generally supportive of deficit elimination and to co-opt special interest groups such as trustees and teachers into the decision-making process. Lisac (1995) focuses more on the ideological process and effects, stating, 'Officials and cabinet ministers controlled invitation lists. They controlled the agenda. They controlled the information booklets normally sent out to participants ... Control was built in at every level. What this structure did was create a mythic voice of Alberta – a united, one-dimensional Alberta' (144–5).

Government-sponsored roundtables on education were held in Calgary and Edmonton in October 1993. While the stated purpose was to talk about the future direction of education in Alberta, the proposed 20 per cent spending cut framed the roundtable workbook produced by Alberta Education. Within this fiscal framework, roundtable participants were asked to discuss what should be offered to students as part of a basic education; how education should be funded; how the results of the education system should be assessed to ensure quality, effectiveness, and efficiency; and how services should be delivered to students (Alberta Education 1993c). Quotations from *A Lot to Learn* (Economic Council 1992), *Reinventing Government* (Osborne and Gaebler 1992) and *Tough Choices* (Alberta Education 1993b) were scattered throughout the report. *Tough Choices* was produced from consultations held in August–September of 1992 with fifteen municipal leaders, school board administrators, and businesspeople, along with half a dozen other representatives of education groups. The stated purpose was to examine the fiscal challenges facing the education system.

The *Tough Choices* report appears to have provided the framework for the roundtable workbook. It supports the theme, also present in the roundtable workbook, that a fundamental restructuring of education is required. Recommendations from *Tough*

Choices found their way into the workbook as topics related to funding (defining and funding a basic education, linking funding to results, distributing funding through a voucher system), roles and responsibilities (amalgamating school boards, changes to legislation), and more flexible delivery of education (year-round education, differentiated staffing, assistance from the private sector). Thus, the parameters for roundtable discussion and for subsequent reforms had already been established through previous consultations with a more *select* group of stakeholders. This confirmed the feeling voiced by roundtable participants that 'the government had already made essential decisions about what programs to cut' (Alberta Education 1993d: 3).

Roundtable results were communicated in a report, *Meeting the Challenge* (Alberta Education 1993d). Most participants resisted the idea of identifying programs and services as 'basic.' Several expressed concerns about the constraints of limited time and information as well as the deficit-reduction mandate. In terms of funding cuts, it was felt that 'the quality of education must be preserved, the issue of fiscal equity must be addressed, and cost-savings should occur in areas furthest away from the classroom' (9). Report recommendations include: ensuring equal access for all students, increasing decision-making at the local level, looking for alternatives to cutting education spending, expanding the use of technology, exploring new ways to provide classroom instruction, and involving parents and the business community more in education. Since the workbook was framed in terms of increasing the efficiency of the education system, these recommendations are not surprising.

If roundtable participants in general were sceptical about whether their input would be considered seriously by government, representatives of teachers and parent groups were particularly concerned. As a result, the ATA and the AHSCA sponsored *alternative roundtables* across the province, which took place a short time after the government roundtables in October 1993. The ATA workbook for alternative roundtables was entitled *Challenging the View* in response to the government's *Meet-*

ing the Challenge workbook. While the welcome from Education Minister Halvar Jonson in the government workbook begins from the premise that there is a need to cut education spending, the welcome from the president of the ATA begins: 'The talk [about deficit reduction] currently centres on spending cuts as the only way to solve the problem ... It is time to begin talking not about cutting education funding but about what kind of a public education system Albertans wish to see in the future. The issue has become one of values and has implications much broader than simply balancing a provincial budget (ATA 1993a: 3).

The ATA workbook, like that produced by Alberta Education, then goes on to identify questions for discussion, including:

What is a basic education?
Is the main purpose of public education to prepare students for the workforce?
How can the current public education system be made more efficient?
What are the costs of underfunding public education?
Are we prepared to pay for an efficient public education system?

These questions and the accompanying background information try to reframe debates over education in Alberta by arguing, on the one hand, that education is investment and not an expense, and on the other, that there is more than one way to reduce the deficit. Quotations from *USA Today*, the *Globe and Mail* and *Fortune* magazine suggest that educational problems reflect broader social problems which have been 'dumped on [schools] by social agencies and parents' (ATA 1993a: 18). The need to invest in education is supported using a report by the Child Poverty Group in Edmonton stating that 'for every dollar spent on Head Start, five to seven dollars are saved later in remedial education, criminal justice, and welfare costs' (20). The workbook goes on to juxtapose Alberta's 'attack on funding' with the more moderate deficit-reduction approaches of other provinces. Quoting a report by two economists at the University of Alberta, which proposes a more balanced approach to deficit-reduction, the ATA message is that there are alternatives to the emerging agenda of the Klein government.

The alternative roundtables report reflects the different framing of issues. The social and economic costs that result from underfunding and privatizing education are emphasized. The report argues that education funding must be maintained if the country is to remain competitive in a global, information-based economy. In support of this view, roundtable participants indicated a willingness to pay higher taxes or to support other revenue-generating activities by government.

Government and ATA roundtable workbooks provide an interesting juxtaposition. Both were ideologically constructed to provide questions and background information that encouraged participants to focus on very different aspects of educational debates. Workbooks therefore engage in a degree of 'push-polling' of participants. The roundtable process ultimately represents a battle over public opinion – which group could claim to represent more Albertans. The ATA argued convincingly that public opinion was not aligned with a 20 per cent cut to education funding, and it organized a consultation process that was more open and potentially inclusive than that undertaken by the government. At the same time, since alternative roundtables occurred *in response to* the government workbook, it was impossible to ignore the government frame. Both workbooks focus on the economic importance of education, albeit with differing conclusions. The government workbook argued that education cuts were necessary for fiscal stability and competitiveness in the longer term, while the ATA workbook argued that the government must maintain educational funding in order to ensure future labour force competitiveness. The government's adoption of a reinvented human capital theory – also adopted in Prosperity Initiative and Toward 2000 Together documents – was challenged by the ATA using the human capital theory associated with expansionary economic policy in Canada during the 1950s and 1960s. We later see this tension reflected in public opinion where data indicate majority support for deficit reduction at the same time as cuts to education are viewed with ambivalence (Archer and Gibbins 1997).

Despite Education Minister Halvar Jonson's assertion that the roundtable report would play 'an important part in our planning and budgeting for education in the months and years to come' (Alberta Education 1993d: preface), there are discrepancies between the roundtable report and the three-year business plan for education released a few months later.

Government Restructuring and the Three-Year Business Plan

The book *A Government Reinvented* (Bruce, Kneebone, and McKenzie 1997)[5] helps to place education reforms with the government's broader restructuring agenda. Interviews with politicians, civil servants and bureaucrats, and various other stakeholders in Alberta inform the authors' analysis of Alberta's deficit elimination program. Authors argue that the forces that came together in Alberta to permit fundamental change included (1) the perception of fiscal crisis; (2) the presence of a relatively centralized, hierarchical political system able to move quickly; (3) strong and determined leadership; (4) the basic elements of reform prepared in advance; (5) an electorate that is receptive to change; and (6) an opposition that is fragmented (Kneebone and McKenzie 1997: 201).

Discussion in Chapters 2 to 4 presents some of the elements of educational reform, and argues that groups beyond Alberta promoted them. The construction of educational crisis and the development of reform solutions were taken up by the Alberta government in alliance with Joe Freedman, Albertans for Quality Education, the Alberta Chamber of Resources, Chambers of Commerce, and the Conference Board of Canada, to name a few. Efforts to obtain popular consent were made through the Prosperity Initiative, Toward 2000 Together, and, later, through government roundtables. There were also struggles over the direction of reforms as exemplified by the alternative roundtables. However the plan that emerged favoured the unhappy parent/dissatisfied employer alliance. Alberta Education's three-year business plan for education therefore represents a point of hegemonic settlement in education.

The discourse of fiscal crisis was fundamental to this settlement. Politicians in particular felt that a large cut was required to force structural change, and after being convinced that the government was serious about reform, most bureaucrats reportedly 'bought in' as well (Kneebone and McKenzie 1997: 204). Funding cuts gave politicians and bureaucrats the excuse to restructure and implement pet reforms. Conservative party members and the party caucus were also firmly behind cuts and reforms. Given the history of Tory dominance in Alberta since the early 1970s, it is not surprising that the party had the apparatus in place to move quickly once decisions were made. In addition, Premier Klein and Treasurer Dinning provided strong leadership. Interviews with ministers and MLAs confirmed that Klein's leadership style was crucial in maintaining the party's resolve during the budget-cutting process, while Dinning pushed ministries to make structural changes as well as spending cuts. Treasury played a key role in setting the budget agenda and establishing performance measures and three-year business plans (Kneebone and McKenzie 1997).

Another element that facilitated government action was the preparation of basic reforms in advance. Interviews with bureaucrats and senior officials confirm that the basic elements of a reform package for education were in place before 1992 (Kneebone and McKenzie 1997). This supports the view that the government roundtables were held more to manufacture consent and gauge the strength of resistance than to consult with various stakeholder groups. The growing public awareness and acceptance of the discourse of fiscal crisis undoubtedly had made the electorate more receptive to the restraint and restructuring promised by the Klein Conservatives. But while the 1995 public opinion poll undertaken by Archer and Gibbins (1997) did indicate general public support for deficit reduction, the majority of respondents also felt that cuts to education were too large and they had concerns over specific reforms.[6]

Therefore we cannot assume general support for educational reforms and cuts. More to the point is the suggestion that opposition has been fragmented. The fact that the provincial Liberal party also ran on a platform of deficit elimination in the 1993 election campaign made it difficult for them to oppose government cuts later, while the New Democrats' complete lack of representation in the legislature after the 1993 election presented a major obstacle. Aside from political parties, Kneebone and McKenzie suggest that the civil service and teachers, among other groups, have 'not been able to mount rigorous opposition to the changes' and have been 'remarkably passive in the face of widespread wage cuts and lay-offs' (1997: 204). However, interviews with representatives of education groups found that they were *not* passively accepting government changes. Mackay and Flower's (1999) documentation of ATA activities between 1993 until 1998 suggest this group sustained its opposition to several aspects of educational reform. But, admittedly, while the attempt was made by labour and social activist groups to develop a 'common front' to oppose government restructuring, its effectiveness in changing the government's course was limited.[7]

In retrospect, we see that a number of elements came together to form the terrain on which a new politics could be developed in Alberta. The roundtables were followed by the budget process, whereby each department was required to justify to Treasury why it should not face cuts in funding of 20 per cent or more. Four Standing Policy Committees were introduced by Ralph Klein to oversee the government's sixteen departments. These committees monitored and reviewed government policy and encouraged 'horizontal competition and policy diffusion' across ministries, since all MLAs were assigned to a committee (Kneebone and McKenzie 1997: 196). Another change introduced by the Klein government was the introduction of three-year business plans for departments to encourage longer-term fiscal planning and performance assessment. Each department and agency was asked to establish measurable performance indicators as part of its three-year plan. The themes of measurable outcomes and accountability were therefore to guide reforms in all departments.

Alberta Education's 'business plan' was released about a month after the provincial budget announced a cut of 12.4 per cent in education funding in February 1994. A key message of the plan was that funding cuts would not cause a decline in educational quality provided that other reforms were introduced at the same time: 'We can provide the quality education our students need despite reduced resources by restructuring the education system. This means setting a strong provincial direction for education, reducing layers of administration and allowing schools and their communities to make decisions that directly benefit students ... By making the system more efficient and accountable, savings can be redirected to the classroom' (Alberta Education 1994a: 3). This message is reinforced a number of times throughout the twenty-page plan.

The keywords of restructuring were *efficiency, accountability,* and *choice*. Although focus has tended to be on cutbacks at the local level, the number of people employed at Alberta Education declined by almost 60 per cent between 1992 and 1998 (Peters 1999). The cost of services provided by the department also decreased by almost one-third. Education funding was centralized and a new framework that would help equalize funding across school boards was introduced.[8] While the new framework did distribute funds more equitably, urban boards were particularly hard hit by the redistribution that took place, in part because of their disproportionate numbers of students with special needs and those studying English as a second language – since provincial grants tend not to cover the actual expenses of educating these groups (Alberta Education 1998). The funding formula directed boards to reduce spending on administration and capital by specifying how much money could be spent in these areas.[9] Boards were also encouraged to move towards school-based budgeting and decision-making. Superintendents were to be appointed jointly by school boards and Alberta Education, and the number of boards was to be reduced by more than 50 per cent.

These actions reduced the power of school boards and seemed to contradict the idea of greater local autonomy. Alberta Education's attempts to steer at a distance are partly explained by the department's distrust of school boards. For example, a senior bureaucrat expressed the concern that 'cutting grants to boards without controls would result in certain boards simply "offloading onto taxpayers" by increasing local taxes' (Kneebone and McKenzie 1997: 189). The department's solution was to reduce significantly the ability of boards to raise money through local taxation.[10] Directing how boards could spend funds also prevented them from protecting the administrative area and downloading budget cuts to the classroom level.

While power was being taken away from school boards, individual schools were gaining budgetary autonomy through school-based management. Greater parental choice and involvement in schooling were encouraged by charter school legislation, the removal of local attendance boundaries, and mandatory school councils. Business people were also to have more say in education as the roles of Alberta Education, business and educators were redefined: 'The province will define acceptable and excellent standards of student achievement. Business will be a key player in defining the specific learning requirements of industry. Schools, school jurisdictions and the province will audit and report on the full range of student learning' (Alberta Education 1994: 6). The goal of public accountability was to be achieved by redefining roles and responsibilities, establishing standards, and measuring results.

Five MLA teams were established by the minister of education in March 1994 to assist in the implementation of the different components of the three-year business plan. These were to address the amalgamation of school boards, the new funding framework, redefining roles and responsibilities, developing performance measures, and improving business involvement and technology integration. Teams were to refine the business plan and make recommendations through further consultations with stakeholder groups. By 1996 all of these teams had completed their work and reported findings and recommendations.

Despite talk of further consultations, the direction for government reforms had been set. Increased *efficiency* was encouraged through greater provincial control over board spending as well as mandated reporting of board spending compared to the provincial average (Alberta Education 1995). Accountability was encouraged through the development of a province-wide student information system, increased standardized testing, and the involvement of 'partners' in developing standards and expectations for schools. Standardized reporting of results, open boundaries with funding following students, and charter school legislation encouraged competition among schools. As Bruce and Schwartz (1997: 392) note, few provinces in Canada have 'more avidly' received the message of the Economic Council report, *A Lot to Learn*, than has Alberta.

The Effects of Restructuring

> By the middle of 1994 Alberta was a society splitting nearly in half. The myth of a united voice on the province – a silent majority talking to members of the government in the privacy of roundtables – could not stand up to close examination. The only way it could be made to stand up was to tell dissenters they did not count: they were whiners, they were out of touch with reality, they were defenders of stale privilege, they were selfish special interests. They were not real Albertans ... [T]he lack of debate over specifics meant there could be only two options for anyone who cared. The only subject left for debate was the idea of the revolution as a whole and the only arguments were Yes and No.
>
> (Mark Lisac, *The Klein Revolution*)

The Klein government's approach to restructuring did result in increased social polarization. Within education, the government's redefinition of its *policy community* raised the status of 'consumer' groups (e.g., Joe Freedman, business groups) and diminished that of 'producers' (e.g., teachers' unions, schools boards) (cf., Ball 1990). Journalists played a role in the public relations wars that were waged as different groups claimed to represent the *public interest*. An Angus Reid poll found that 31 per cent of

Albertans mentioned education as an important issue on the public agenda in the spring of 1994, compared to 10 per cent at the beginning of 1993.

As ex-Minister Roger Douglas from New Zealand advised, the Klein government 'stayed the course' despite challenges from public sector workers and the broader public. Part of this agenda involved downsizing government. In his first four months in office, Premier Klein eliminated 1,800 full-time government jobs and reduced his cabinet from twenty-six to seventeen members (Laird 1998).[11] The September 1993 budget plan called for a decrease in program expenditures of almost three billion dollars or a decrease of 21.7 per cent over four years (Mansell 1997). Accounting for population growth and inflation, this translated into a decrease in real per capita program spending of 27 per cent (McMillan and Warrack 1995). In addition to downsizing government, the Tories reinvented government in ways that were consistent with the Canada West Foundation. This included rationalizing and restructuring departments, introducing greater discipline through performance measures and legislation,[12] privatizing 'non-core' areas and introducing competition into 'core' areas, decentralizing decision-making, and generally lowering public expectations about government-provided services.

Some of these elements appear in the three-year business plan for education. But the role of government within quasi-markets was problematic. For example, there appeared to be a tension between decentralizing decision-making through school-based management and stronger school councils while centralizing funding to boards and reducing their autonomy in budgetary decisions. There was also a contradiction between government attempts to introduce competition through open boundaries, funding following students, and charter schools, while trying to coordinate and ensure public accountability. Commenting on the Alberta model, Trebilcock (1997: 213) suggests that such tensions were evident across government policies: '[Kneebone and McKenzie's] description of these institutional changes [in government] suggests some significant measure of confusion as to the respective roles of competition and co-ordination among the decentralized institutions, or to put the issue another way (following Albert Hirschman), the respective roles of exit (choice) on the part of citizens (the discipline of competition) and the role of voice on the part of citizens in holding these public-sector institutions accountable for their performance.' He concludes that more careful thinking is required as to 'the respective roles of competition and coordination, and citizen choice and citizen voice, in publicly financed or operated institutions,' since these had not been clearly worked out in the policies of the Klein government.

Reforms designed to make schools more responsive to business and parents are certainly not unique to Alberta. In his introduction to a 1992 White Paper, British Prime Minister John Major comments that 'Our reforms rest on common sense principles – more parental choice, rigorous testing and external inspection of standards in schools; transfer of responsibility to individual schools and their governors ... and a common grounding in the key subjects' (see Chitty 1992: 89). Magnet schools, charter schools, and voucher systems have been introduced in different areas of the United States. Within Canada, the Tories under Premier Harris in Ontario followed Alberta in centralizing education funding, significantly cutting government funding, amalgamating school boards, and increasing provincial testing in the mid-1990s. In 1997 the introduction of Bill 160 – which centralized significant areas of decision-making and authority and restructured the work of secondary school teaching – led to protests by 126,000 Ontario teachers.[13] The government also cut millions of dollars from the education budget. Governments in New Zealand and Australia have also introduced education reforms towards the privatization, rationalization, and marketization of schooling (Spaull 1996; Douglas 1993). Reforms in Western industrialized countries more generally in recent years have emphasized the local management of schools, markets, and choice programs, and increased use of large-scale student assessments.

Concluding Comments

> The 'business plan' of Alberta Education outlines the most com-
> prehensive changes ever introduced to a provincial education
> system. It promises that the reforms will 'substantially alter the
> character of the education system, ushering in an era in which
> "schools and businesses can work in partnership with parents
> and the community" to "ensure our competitiveness in a global
> economy."'   (Maude Barlow and Heather Jane Robertson, *Class Warfare*)

The plan included budget cuts along with centralized funding,
amalgamation of school boards, mandatory school councils, legislation permitting charter schools, and other vehicles for increasing parental choice, site-based management, and increased
reporting and standardized testing. Reform keywords were standards, accountability, and choice.

The business plan arguably represents educational settlement.
While Kneebone and McKenzie accurately identify some of the
forces that facilitated the Klein government's restructuring between 1993 and 1995, they tend to ignore national and international influences. For example, the hegemonic work undertaken
by the federal Progressive Conservative government in the Prosperity Initiative and corporate leaders through the Conference
Board, as well as the work of the Alberta Chamber of Resources,
Joe Freedman, Andrew Nikiforuk, and Albertans for Quality
Education informs our understanding of educational restructuring in Alberta. Models from Britain, New Zealand, Australia,
and the United States should also be acknowledged (Whitty,
Power, and Halpin 1998). Solutions in Alberta and elsewhere
have been neoconservative in their emphasis on traditional values and neoliberal in their emphasis on a revised human capital
theory that draws simultaneously on the discourses of education for economic prosperity and the fiscal crisis of the state.
Reformers joined forces and became partners in formulating
and disseminating their vision for education. The objective of

this ideological work was to achieve internal consensus, draw in potential allies, and convince both politicians and the public that action must be taken.

In Alberta the government was receptive for several reasons. First, there was an ideological affinity between conservative politicians and the alliance of dissatisfied parents and employers. Key politicians such as Ralph Klein, Jim Dinning, and Stockwell Day[14] managed to 'unite the right' and manage tensions within the Conservative party, perhaps because of the neoliberal/neoconservative alliance that had formed. Therefore, the vision promoted by unhappy parents and dissatisfied employers has been consistent with the broader restructuring agenda being developed by the newly elected Klein government. Second, Alberta historically has been a 'corporate' province in its blurring of lines between business and politics (Newman 1998). Finally, certain bureaucrats had been frustrated in achieving their own agendas and were receptive to opportunities that might bring them to fruition. These factors help explain government actions in this period.

While Chapters 2 to 5 focus on the hegemonic work that led to educational restructuring in Alberta, hegemony involves struggle and is never complete. Chapters 6 to 10 therefore explore the different responses of stakeholder groups, including business people, teachers, trustees, administrators, parents, and community representatives. Interviews with these individuals demonstrate that reforms to education and their underlying assumptions were not universally accepted.

CHAPTER SIX

The Corporate Alliance

The Corporate Alliance

Chapters 2 to 5 acknowledge the role played by business in educational reform discussions at national and provincial levels. Evidence suggests that business people were key players in achieving the education settlement reflected in Alberta Education's three-year business plan. Of course, increased business involvement in education is not restricted to Alberta. A booklet by the Canadian Chamber of Commerce (1990) suggests that although business leaders tended to be distant from schools in the mid-1960s to the late 1970s, they later began re-establishing connections in order to bring about educational change. They were particularly motivated by projections of a shortage of the skilled labour needed for the development of a 'high productivity, high wage economy' (Canadian Chamber of Commerce 1990: 3). In recent decades in the United States we see evidence of this renewed interest in the work of the Conference Board of Canada, the Business Roundtable on Education, and the National Alliance of Business, as well as the growing interest in 'adopt-a-school' and work experience (e.g., tech prep) programs. In Britain, the Technical and Vocational Education Initiative (TVEI) was introduced as a pilot project in 1983 to 'stimulate work-related education, make the curriculum more relevant to post-school life, and enable students to aim for nationally recognized qualifications in a wide range of technical and vocational subject areas' (Chitty 1992: 29). The goal was a differentiated secondary curriculum that would prepare students for their different places in the workforce.

In Alberta, interest in the vocational role of education has also grown. Concerns over the futures of non-college-bound youth were partly addressed in 1989 with the development of a registered apprenticeship program (RAP) for high school students and a new practical arts curriculum. This new Career and Technology Studies (CTS) curriculum was later introduced as part of the three-year plan in 1994. A growing alliance between business and education leaders is also evident from the 1991 *International Comparisons* study (co-sponsored by the Alberta Chamber of Resources and Alberta Education), the 1991 survey of senior executives co-sponsored by the Alberta Chamber of Commerce and Alberta Education (Meanwell and Barrington 1991), the references to business models and partnerships within 'Vision' reports in the early 1990s, and, finally, in the three-year plan itself. The fact that one of the five implementation teams ('I-teams') established to carry out the plan was the team on 'business involvement and technology integration' confirms that it was a key component of the plan.

This chapter explores the response to the business plan by members of what could be described as a 'business-in-education' network in Calgary. The first theme focuses on the interconnections and tensions within the network. Since participants in this network interact with each other and have been involved in discussions around educational reform at the provincial and federal levels, we might expect a high level of inter-group political cohesion. Interviews with participants suggest that this is the case. However, there are also divisions, based in part on participants' location within the network and within different types of organizations. A private school operator may have somewhat different interests in education than an executive with a large petroleum company. To some extent participants and groups are competing for recognition within the government's policy community. The second theme examines the solutions to educational 'crisis' suggested by participants, and their response

TABLE 6.1
Business Participants

Dan Williams, Alberta Chamber of Commerce	March 1994
Jennie Thompson, small-business person	May 1995
Andrew Markham, Monarch Corporation [oil and gas sector]	April 1994
Gary Baldwin, Panorama Corporation [oil and gas sector]	September 1994
Mike Popiel, [partnership foundation]*	February 1994
Andrea White, [science foundation]*	May 1995
Lawrence Grant, Conference Board of Canada	July 1993

* Pseudonym.

to government actions. There is evidence that although participants generally are favourably disposed towards government restructuring, they are concerned that the cuts to education funding may be too great. If so, business may be called upon to compensate for deficiencies. The final theme explores the roles played by different participants in achieving educational settlement. Participants were involved in educational reform as strategists, emissaries, organic intellectuals, brokers, and cheerleaders.

Interview Participants

Seven participants in the 'business-in-education' network within Calgary were interviewed. Some attempt was made to include representation from diverse organizations in terms of type, size, and industry sector. Table 6.1, above, lists interview participants by pseudonym, affiliation, and date of interview.

Dan Williams is an administrator of a private educational institution in Calgary who is prominent in educational and business circles in Calgary. He was involved with the Chamber of Commerce provincially and locally, was on the board of a local school-business partnership foundation, and was cited regularly in popular and business presses such as the *Calgary Herald*, *Alberta Report*, and *Calgary Commerce*. The second participant, Jennie Thompson, had been a supervisor for just over a year with a small manufacturing company based in Calgary. Before this, she worked briefly as an elementary school teacher in

Calgary. At approximately twenty-five years of age, she was noticeably younger than the other participants.

Andrew Markham is an executive with a large corporation in the oil and gas industry in Calgary. He was also on the Corporate Council on Education of the Conference Board of Canada and his company, Monarch,[1] was partnered with a local high school. Gary Baldwin is an executive with Panorama, another large Calgary corporation in the oil and gas industry, with several connections to the education system. Baldwin's boss, Joseph Sanders, had worked with a local school board and with the Calgary Chamber of Commerce and was also on the Conference Board's Corporate Council. Sanders's involvement with the *Employability Skills Profile* led him to take an interest in developing a system-wide initiative, which was coordinated by Baldwin. Chapter 7 provides a more in-depth look at the Monarch partnership and the Panorama employability skills initiative.

Mike Popiel is a high school teacher who was seconded to a business-education partnership foundation a year after its formation in 1992. The foundation, is located in the building of one of the organization's sponsors – a medium-sized company in the oil and gas sector in downtown Calgary. Popiel is included in this discussion of the Calgary 'business-in-education network' because, according to the foundation's business plan, one of its goals was to 'increase the active involvement of the business community in the activities of the Calgary and area school board.' A former trustee and teacher, Andrea White, represents a provincial science foundation located in a downtown Calgary office building. The science foundation, an example of a provincial partnership funded by provincial and federal governments and the private sector, was the brainchild of oil executive John Smith, whose company housed the partnership foundation. Smith chaired the science foundation between 1991 and 1995. Like the partnership foundation, the science foundation sees itself very much as an organization that promotes business-education partnerships. Information about this organization stated that the foundation could partly respond to the 'need to develop a more enriched, competitive economy in a future in-creasingly dependent on science and technology.' The foundation was described as 'a change agent in popularizing the need to change the economy' and helping to bring about that change.

The final participant, Lawrence Grant, was introduced in Chapter 3 as a researcher with the Conference Board of Canada, an organization whose members include the 100 largest corporations doing business in Canada. It is worth noting that five of the seven participants are male and all participants are white. This proportion of women is higher than in the survey of business executives, where it appears from the list of names that sixty-two males and only three females (4.8 per cent) were interviewed (Meanwell and Barrington 1991).

Our Network

Interviews support the idea that a business-in-education network existed in Calgary, which served to facilitate the development of an ideologically consistent view of problems and solutions in education. This network also encouraged business people to collaborate on educational reform initiatives. Despite the Calgary focus, the activities of interview participants for the most part transcend the local level because of their national and international connections. We might therefore expect that similar and overlapping networks exist in other Canadian cities. An examination of how the network has been defined in terms of insiders and outsiders provides a sense of the alliances that have developed. In keeping with the notion that hegemony is never complete, tensions within this network are also explored.

Insiders and Outsiders

Key insiders in the business-in-education network are connected with the Conference Board, Chambers of Commerce, and/or the Alberta Chamber of Resources in ways that deserve mention. The CB's influence in education stems largely from its ability to bring together key leaders from business, education, and government across the country. As well as provincially and nationally, this influence can be seen at local levels where affiliation with the CB legitimates participants' membership in local business-education networks. In Calgary several of the CB's corporate affiliates are partnered with local schools and/or have a system-wide presence in education. As mentioned, of my seven interview participants Gary Baldwin's boss and Andrew Markham are members of the CB's Corporate Council on Education, while Lawrence Grant is a researcher with the CB. Markham explains his involvement with the CCE as follows: 'Well, [Monarch] is a national company. And maybe because I've lived in other parts of the country and I've lived outside of the country, I'm adamantly opposed to regional, parochial points of view. And maybe that's why I don't participate at the provincial level, and choose to stick at the broader level. I don't like parochial[ism] or regionalism' (Interview 23).

Although Markham states that he 'doesn't participate at the provincial level,' he later noted that he had been part of a provincial group that looked at whether Alberta should establish a labour force development board in the early 90s, and was invited to the government's education roundtables in the fall of 1993. But Markham's view that his interests transcend provincial boundaries is noteworthy.

The local partnership and science foundations also have connections with the CB. A public school administrator who was prominent in the CB's National Council on Education was also a key player in forming the partnership foundation. It was established to promote the partnership concept at a system level by seeking out potential business partners for schools, encouraging business-education dialogue, and providing an organization through which business could supplement the educational resources of Calgary and area schools. Six of the eleven foundation board members were from business, as were the president and treasurer. At the time of my interviews, the foundation's board and executive included at least four representatives of companies affiliated with the CB. Foundation representative Mike Popiel had participated in the business-education conferences organized by the CB, as had Andrea White of the science foundation. White also mentioned participating in activities of the CB's Corporate and National Councils. In 1996 the CB presented a National Award for Excellence in Business and Education Partnerships to the partnership foundation.

Participants also have connections with Chambers of Commerce. There was evidence of mutual support between the Calgary Chamber of Commerce and the local partnership foundation since the president of the local chamber was on the board of the partnership foundation and Mike Popiel from the foundation had done some education work with the chamber. At the national level, connections between the Canadian Chamber of Commerce and the CB were acknowledged by Lawrence Grant, who commented that the chamber's education committee helped the CB market its business-education conferences. Grant suggested that the collaboration between the Chamber of Commerce and the CB would encourage smaller businesses to become 'connected to some broader plan' for education. Again, the potentially mutual benefits of this alliance were stressed.

Another key player in educational reform in Alberta is the Alberta Chamber of Resources. It will be recalled that the ACR cooperated with Alberta Education to produce the 1991 *International Comparisons in Education*, a study initiated by Joe Freedman. Also, in the early 1990s, the ACR piloted an initiative to encourage non-college-bound students to consider careers in the trades, which led to the partnership called Careers: The Next Generation that included government, educators, and employers. By 1998 twenty communities across the province were participating in this industry-driven, private-public partnership and a CNG foundation had been established. This foundation took on the role envisioned for the career education foundation that was recommended in Alberta Education's *Framework for Enhancing Business Involvement in Education* (1996a).

Although interview participants were primarily located in Calgary, a number of connections with the ACR were evident. First, the companies represented by Baldwin and Markham were among the 130 resource companies that belong to the ACR.

Second, Andrea White mentioned the mutual support expressed by key people within the ACR for the science foundation. Third, the CNG initiative was showcased by the Alberta Minister of Advanced Education and Career Development at a CB business-education conference. Fourth, in July 1998 a representative from the partnership foundation suggested to me that his organization is supportive of CNG, and that he networks with that organization.

As well as their connections to national and provincial business groups, interview participants overlapped in terms of their knowledge and involvement in one another's organizations. As mentioned, Dan Williams was on the board of the partnership foundation. The partnership and science foundations collaborated on a 'teachers in business' project where teachers were to update their skills in a business setting. Andrea White had served on the board of the partnership foundation. Andrew Markham's company had financially supported the partnership foundation, while Gary Baldwin's company was collaborating with it on an employability skills project. His company had also supported the science foundation financially.

The preceding discussion provides a sense of some of the 'insiders' in the Calgary business-in-education network, and suggests that this alliance is based in part on individuals' affiliations with particular business groups that are involved in education reform (locally, provincially, and/or nationally) as well as the personal links that have developed through a recognition of mutual interest and potential benefit. Interview participants also acknowledged the political activities that draw like-minded people together in an effort to expand their sphere of influence. For example, oil executive and prominent Calgary businessman John Smith was mentioned as a key player in both partnership and science foundations. Smith's assistant was elected as a trustee in 1992 and then as an alderman in 1995. Similarly, Mike Popiel ran for alderman in a previous election. Trustee Marcia Jensen describes Smith's sphere as follows: '[Science foundation person Andrea White] used to be [a trustee] and ran as mayor. And [John Smith] hired her for the [foundation]. If you look at its funding, very political kind of funding. Then he has [his assistant] run as trustee. Then he had a person run as alderman out of his office, one of our partnerships people ... And [John Smith] is super conservative, I mean, he's a Progressive Conservative party person' (Interview 30). 'Whether or not the individuals in this network have overt political affiliations or not, they appear to share a particular perspective about problems and solutions within education, as we will see. They also share, to some extent, a particular view of outsiders.

For example, while business executives generally had no qualms about being associated with the Conference Board of Canada, they were less willing to be associated with prominent parent reformer Joe Freedman. When asked to comment on Freedman's activities, Dan Williams replied, 'I've seen Joe moderate over the last two or three years. When he started out he was very, very single-focused on curriculum and one method of curriculum delivery, which I happen not to agree with. Now as Joe has matured in his thinking, I think he has moved away from this curriculum model that he has (as a single focus) to the idea of choice, and I think he's got a very well-thought-out position paper on charter schools. [But] Joe's reputation was made on this issue over here, and I have a little hesitation in associating myself with him because there's still that perception' (Interview 11). Markham also expressed interest in some of Freedman's ideas but added that he 'scares me a lot' (Interview 23). While both men appear conscious of the need to enlist allies in hegemonic struggles over educational reform, they are uncertain that individuals like Freedman will be helpful in generating the broad-based public support that is required.

Williams in particular, is quite Machiavellian in his assessments of various groups and their potential influence. He disparages the Alberta Home and School Councils Association (AHSCA), a provincial parent organization, as ineffectual – 'a group of stay-at-home mothers who want to feel good about doing something, and they get together and they feel good about doing something that amounts to absolutely nothing' (Interview 11). On the other hand, Williams dismisses the Alberta Teachers' Association because he feels they have *too much* power. As he states, 'we cannot accomplish in education what we must accomplish by having that very strong influential group say "no" to everything.' He hoped that 'nothing would have to be done with the ATA,' – that is, splitting it into bargaining and professional divisions – but that it would 'wake up and understand that changes are necessary.'

Baldwin and Markham share this view of the ATA to some extent. Both corporate executives question whether it is 'representative' of all teachers and ask how credible the organization is as a result. These comments are echoed by approximately 13 per cent of the sample of senior executives interviewed for Alberta Education, who expressed strong negative views about the 'union mentality' perpetuated by the ATA amongst members (Meanwell and Barrington 1991: 33).

This challenging of the ATA as a legitimate participant in discussions over educational reform raises the question of who *should* be participating in the policy process. Dan Williams responded to this question as follows: 'Everybody, parents, students ... However, I think parents and students in a different way than the business community, and teachers, and educational administrators. Because the education system in my mind, should reflect the needs and values of society. So everybody in society has to be part of that change. However ... what I was going to say was going to sound terribly elitist. Let me say it and then come back and probably take it back (laugh). Not everybody in society is cognizant of the role that education could play in helping us maintain a viable economic order. And if you get too many people involved who don't understand that, we could quickly lose our quality of life. Now I know as soon as I say that, that sounds very elitist, and I want to retract it (laugh)' (Interview 11). Note that Williams's initial adoption of a rhetoric of inclusiveness is quickly revised to a version of participation that seems to be primarily based on manufacturing consent. His comments are reminiscent of discussion in Chapter 4 of the consultation processes involved in the federal Prosperity Initiative and Alberta's Toward 2000 Together.

Tensions within the Network

Discussion of insiders and outsiders in the business-in-education network may suggest that interview participants are aligned
on every issue, which is not the case. They have different perspectives that appear to be at least partly rooted in their location within the corporate class. Michael Useem (1980) suggests
that there are two main divisions within this class: the cleavage
between major business sectors and the schism between large-
and medium- to small-sized firms. We see evidence of these
divisions in some of the comments of interview participants.

For example, Dan Williams works within the for-profit education sector in a medium-sized organization and tends to align
himself with other small- to medium-sized companies. Not surprisingly, he complains about the exclusion of small- and medium-sized businesses from membership in the Conference
Board and concludes, 'this isn't grassroots. It's big business buying research' (Interview 11). In contrast, CB representative
Lawrence Grant speaks of the involvement of large companies
in education as being more 'strategic' and focused on objectives
compared to the more ad hoc activities of small businesses. Executives Gary Baldwin and Andrew Markham work for large
corporations within the oil and gas sector and decry 'parochial-
ism.' They tend to associate themselves with a dominant stra-
tum of corporate elites who are able to move beyond their
company's interests to those of the industry and perhaps even
to those of the corporate property class as a whole (cf., Mills
1956).

Williams continues to elaborate his disaffection with a big
business approach as he distinguishes between the Alberta
Chamber of Commerce and the Alberta Chamber of Resources.
The *International Comparisons* study indicates to him that the
ACR is also guilty of 'buying research,' rather than building
support for its positions through the voluntary work of its members. He concludes, 'that's why a Chamber of Commerce has
much more political recognition than a Chamber of Resources.
Because, again, it's grassroots rather than purchasing informa-

tion' (Interview 11). Williams's comments indicate that he sees groups like the Conference Board, the Chamber of Commerce, and the ACR as competing for political acceptance and influence.

Divisions within the corporate class based on the cleavage between major business sectors are also evident in the comments of Gary Baldwin. Speaking about the ethics of school-business partnerships, Baldwin comments that these relationships are not intended as 'commercial enterprises' where 'a business gets in there to put their logo on the hallways and sell more of their product' (Interview 33). His own company's interest in education is as 'a supplier of the future workforce.' From this vantage point, the legitimate role of businesses in partnerships is to promote their interests as purchasers of labour, not to market products. This perspective no doubt differs from that held by Jennie Thompson's company, whose market is heavily dependent on sales of products to schools, and from that of Williams, whose business is education. The survey of business executives also found sector-based differences in their responses to a question about the skills they want students to possess. Executives affiliated with 'commercial' industries (tourism, hospitality, etc.) had higher expectations regarding the 'writing skills and enthusiasm' of students, whereas employers affiliated with the 'industrial' group (resources, manufacturing, etc.) were more interested in 'computing, science, business and learning' (Meanwell and Barrington 1991: 13).

In addition to tensions among business elites, there are also potential tensions among nonprofit organizations that are competing for corporate donations. Mike Popiel suggests that when the partnership foundation first started, representatives of Junior Achievement were concerned 'about us tapping into corporate funding that they were getting.' Perhaps, as a result, the foundation lets JA know what they are doing so 'we don't get in each other's way' (Interview 8). While we can expect that the preceding tensions within the network present obstacles to collaboration in educational reform, the overlap in interview participants' views of problems and solutions in education suggests that a significant degree of inter-group cohesion remains.

As Williams notes, '[Y]ou know, I think the fact that so many agencies and governments, and private groups and public groups are calling for reform, and in many cases the same kind of reforms, gives credence to the fact that those of us who are kind of on that bandwagon right now are not wide-eyed radicals' (Interview 11).

Solutions to Educational Crisis

The discourses of *fiscal crisis of the state* and *education for economic prosperity* (discussed in Chapter 2) predominate also in the comments of interview participants. Educational change was unanimously viewed by participants as inevitable because of fiscal pressures on the state. But while fiscal pressure translated into cuts to education spending, it was believed that these cuts could be offset by reforms that made the system more efficient. Reforms that involved tightening the relationship between industry and schools were particularly attractive solutions to educational crisis. Participants' vision for education was tied to their economic vision of a globally competitive province based on flexible and productive, high-skill, high-tech workers. The images that recur in discussion are those of 'education in crisis,' 'the lessons from business,' and the 'silver lining of reforms.' The seemingly shared view of interview participants that educational restructuring was inevitable appeared to be rooted in the belief that the public sector was simply following behind the private sector, where most businesses had undertaken restructuring in the 1980s and 90s to varying degrees in order to remain competitive. As CB researcher Lawrence Grant comments, '[There is] growing awareness that there is a real financial, economic constraint imposed on everybody right now. The larger businesses in Alberta have downsized to stay alive, and that's a painful process to go through ... So there's pressure on the business people and now we're seeing a pressure in the public sector, for governments to cut their spending – locally, provincially, and nationally ... And that's providing this reality check outside. So my thinking is that it means change. Necessity is the mother of invention truly and change is going to come' (Interview 3). The ideological effect of such comments is that change is constructed as natural and 'opposition is merely negativity left over from the old unenlightened paradigm' (Barlow and Robertson 1994: 9).

Andrew Markham, Gary Baldwin, and Dan Williams also argue that the push for educational change in Alberta is rooted in 'fiscal realities.' Partnership foundation representative Mike Popiel adds that the education system has previously been 'insulated from the "real world" or the rest of the world' and that, 'for the first time ever, educators are feeling what the rest of society has felt with the downsizing and global markets' (Interview 8).

But while educational change is described by these participants as *inevitable* because of the fiscal crisis of the state, they also talk about why reform is *desirable*. Popiel, in particular, suggests that schools need to foster self-reliance and build communities as a way of combating the 'garbage bear syndrome' that has developed. He says, 'Society has become so dependent on government hand-outs that we've forgotten how to, and I'll use the analogy, how to "forage," and although we exist like a garbage bear, we're not a healthy animal. We're no longer innovative, we're no longer creative, we no longer take ownership for our own problems. We need to start building some of our own barns again, as a community.'

Popiel's comments parallel those of senior executives in the survey conducted for Alberta Education where 'Six executives (10 per cent) expressed their concern about a need for a greater sense of purpose and motivation in young people. Many executives believe graduates (and high school students) are less ambitious than previously. They attribute this to a growing feeling in graduates that if things don't work out, government support systems or parents will be there to help. This in turn is attributed to what is perceived to be the increasingly socialistic tendencies of teachers' (Meanwell and Barrington 1991: 22). Educational reform is desirable therefore in response to the social and economic crisis that has resulted from lax schools and left-wing teachers. Reform is also needed because of the lack of responsiveness of the 'huge school bureaucracies that have built up,' according to Dan Williams (Interview 11). In the preceding comments we see the overlap between the discourse of the *dissatisfied employer* and that of the *unhappy parent*, like Joe Freedman who also criticizes the bureaucracy of the system and its mediocre outcomes.

School reform is also necessary because of the poor global performance of Canadian students according to Dan Williams: 'We are truly living in a globally competitive world marketplace ... And if you look at what's happening in Korea, and Japan, and Singapore, and in Germany, for example. They have much different kinds of educational systems, and those education systems are producing different kinds of educated citizens, and different kinds of educated workers. And I have a real concern that we are quickly falling behind in our competitive ability when it comes to the educational product. If we fall behind in the educational product, the margin is very thin ... And we could also say what makes this profit is the "knowledge margin"' (Interview 11).

Andrew Markham reiterates the human capital theme underlying Williams's comments when he suggests that his company's success is dependent on the level of skills and education of the people who 'will make Canada productive and competitive' (Interview 23). He later makes the connection between educational reform and economic competitiveness when he says, 'ultimately we are the employers of these young men and women, [and therefore] I think we have a place at the table to engage in that dialogue as to what those skills are that are going to be needed.' Baldwin also emphasizes the role of employers in schools: 'You come down to it and you say, why are schools there in the first place? And I think what happens is a lot of the teaching faculty generally thinks, well they're there to teach and to make kids broad thinkers and so on. And I think that's good and I think *that's half of it*. But the other half is to help people to learn and eventually pursue avenues when they get older that are going to be self-supporting, either as entrepreneurs or business people or industry people, or teachers, or something. So when you think of it, education is like an industry. *It's just another supplier.* And they're a supplier of the future workforce. And have the educators really gone out and asked *the purchasers, being the employers,* what do they really want?' [my emphasis] (Interview 33).

In terms of how education should be restructured, Baldwin and Markham draw on their industry experience and suggest that the education system has to look at 'whether or not this model that's been used for the last 100 years in Canada is still the right model' (Interview 23). Markham goes on to suggest that some of the ideas associated with business restructuring could be applicable to education: for example, more efficient use of facilities, greater use of cost-effective technologies, and bench marking 'best practices.' Baldwin also makes a number of recommendations based on his business experience:

I think quite frankly that we're going into a kind of industrial revolution in the way of education, and the way we will be delivering teaching and programs in the future. I think we're going to see more long-distance learning. Maybe schools won't even resemble schools as we currently know them in the future. I've read some things where in some cases, some companies are maybe entertaining the thought that you could bring your kids to work. We're hearing a lot about schools opening twelve months of the year. I think there are also going to be very dramatic changes in the way teachers are probably rewarded. People in industry and business – for many years now their pay practices have been more performance-related, where you set objectives and you're measured against them. Whereas teachers tend to [emphasize] seniority and their unions are so strong, etc. And I just don't know that the mechanism's there to reward the really good teachers. And so I think there are going to be revolutionary changes there. I think schools themselves, even at the public level, are going to become almost competitive little enterprises, where maybe parents can pick and choose what school they want to go to, based on what's got the best reputation, the lowest dropout rates, and so on. And I think it's good and healthy to have competition. (Interview 33)

Markham's and Baldwin's comments echo those of the chair of the Calgary Chamber of Commerce Education Committee, who writes that the education system can increase its efficiency by using 'technology, training and empowerment to improve its position' just as industry has done (Gregor 1994: 35).

These corporate executives believe that education needs to be more efficient and that greater efficiency will offset funding cuts. This revised human capital view – that there is some fat in the system that can be trimmed without impacting on educational quality – is also expressed by Popiel, White, and Williams. Their comments suggest that educational efficiency may be attained by adopting business management practices and/or a market model of open competition. Popiel takes this line of thought further when he talks about the private sector opportunities that restructuring presents in the following exchange: '[T]here's going to be a ton of money to be made somewhere [in the private sector]. And I really see that with the government's push for business and education partnerships, there are going to be opportunities to help Albertans in rural areas expand that program, whether it be for the government or private. So those with the knowledge are going to be called upon' (Interview 8).

This reference to the silver lining of reforms suggests that at the heart of educational restructuring in Alberta is a reassertion of private sector authority over government. But although governments appear to have placed their faith in the business community to fill in the gaps created by its retrenchment, Markham suggests that this may be misguided. I asked how he saw provincial cutbacks affecting school-business partnerships, and he responded, 'The first thing [schools] will do is start leaning on their partners to get funds and computers and resources that are no longer available in the system. I don't think that's a good thing, and I don't like to see funding being a part of a partnership. [W]e're not in a hell of a lot better shape these days than what governments are. I mean [schools] may be in for a rude awakening when we say that the partnership is not about us funding you. I mean, everybody's turning to business thinking that's the salvation' (Interview 23). The CB also prefers that partnerships be based on an exchange of human resources rather than financial donations from corporations to schools. Its 'ethical guidelines' for school-business partnerships states that resources from business partners should complement and not replace public funding for education.

The argument that educational restructuring is necessary because of fiscal crisis and the need to produce workers with skills that will make the country competitive raises questions around where jobs are being created, what skills are associated with these jobs, and what is the role of education in preparing students as potential workplace entrants. The responses of interview participants to these questions indicate a shared way of thinking about labour market demand and supply.

Participants tend to talk less about the existing job market that they do about creating the right climate for economic growth, which in turn is assumed to create jobs. Of the various labour market forecasting methods, participants tend to adopt a *futurist* approach, basing labour market projections on a scenario that they have developed, rather than extrapolating from past trends or surveying employers about their future needs. This approach is clearly based less on the current labour market situation than are the other two approaches, and is therefore more difficult to challenge.

Comments made by Lawrence Grant and Dan Williams provide a sense of their economic vision. Grant uses the example of Silicon Valley: '[T]he economy isn't static and you can actually grow it. The correlation, for example, is the famous case in the 1980s in California, 70s and 80s with Silicon Valley ... Now the idea is the same in Canada, if we keep building the number of educated people who have those generic employability skills plus specialized skills. And if you create more and more people who fit in there, you're going to create more and more products that you can sell to people, including the market abroad, so you actually grow more jobs' (Interview 3). More specifically, Grant

refers to the need to educate people in the new growth industries of electronics, telecommunications, software production,
and so on.

When I asked Williams how the vision of the need for a highly
skilled workforce related to his knowledge of current labour
market demand in Calgary and Alberta, he replied, 'See, we get
into the chicken and egg syndrome here. Right now we have
more educated people in this province than we have jobs for,
that's on the one hand. On the other hand, we will never attract
the business and industries here that will be competitive in the
global marketplace if we don't have more educated and trained
people. So I guess I'm one who believes that we've got to bite
the bullet and build the labour force as part of attracting industry ... In coordination with that we then need to create the right
business climate which will attract business, which means low
taxation, little regulation, and then giving business the freedom
to run their organization ... and I think this is what Ralph [Klein]
and his company are trying to do' (Interview 11). Andrea White
also talked about education as a 'value add' component in a
province seeking to attract businesses in high-tech industries.
Participants generally agreed that future jobs will require greater
levels of education, that the greatest growth would be in high-
tech industries, and that it is most important to train future
workers to be flexible, adaptable, and entrepreneurial to meet
constant labour market changes.

Tensions within the Vision

The vision that is presented by interview participants is not
without its contradictions and challenges. Recall that in Chapter 2 I discuss tensions within arguments around fiscal crisis
and education for economic prosperity that have been challenged
by the Canadian Centre for Policy Alternatives, Barlow and
Robertson, and others. Interviews with business-affiliated participants also suggest tension.

For example, some participants expressed ambivalence about
the extent to which increased efficiencies in the education sys-

tem could actually offset government funding cuts, despite the rhetoric of doing more with less. Science foundation representative Andrea White suggests that 'there is some point at which you've pared away so dangerously that you have a truly anaemic cadaver there' (Interview 39). Gary Baldwin echoes the sentiment that cuts may be doing more than eliminating excesses in the system. Mike Popiel and Jennie Thompson comment on the potentially negative impact of funding cuts on teachers and students in classrooms. It therefore appears that while participants generally adopt the rhetoric of efficiency in education, they are not entirely certain of the results. Perhaps because of their involvement with educators – and in the case of Popiel, White, and Thompson, their experiences as former teachers – they are aware of the impact of cutbacks at the level of the school. This encourages reflection on the question of 'how much is too much' when it comes to funding cuts. As Markham's earlier comment that 'business is not the salvation' suggests, this relates also to the extent to which business people are willing to step in and fill the gaps created by government retrenchment.

A second tension involves the idea of solving social as well as economic problems through the privatization of public services such as education. Specifically, Mike Popiel's comments that we need to get rid of 'garbage bears' and build communities can be juxtaposed with his references to the private sector opportunities in education created by restructuring and cuts. Certainly the issue of a loss of community is a popular theme for people who would locate themselves at different places on a political spectrum. However, the solution of cutting government services in order to force people to cooperate and find creative solutions to community problems raises issues around who is to bear the cost of retrenchment and who will reap the benefits. The tension between the goal of building community (usually associated with collective action based on the common good) and the goal of solving economic crisis through privatization (associated with the commodification of the public sphere and individualized consumption) is clear. Given this juxtaposition, the desirability of seeking out lessons from business for the education system also becomes questionable.

The third tension revealed in the comments of interview participants is between the high-tech vision of labour market demand that they promote and their implied claim to represent the interests of all employers. Again, cleavages between large and small employers and between firms in different industrial sectors are evident. When we consider current labour market data, it appears that participants are proposing a vision for education based on labour market projections that are quite self-interested. Participants' own employment practices also challenge their labour market projections.

The emphasis of corporate employers Baldwin and Markham on students' technical skills contrasts with small business representative Jennie Thompson's observation that her firm tends to look more at the motivation, enthusiasm, and interests of potential workers than at their actual qualifications. According to Thompson, several of the company's current employees would not necessarily have stood out 'on paper' (Interview 38). Her comments are echoed in the survey of senior executives where respondents expressed more concern over students' poor work ethic than over their levels of general skills (Meanwell and Barrington 1991: 12, 19). As mentioned earlier, executives in different industrial sectors also disagreed over what skills were most important. The way different employers prioritize workers' skills and attributes therefore varies, and presents an area of tension. In sum, the statement 'We need to build a highly educated, highly skilled workforce' addresses the labour needs of some employers more than others.

Further, this statement does not necessarily coincide with either employers' past hiring practices or with the current labour market. For example, while Andrew Markham states that 'we are the employers of young men and women,' he also acknowledges that his company's recruiting has been on the decline since the late 1980s (Interview 23).[2] Markham's comment 'We are the employers' is also useful to consider in light of Appendix B, Tables 2 and 3, which list Calgary's major private sector and public sector employers. These tables indicate that the top three public sector employers employ more people than the top fourteen private sector employers. Energy companies represented approximately half of the top twenty private sector employers. Markham's selective perception is also evident when he suggests that the tremendous growth in the high-tech intellect industry in Calgary has been spawned to a large degree by the downsizing and contracting out practices of companies like his own. In these cases, employees who have been laid off begin their own businesses or join other small firms that are selling services back to their previous employers. Describing the displacement of workers from presumably well paid secure jobs to insecure jobs as 'growth in the labour market' is clearly something of a misnomer.[3]

In fact, a 1992 report by consultants Nuala Beck and Associates classifies crude petroleum and natural gas as 'old economy' industries where jobs are most at risk. In the same report, the top four industries in Alberta's new economy, where the greatest growth in jobs was expected, included retail trade (with 17.3 per cent of current jobs), education (with 13.4 per cent), health services (12.9 per cent) and accommodation and food services (9 per cent). A labour market pamphlet from the Calgary Human Resources Development Centre, also suggested that Alberta occupations expected to provide the largest job increases by the year 2000 were 'salespersons, secretaries, managers, nurses, bookkeepers, cashiers and tellers, chefs and cooks, systems analysts, child care workers, and financial officers' (CHRDC, May 1993). These occupational projections cause one to question the stated primacy of the need for more education in high-tech areas.

Further, statistics around the growth in high-tech employment are not entirely convincing. A 1994 article in *Calgary Commerce* states that more than two-thirds of Alberta's advanced technology companies are located in Calgary and employ 25,000 employees (CCC 1994). But this represents only about 4.6 per cent of total employment in Calgary (based on population and participation rates). Coupled with the fact that Calgary already had more than double the national average of employees in sciences, engineering, and mathematics according to the same article, calls for more technical training seem redundant unless the objective is to develop an oversupply of these skills.

Roles in Hegemonic Work

Hegemonic work has been described in terms of the establishment of a dominant alliance of forces, the development of a set of solutions to capitals' educational needs, and the recruitment of popular support for these solutions. Interview participants individually and collectively have played active and often complementary roles in this work. CB researcher Lawrence Grant, for example, was involved in all three stages of hegemonic work at the national level. Chapter 3 argued that the CB serves as a forum for harmonizing the interests of corporate members through the development of a unifying vision and the production of research that supports that vision. The CB has acted also as a national-level broker, identifying and bringing together key stakeholders from business, education, and government in order to broaden the dissemination of a corporate-driven vision for education. Grant was involved in selecting conference participants and balancing groups according to 'how significant they are' in education (Interview 3). Representation from organized labour has been noticeably lacking at conferences and in other CB activities. When asked about this, Grant suggested that labour's historically adversarial approach may be irreconcilable with partnership initiatives that are based on collaboration (1-3: 9). As mentioned earlier, there are *insiders* and *outsiders*.

In addition to his work on conferences, Grant helped to plan and coordinate NCE and CCE activities. He played a strategic role in developing the CB vision for education by acting as advisor to these groups, writing reports, and generally working to ensure ideological consistency. Chapter 3 notes Grant's interest in using business-education conferences to move stakeholders in the direction of educational change and to connect all CB activities into a strategic plan.

Closely linked to this strategist role is the dissemination of the CB vision through meetings, conferences, reports, and press releases. Ultimately, the goal is to generate public support for the CB vision and thus act as a 'catalyst' for change. As Grant says, 'The people on that National Council are conscious of this difference between what they can do as a national group of leaders and what can be done locally, or in a classroom, or in a home. They know that they can't actually do it – all they can do is get people to want to do it. They can give the right signals, get people to actually pay attention ... The only thing that constrains it is the economic reality, and if people really truly believe that the education part of it is key, then something will happen. Education has moved up a bit in the latest polling I've seen. Sometimes it gets in the top ten issues. It didn't before; it was never in the top five.'

As representatives of CB member corporations, Andrew Markham and Gary Baldwin act as emissaries, disseminating the CB vision to local educational constituents. For example, CCE member Markham spoke to the parent advisory council at his company's partner school about the development of the employability skills profile (ESP), and Baldwin's company undertook an initiative aimed at extending the work of the CB by introducing employability skills portfolios in Calgary-area schools. Both companies had partnerships with high schools: Monarch had been partnered with an 'academic' high school since 1989 and Panorama was partnered with two high schools that emphasized academics and science. Activities in these partnerships included job shadowing, providing speakers for classes, and participating in Junior Achievement programs. Through these activities, Monarch and Panorama had opportunities to articulate the CB vision at the local level. At the same time, Baldwin and Markham's roles as CB emissaries raise the question (addressed in Chapter 7) of whether, and to what extent, they are able to transcend the specific interests of their companies in promoting a vision that goes beyond these interests to those of the capitalist class as a whole.

If Baldwin and Markham are members of a corporate elite that spans provincial and national borders, Dan Williams is arguably more focused on the provincial context. Of all seven participants, Williams is the most overtly political in terms of the Alberta scene, largely because of his involvement with the

Alberta Chamber of Commerce (ACC). Williams discusses the appeal of the ACC as follows: 'And I can tell you that's why I got involved with the Chamber of Commerce. Because I saw it as an organization that is outside of education that could influence education. And I also saw it as a group of people that, for whatever reason, were listened to. So it was a way to, first of all, influence the thinking of the Chamber of Commerce, and then having the Chamber behind some of my thinking' (Interview 11).

Williams is obviously strategic in his practices and has constructed himself as an *organic intellectual* for the ACC. As he says, '[E]very group needs a spokesperson, every organization needs someone who can articulate positions. And, if they're not ready to embrace those positions, they will not embrace them. A group of people can be ready for something but they need somebody to pull it together. I saw that as a possibility at the Chamber.'

Williams emphasizes that the ACC is a 'grassroots' organization, representing 'every kind of business from the very largest to the very smallest'[4] and 'every kind of community' from small rural communities to Calgary and Edmonton. In contrast, the CB can be viewed as a corporate organization with connections to an urban educational elite. According to Williams, the ACC's broad-based business support gives the group greater political clout in the province: 'So we try to influence events through our policies and through conversations we have with government officials, reacting to policy positions they have put out, and providing input prior to their making policy positions.'

Williams was a regular participant in government consultations and participated in the teams that developed the government's education roundtable workbook and process. Earlier, he was involved in a consultation that led to *Tough Choices* (Alberta Education 1993b) and participated in the committee to structure the Career and Technology Studies curriculum. Nevertheless, Williams underplays the ACC's political impact: 'Do I think that because the Chamber advocated, the government does it? No. I think it's simply a matter that what we're saying, in many cases in this area of education, is similar to what they're thinking. So we become, in my mind, supportive of what they're trying to accomplish. It isn't that we have influenced them to think that way.'

Despite this statement, Williams has been an influential player in educational reform in Alberta. Like Lawrence Grant, he shares the view that there needs to be a strategic plan, and that each educational initiative represents 'one leg of a many-legged platform.' While he also agrees with some of the recommendations made by Markham and Baldwin, such as year-round schooling and greater use of technology in schools, he is critical of the tendency for business people to 'lose sight of the forest for the trees' through 'feel-good' initiatives with schools. Williams adopts a more confrontational approach towards public schools than that endorsed by the CB and its affiliates. His approach is supported by a February 1994 letter to the minister of education from the president of the ACC, which concludes that the education system must be 'overhauled and restructured,' since, like the North American car industry in the 1960s and 70s, it is 'out of date,' 'out of touch with reality,' and 'far from competitive' with systems in Europe and Asia.

One of the areas that required restructuring according to Williams was the role of school boards. He elaborates: 'It's my view that funding has to bypass the school board. And I'm not saying that school boards won't exist. I think they could exist, but they'll serve on a contract basis to the schools that want their services. So they'll contract out purchasing, accounting, transportation, if it's their choice to do that ... to contract out curriculum development if they want that. But what it does, it completely reverses it doesn't it? The power structure is here at the school level.' Presumably Williams would agree with the New Brunswick decision in 1996 to eliminate elected school boards and replace them with a new parent-driven governance structure. Such changes are consistent with his interests as a private educator, because, in eliminating or minimizing the role of elected school boards, another of the distinctions between public and private systems is eroded.

My interview with Dan Williams was the most interesting of all participants from the perspective of studying hegemonic work because he was so consciously strategic. Through his involvement in the ACC and local groups like the partnership foundation, he had succeeded in establishing a dominant alliance of forces that was politically influential. With the backing of the ACC and other allies, he proposed solutions to educational crisis that promoted greater privatization of education – funding following students, charter schools, a minimal role for elected school boards, and so on. He also recognized that there was an opportunity to generate public support for these solutions because of the public perception (accurate or not) of educational crisis: '[The impetus for reform comes] from a view that something is wrong with our schools ... Now that works very well for me in my beliefs that there is something wrong with the education system. And I know this sounds manipulative, but I mean, it's how you get things done. To use that discontent that exists naturally in society to in fact change a system that I know can be changed to be so much more effective and efficient at the same time.'

Two organizations that have sought to change the education system in subtle ways are the partnership and science foundations, and their roles in hegemonic work should be acknowledged. Like the CB at the national level, these foundations act as local level brokers, bringing stakeholders from business, education, and government together. Lies and Bergholz (1988) discuss similar organizations in the United States, and conclude that effective brokering requires broad community credibility, entrepreneurial style, an ability to work well with educators as well as business people, and a finely honed political sense. On the basis of these criteria, the partnership and science foundations are very effective. Andrea White notes that corporate leader John Smith's vision for the science foundation was motivated by concern about science literacy in general and about the future labour pool for science and technology jobs in particular. Smith saw the foundation as a 'way of bringing science into the popular culture' (Interview 39). The foundation concept was undoubtedly attractive for employers who shared Smith's concerns about the future labour pool and who could achieve some control over their investments in education through participation on the foundation's board and/or as partners in specific ventures. It was also attractive to politicians, according to White: '[T]he province was supportive [from the beginning]. And when I say that, I think there were some key politicians who were supportive whose ear [John Smith] had. And they believed in the concept that he was espousing, so the support came from them. And it was lottery money that we used. The key people that I think were supportive were Fred Stewart who was Minister of Technology, Research and Telecommunications ... Jim Dinning who was then Minister of Education, the Premier, more because of the personal relationship he had with [John]. And eventually Ken Kowalski [Deputy Premier] did become supportive of what we were doing.' This quotation suggests that founders had political connections in addition to a finely honed political sense.

White comments that the foundation focuses on people and programs at the community level and is 'interested in staying as an informal influence on the formal education system.' At the time of our interview, its activities fell into three main areas: a grant program to reward innovative community science projects, exhibition development and touring, and interface with the formal education system. White talks about a few initiatives in the latter area: 'We have been authorized by the provincial department of education to draft the implementation guides that will go along with the new elementary science curriculum. So we're the ones that worked and selected teachers to work on drafting them. We're doing the design and formatting and publishing and all that sort of thing. We run a competition for division two and division three students in the province called our "yellow box program" where they design a science experiment that will fit in a box. We do institutes for elementary science teachers in the summer. We have a program that we've developed called "science under seven," we sell activity books and kits to daycares, nursery schools, kindergartens, some division one classes. So there's quite a variety.'

The science foundation became more than an 'interface' with the education system when its charter school opened in the fall of 1999. This school focuses on science and math and offers a curriculum that emphasizes the interrelationships between the sciences, mathematics and technology, and the arts and humanities. According to an information pamphlet, one of its goals is 'to serve as an excellent preparation for students intending to study in the International Baccalaureate program and other college-preparatory high school programs.' While it began by enrolling students in grades four to six (who demonstrated grade level literacy and math competency), it planned to extend the program to grade nine. This initiative undoubtedly increases the influence of the science foundation within the school system.

At the time of the interview with Ms White, the science foundation was looking to develop revenue streams based on their products and services that would offset reductions in government funding. White commented that a 'huge market for in-service' existed, for example, in the implementation of the new elementary science curriculum. Another project that the foundation was working on with the federal and provincial governments was the provincial roll-out of SchoolNet. White had met with the deputy minister of education to explain her plans and enlist his support. Part of these plans involved looking for partnerships with the private sector that would speed up the implementation. These activities demonstrate the entrepreneurial character of the foundation and its ability to mobilize private sector funders.

Since my interview with White, it has become clear that Alberta Education is very interested in the partnership and science foundation models. *Framework for Enhancing Business Involvement in Education* (Alberta Education 1996a) recommended the establishment of a provincial Career Education Foundation modelled on the science foundation. It also recommended that business partnerships and community resources be used to support technology integration in schools. Alberta Education itself entered into exclusive arrangements with telecommunications companies and software providers to supply schools with software and training at discounted prices. It also recommended creating a business-sponsored and administered technological investment fund to assist schools to get online (Alberta Education 1996b). These examples suggest that the science foundation has indeed been an effective broker.

The partnership foundation has also been effective in this role. According to its 1993 business plan, it was initiated by a Calgary school administrator in order to 'better prepare students for their future by building powerful relationships between businesses and educators in a way that results in proactive activities.' Former teacher Mike Popiel was probably seconded because of his entrepreneurial sense and his comfort with both educators and business people. Despite the fact that business people comprised half of the board of directors, he constructed it as broadly representative and credible in the community. Like the science foundation, it received support from governments as well as corporate funding partners. In fact, the 1993 Business Plan indicated that the majority of funding came from the five school districts in the Calgary area.

Also like the science foundation, the partnership foundation had a high level of provincial support. When I asked Popiel if he thought the foundation would be affected by the cuts to education in the 1994 budget, he replied, 'I think everything's up for grabs. But my sense would be "no." My sense is that this is a value-add. In many ways if this organization did not exist, the students that we serve in five different districts would not have opportunities to do the things that we're offering through the board because of the budget cuts. So I would see this organization growing. The provincial government is really behind the concept of partnerships. Right from the very inception, [former education minister] Jim Dinning has been a big supporter of us, and we receive money from Alberta Education' (Interview 8).

The partnership foundation's vision statement in its 1993 business plan suggests that it too is interested in becoming more than an informal influence on schools – it says that the foundation would like to contribute to the 'fundamental restructuring of education in Alberta.' When I asked Popiel what that meant, he joked that his organization was not advising the premier. However, he did see a need for change in the system: 'If you look at five, six years ago, business was not allowed anywhere near the schools to any real extent. Well, [the foundation has] opened that door and as you introduce people to one another and the synergies begin to develop, friendships occur, the old wall, the Berlin wall between education and business is coming down. And I think we're a good deal responsible for that.'

The foundation initiated a number of system initiatives, including student conferences, 'stay-in-school' initiatives, teacher internships in business, and the distribution of corporate donations to schools. Like the science foundation, it was beginning to demonstrate entrepreneurial style by marketing the employability skills materials developed by Panorama. Its 1994 student conference also encouraged this spirit in students by inviting successful entrepreneurs to talk to students about their experiences and to act as role models. In sum, the partnership foundation, like the science foundation, exhibited the characteristics of an effective broker: it developed broad community and government support, displayed entrepreneurial style, and worked well with educators and business people. Its ties to the CB enabled it to articulate the CB vision for education at the local level and to draw educators into this vision.

Discussion of the different roles in hegemonic work has so far included reference to strategists, emissaries, and brokers. However, this discussion would be incomplete without reference to people who play more of a supporting role in the business-in-education network. Small business representative Jennie Thompson appears to play this kind of 'cheerleading' role. Thompson was interviewed because of her company's involvement in the employability skills project initiated by Baldwin's company. According to Thompson, her company was very interested in this project as a way of becoming more involved with schools, and it promoted itself to Panorama.

Therefore, it is not surprising that she echoes the CB rhetoric of encouraging stronger links between schools and businesses so that students develop employability skills. As a producer and marketer of products for schools, Thompson's company has an additional motivation for becoming involved in education, and has initiated activities with schools that include job shadowing, providing guest speakers, and conducting marketing. She elaborates: 'So we'll go in and we'll work with kids. And sometimes it's just a one-class thing and sometimes it's a series where they're becoming involved in their school. Like if we're doing [product days] in their school and they become involved in some of the business aspects of it. Like, what needs to be done to make this happen, how can we promote in your school? And getting them to help us do some of the promotion. And sometimes this is "for-credit" work as well, because it's like a mini-project within their school' (Interview 38).

The advantages of such initiatives for the company are clear. After all, who would know better how to market the product than the potential customer? Thompson reiterates the view held by Baldwin and Markham that schools can learn from the business model. She talks about 'making schools more aware financially so that they can do some of their own financing' and structuring schools so that they run 'a bit more like a business.' In this way they can run 'more efficiently.' Thompson's comments about the need for school-business links, employability skills, and greater efficiency in education therefore support the CB vision for education. Thompson's company, as a relatively new and growing small business, appeared eager to get a 'piece of the action' by becoming more involved in the Calgary business-in-education network.

Concluding Comments

Common interest, cutting across the lines of all separate [subgroups], tends to hold the community structure intact. [One respondent] said, 'If you want to know what is going on, you have to be where the money is. It is capitalism, I suppose you would say. The men who make things move are interested in the larger issues – making money, keeping power.' (Floyd Hunter, *Community Power Structures*)

The business-in-education network in Calgary also suggests a high degree of interaction and cohesion among participants. However, there were also tensions. Williams's interest in education, as a private school operator, was somewhat different from that of oil executives Baldwin and Markham. The 'men who [made] things move' in Alberta in the early 1990s were aligned with groups that could best help them achieve their goals: the Alberta Chamber of Commerce, the Alberta Chamber of Resources, the science foundation, the partnership foundation, and the CB. To some extent, these groups were competing for government favour. Interestingly, the two women who were interviewed played the supporting roles of broker and cheerleader. The sexism within the network is evidenced further by Williams's comments about the AHSCA as a group of 'stay-at-home mothers.'

Although tensions could threaten cohesion over the longer term, participants' views on educational reform were quite similar. Despite ambivalence about the extent of education cuts, all seven participants adopted the discourse of the *fiscal crisis of the state*. They also supported the restructuring of education in the three-year business plan.[5] Williams, Markham, Baldwin, and Popiel expressed 'revised human capital' ideas also featured in the visioning reports of governments (see Chapter 4). Williams strongly supported the view of the private sector as the engine of growth and government's role in creating the conditions for this growth – key themes in the Toward 2000 Together process. Popiel's discussion of the 'garbage bear syndrome' is reminiscent of the government's emphasis on making Albertans more 'self-reliant.' Finally, the priorities placed by federal and provincial vision reports on developing partnerships and encouraging excellence in science and technology were echoed by most participants.

One topic that did not occur to the extent one might expect was the focus on skilled trades. Although Popiel suggested that more vocational streaming should occur in schools in grade nine, and Williams lamented the lack of value given to technical and vocational work in our society, there was not the same level of interest in 'non-college-bound youth' as was expressed in documents of the ACR and the Economic Council. This might be explained by the fact that participants were located in Calgary, as opposed to a place like Fort McMurray where expansion projects related to oil sands development have raised concerns about labour shortages. The ACR joined with other partners in 1994 to launch the CNG pilot project, after working for some time with communities and the government to raise public awareness of this concern. Like the CB, CNG acts as a catalyst in bringing employers, educators, and the government together to develop strong community partnerships.[6] The influence of the ACR, while not addressed in detail in this study, is evidenced by the attention given to school-to-work transition and attracting students to the trades within Alberta Education's 1996 *Framework for Enhancing Business Involvement in Education.* It was also revealed by the province's decision around 1997/8 to support the CNG foundation instead of establishing its own Career Education Foundation. This influence is clearly tied to economic development and to the traditional political clout of the resource sector in Alberta.

This study attends more closely to national-provincial connections. For example, Grant's work as a 'national-level strategist' for the CB involved constructing and communicating a coherent vision for educational reform that could be disseminated and adapted to the local context by executives like Markham and Baldwin. The science and partnership foundations negotiate differences among participants through their work as local third-party brokers. They have attained legitimacy as community organizations, although corporate sponsors undoubtedly maintain some control. Both foundations bring together key stakeholders from government, education, business, and the broader community to embrace a vision that effectively translates locally the hegemonic work of the CB and draws educators into this vision.

The vision rests on certain images and produces certain effects. Images of education in crisis, the need for fundamental change, the lessons from business, and the 'silver lining' of reforms serve to rationalize the inevitability of restructuring, legitimize the advice and wealth of experience offered to educators by business people, and, more generally, increase the propensity to view education as a business. Similarly, constructing relationships between corporations and schools as partnerships perpetuates an image of equality and reciprocity, which masks the underlying corporate interest in schools as 'suppliers of labour' and as 'markets for products.' The notion of community when juxtaposed with that of big government has the effect of obscuring social divisions and masking who wins and who loses as a result of restructuring and cutbacks. The adoption of a futurist discourse of high-tech employment evades challenges based on existing labour market demand and the projections of employers.

The underlying thrust, however, is towards the marketization of education. The public sector is to behave more like the private sector though the devolution of financial and managerial control to local levels, along with increased accountability, promotion of parental choice and competition among schools, and greater adoption of management practices within schools. In their study of educational reforms in England and Wales, New Zealand and Australia, the United States, and Sweden, Whitty, Power, and Halpin (1998) identify similar developments based on a strong state that steers at a distance and an increasingly marketized civil society. This is consistent with views expressed by participants in the business-in-education network in Calgary. Chapter 7 looks more closely at the relationships that have developed between specific Calgary corporations and schools.

CHAPTER SEVEN

Partnerships as Sites of Struggle

Partnerships between businesses and schools have been promoted by the OECD as well as by federal and provincial governments. An OECD (1992) report on partnerships suggests that they have grown out of a movement to widen the range of stakeholder involvement in education, which in turn developed because of the perceived failure of state-run education systems. Employers were expressing concerns over declining standards in education, the relevance of much academic education, and the general skill levels of students. Greater input of business through partnerships responds to these concerns by forging closer relationships between schools and the workplace and ensuring that schools are more accountable for student employability. The OECD report suggests that these relationships are most successful when they act as a 'catalyst for existing reform movements supported or initiated by governments' (7).

Federal and provincial governments in Canada have taken this recommendation seriously. The federal government described partnerships as a key part of educational reform recommendations in Prosperity and Economic Council reports. Shaker (1998) writes that the 1994 education statement by the Information Technology Association of Canada (ITAC) also stressed the importance of partnerships in developing a new approach to education. The ITAC statement voiced concerns that children were not acquiring the skills and knowledge needed in the global economy; employers were worried about finding qualified workers, and the federal government was worried about the country's ability to remain competitive. ITAC recommended that the Council of Ministers of Education, Canada develop 'joint education/industry/parent bodies to make decisions about the role of schools, skill sets, knowledge requirements, and curriculum needed to take students into the 21st century' (Shaker 1998: 20).

Partnerships have been consistent with Alberta Education's direction since the early 1990s. 'Vision' reports encouraged school-work linkages and partnerships with business, and Alberta Education's three-year plan described business as a key player in defining learning requirements. This was reflected in the 1996 *Framework for Enhancing Business Involvement*, which supported school-business partnerships, system-wide partnerships, and greater involvement of business people in policy-making at all levels. Promoted by groups like the Conference Board and the Alberta Chamber of Resources as a 'win-win' solution for educators and business people, partnerships provide attractive models for bureaucrats and politicians in a time of retrenchment.

School districts increasingly have become interested in the concept also. Influenced by adopt-a-school programs in the United States, school boards across Canada have developed partnership programs and hired coordinators to oversee them. This chapter examines two school-business partnerships involving the corporations Monarch and Panorama [pseudonyms] and their partners. It extends the analysis (in Chapter 5) of the business-in-education network by moving beyond the rhetoric of business to explore interactions between business and school partners and the struggles involved in such relationships. This analysis serves as a reminder that hegemonic settlement 'must continually be renewed, recreated, defended and modified' (Williams 1977, quoted in Eagleton 1991: 115).

The 'Courtship of Business'

The Alberta Teachers' Association conducted a survey of its members across Alberta in relation to business involvement with education in early 1999. Some of the findings (based on 1,104 responses) are as follows:

- 37.8 per cent of respondents said their school had a partnership with a local business (24.5 per cent said their school had a partnership before 1995)
- 33.5 per cent said their district had a system-based partnership
- 56 per cent said they were supportive or very supportive of partnerships between businesses and schools, and 18.3 per cent were not supportive (25.7 per cent were in the middle)
- 40.1 per cent rated the importance of partnerships as very high or high
- 41.6 per cent thought there was pressure exerted on schools to negotiate or increase business sponsorships

Regarding the last finding, by far the most commonly cited source of pressure was the government's underfunding of education. The growth in partnerships since 1995 may be related to this budget pressure and to growing competition between districts and schools. Results indicate that interest in partnerships is quite high across Alberta, and not just in urban areas where partnership programs have been established for some time. The type and range of partnerships will, of course, depend on the major employers in the jurisdiction. Calgary, Alberta, is a corporate centre that has embraced school-business partnerships since the mid-1980s.[1]

Partnership liaison Donna Black described the development of the program within the Calgary Board of Education as follows: 'We had been thinking for a long time that there would be value in establishing a means for business to have greater involvement in schools, that there would be real benefits for our students ... So, anyway, the time was reached in 1984 when some of our senior leaders had been at conferences ... where people were talking about what was happening in, what they called in the U.S. "Adopt-a-School" programs. And we decided that the time was right for us to examine the idea more closely, and so we actually had someone visit three programs in the U.S. and take an in-depth look at three different applications of the concept' (Interview 6). The process then involved gaining the moral and financial support of trustees and formalizing the program within the board. According to a report from the CBE, it was one of the first school districts in Canada to establish a partnership program (CBE 1993: 2).

Ten years later the program had become institutionalized in several respects. Black reported directly to the chief superintendent and was responsible for the partnership program among others. A community relations officer more directly involved in the day-to-day workings of the program reported to Black. There was a Partnerships Advisory Committee which included representatives from the Calgary Chamber of Commerce and partnership foundation as well as individual school and business partners. Each year the board held networking sessions for its business and school partners and organized a conference that sounded much like a mini-CB event. The board established guidelines for participants in its *Partnership Handbook* (CBE 1991). An administrator with the CBE was also instrumental in the formation of the partnership foundation (described in Chapter 6) in the early 1990s.

Business partners were welcomed by the CBE, and, according to Donna Black, were invited to 'become in a sense part of the family': '[W]hen we have meetings on system issues, to do with downsizing and so on, we invite them to participate in the life of the organization in that way. We also invite partners to sit on a lot of key system committees. So their involvement is in the partnership, but once they're part of the group, they're utilized in a lot of different ways in the system. And ... they'll have contact with [the chief superintendent] around something they're concerned about, whatever' (Interview 6).

As Black suggests, CBE leaders were supportive of business involvement within the board. For example, when the chief superintendent was hired in 1990, a *Calgary Herald* writer commented that 'the new head of Calgary's public school system says he wants to forge closer ties between schools and the business community' (17 May 1990: B8). The chief superintendent's message in the *1992/93 Annual Report on Partnerships* stated, 'Public education can no longer operate in isolation. Our ability to graduate students with the skills required to compete in this global economy may be the most pressing challenge we face today. But we cannot do it alone, particularly given the speed with which our knowledge base and technology are changing. We need the support of our parents, the community and business people. An essential component of this involvement is the Partnerships in Education Program, through which dozens of schools and businesses are working together to provide new and innovative learning opportunities to students. Partnerships are creating an important new training ground for students and teachers, making it possible to access information, resources and expertise that might not be available otherwise' (Calgary Board of Education 1993). This quotation repeats the idea that schools must open their doors and encourage business participation so that students can develop the skills required by employers.

The CBE partnership program grew from five partnerships in 1985 to eighty-six in 1994. In the 1992/3 school year, the board estimated that '1,700 corporate volunteers provided over 11,000 hours of service to partnered schools' (CBE 1993: 3). A 1992 evaluation of partnerships by the CBE noted that almost 8,000 students participated in them. By 1995 a *Calgary Herald* article noted that 'the Calgary board [had] wedded more than half of its 215 schools to businesses' (Dempster, *CH* 14 March 1995: A11).[2]

The Calgary Catholic School District (CCSD)[3] also set up a partnership program in 1991. Tracey Borger from the CCSD describes her board's motivation for developing the program as follows: '[T]he public board was really a leader in western Canada and in the country, you could say, in the field of partnerships. And you could imagine that when you have a big board that is actively pursuing this kind of community involvement program, you're going to turn around and say, "Hmm, what is there to this? What's in it for our district as well?"'

(Interview 5). Borger was hired in 1990 to coordinate the cooperative education program for her board and the partnership program was later added to her portfolio.

Like the CBE, the CCSD had produced partnership kits and promotional materials, and had taken steps towards institutionalizing the program. Leaders in the district also recognized the need to become part of the business-in-education network according to Borger: 'You know, it's funny because business people have a certain network that's set up among business people, and educators don't have the same network, you know what I mean? Well, it's changed in the last four years, but when I came on it was like, the superintendent was not going out to lunch with the CEO from Husky Oil, like, they're in completely different circles.' Borger's observation that over time educational leaders have become more aware of the need to network with business leaders raises questions about the implications of this change. For example, Slaughter (1990) reports that the Business-Higher Education Forum in the United States was dominated by business concerns and education leaders were required to articulate their interests within this frame.

Recruiting Partners

Borger referred more than once to the competition for partners between the public and separate boards, adding, 'the reality is there are only so many big companies and medium-sized companies and some of them don't want to participate' (Interview 5). Since the supply of schools appeared to exceed that of business partners, both public and separate boards had a recruitment process. In the proceedings from a partnership conference held at the University of Calgary in May 1993, CCSD representatives described this process as follows: '[The board] had a multifaceted strategy for approaching businesses. The superintendent utilized personal contacts to rally support for the Program. As well, a letter and information package was sent from the District to 5 to 10 corporations a month from the superintendent's office. After 10 days this mailing was followed with a phone call by the Partnership representatives to request a meeting to explore the possibility of corporate involvement. At this point it was up to the Partnership representatives to convince the business to become involved' (Kaulback and McKay 1993: 16).

Since economically healthy companies were more likely to become involved, representatives also monitored the business pages of the newspaper and other business publications. Kaulback and McKay (17) note that the 'actual courting of businesses for their involvement in the program could take months.' Donna Black similarly acknowledged that everyone at the CBE was involved in recruiting partners for the large number of schools that were waiting to be matched. Using the metaphor of matrimony, which seems to pervade the discourse of partnerships, the board appeared to act as matchmaker to entice eligible businesses to 'tie the knot' with schools.[4]

But while schools were expected to appreciate these efforts, Black notes that, in reality, teachers have not always been keen: '[A]s we were in the early stages of the program, there was often, not always but often, a lot of staff resistance to this. I remember one school in particular that we visited when we were trying to place the first five partners, and we were going to match them with an organization that sells pizza. And they had images of golden arches over the school and they were really worried philosophically about what this would mean for their students. And so we spent a long time with them working through that, and they had in the end a very successful relationship ... [By now] we have enough partnerships under way that people can see that that isn't a threat; it isn't really a problem' (Interview 6).

Teachers were not the only ones concerned about the potential for businesses to impose themselves on schools. While CCSD coordinator Tracy Borger was supportive of the partnership concept, she too expressed misgivings: '[L]ately we've been having some corporations who are phoning us up and telling us, "We want a partner. This is what we want. You send in bids [almost], and we'll choose one." You know, and I say, "Oh, doesn't that sound like business" (laugh): You send in some bids and we'll choose a school. Well, they're used to operating like that, aren't they? But that's not how the process should work as far as I'm concerned. And you're only going to have people trying to say, "Well, we don't want to become involved with you if it's a matter of you imposing something on us"' (Interview 5). Borger's comments challenge the CB construction of partnerships as collaborative and mutually beneficial and indicate her unwillingness to be complicit in setting up relationships that allow businesses to dominate.

But attempts to accommodate the interests of both partners are undoubtedly more difficult in times of fiscal constraint. When asked whether she thought partnerships could 'take up the slack' caused by cuts in educational funding, Borger referred to a call that she received from a *Calgary Herald* journalist: 'You can imagine what it's like to be phoned by the media and be asked, which was basically what I was asked, "What do you think about a school becoming Husky Oil's high school, or something?" And he wanted me to say, like, do you think in the end you'll see such incredible sponsorship by business that they might start their own charter school, or some version of it. And I'm saying, "well, that's incredibly speculative" ... I mean, that's not coming out of my lips into the newspaper. But you know, people in the public board, like principals, are saying, "Oh yeah," they can see it happening. Yeah, better you say that than me. Because I don't really think that (pause) that's never been the way that we've dealt with our program' (Interview 6). Borger's comments acknowledge the power asymmetry that often characterizes partnerships.

At the same time, partnership coordinators are presumably willing to overlook some of the apparent tensions because of their belief that programs increase the awareness and support of business people for the public school system in Calgary. Tracey Borger says that the program elicits 'more support for public education, by showing businesses the great things that are going on within your school district' (Interview 5). Similarly, Donna Black comments that business partners have a better appreciation of what goes on in schools and therefore express fewer concerns about the system. This view that partnerships turn business people into advocates for the schools is echoed in discussions of partnerships in the United States also (Farrar and Cipillone 1988). Business partners are seen by Borger and Black as more *enlightened* than the rest of the business community. This construction perhaps points to the success of business partners in distancing themselves from groups advocating neoliberal educational reforms and aligning themselves with education leaders. Business involvement is believed to be good for students, and therefore it is assumed that the goals of business people and educators are converging.

'Good' Partnerships

The preceding discussion of the partnership program in public and Catholic districts raises questions about which organizations partner with schools. Not surprisingly, most partnerships are with businesses as opposed to other organizations. In 1992 the Calgary public board's fifty-one partners included twelve predominantly large oil and gas companies, twelve grocery stores, seven financial/insurance/real estate firms, five technology corporations, four law/accounting firms, three service clubs (including the Chamber of Commerce), three hospitality industry companies, three post-secondary institutions, one hospital, and one transportation company. The board also had ten system-wide partnerships involving nine theatre/arts organizations and the city's Parks and Recreation Department. Within the Calgary board, Safeway stores and oil and gas companies were the most popular partners. Safeway stores were more likely to be partnered with elementary schools because they usually preferred their partner to be located in the neighbourhood.

While any public school could be matched potentially with a partner, companies were more likely to request a high school partner (Kaulback and McKay 1993). At the time of my interview with Donna Black, approximately seventeen of the twenty

CBE high schools had partners. Since most Calgary high schools are considered large, they tend to be matched with larger organizations. And while business people expressed their preferences for partners, often CCSD schools 'verbalized a desire to have the very best corporate partner,' which usually translated into a large oil and gas company (19).

Non-business partners within the Catholic board included a local Rotary club, Calgary Transit, and a local hospital. When I asked Donna Black at the CBE about non-business partners, she said, 'We have the [name of hospital]. We find that, so far anyway, organizations that tend to be volunteer-based are not necessarily the best partners because their needs are so great; they need volunteers you know. And their motivation often has to be, just because of the nature of the organization, a little bit different' (Interview 6). However, with provincial cutbacks to health care, hospital-school partnerships in both boards were jeopardized. Although Black was not favourably disposed to partnerships between schools and volunteer-based organizations, one might expect more egalitarian relationships to occur in these contexts.

Black added that her board has tried to involve organized labour in some way, but that 'it just hasn't worked.' When I asked why, we had this exchange:

D: Partly because the organizations (pause) haven't been able to see how they could be involved, because we've made a lot of approaches.
A: What type of organizations were approached?
D: Oh, mainly the Construction Trades Association. It would make a wonderful partner with one of our non-academically inclined schools, for example.[5]

In contrast, a representative of the Alberta Union of Public Employees (AUPE) suggested that her organization had sent letters to the CBE indicating their interest in becoming more involved in public schools and had received no response (Interview 7).

The lack of organized labour involvement in partnerships suggests that while management representatives were gaining entrance to schools, representatives of workers were not.

In sum, norms of 'successful' partnerships have clearly developed over time. School boards in Calgary constructed *good* partners as successful private businesses in particular sectors of the economy – a conception that is quite narrow.[6] This construction is important because of the recruitment function played by boards and the fact that all schools were expected to enter into these relationships. Efforts to recruit 'successful' companies as partners are likely to set up asymmetrical relationships where powerful business partners can 'impose' their agenda. This issue of the relationship that develops between partners is explored further in the case that follows.

Case 1: Monarch Ltd. and Academic High[7]

In 1989 a partnership was formalized between Monarch corporation and Academic High School in Calgary. Monarch [pseud.] is a large corporation in the oil and gas sector; Academic High has approximately 1,700 students and is in an area described by the assistant principal as 'upper-middle class [with] lots of university professionals as parents' (Interview 16). To learn more about this partnership, seven people from Monarch and Academic High (including Andrew Markham, introduced in Chapter 6) were interviewed and I attended five meetings as an observer.

The Ties That Bind

School and company representatives tended to construct the company as *active* and the school as more *passive* in the partnership. Monarch representative Andrew Markham and partnership liaison Sally Long emphasized the company's role as *benefactor*. For example, during a partnership review held at Monarch in June of 1994, the company's tally of hours invested by partners showed that it had invested approximately six times as much time as the school had in partnership activities. While this discrepancy was not raised as a concern, Sally Long suggests that the company had 'thoughts of divorce' for similar reasons in the past. She explains:

S: Ok, about two years ago (pause) we were very frustrated on the Monarch side, with our ability to (pause). I mean, we felt we were reaching out and nobody wanted us. We were not happy with the responses from the school. I mean, we had some frustrations in that the school – particularly the CALM[8] classes where the school taught recruiting, and taught how to write a resume, and taught how to be interviewed – and we had people here who wanted to do that ... And then they were never invited. So we really had some hard thoughts about, maybe it was time to cash in this partnership and get a school that needed us.

A: And what prevented you from doing that?

S: The principal of the school and [Andrew Markham] sat down and said, 'Ok, let's re-jig this and get it to where we want it to be.' So we came back the following September and tried again. And that's when we started getting a declaration of our objectives. And the school, I think, was a little bit frightened that we would leave, and recognized that they should pursue it to see if there was some value. (Interview 19)

Partnership coordinators at the school also construct the relationship as somewhat imbalanced. The coordinator at the time of interviews, Barbara Phillips, suggested that many teachers were not utilizing the human resources that Monarch had to offer. Similarly, past coordinator Andy Laird suggested that the lack of teacher awareness, interest, and time had adversely affected the partnership. He concluded that 'so far, there hasn't been a lot that we've been able to do for them' (Interview 31). At the partnership review, the principal of Academic High also expressed concern over what the school could do to reciprocate.

This construction reinforces the idea that partnerships need to be transformed from a 'one-way form of aid into a genuine partnership with gains on both sides' (OECD 1992: 36). However, it may also be more difficult to measure benefits accruing to the business partner. While schools often appear to get tangible resources (e.g., computers, class speakers), the benefits for companies may be more intangible (e.g., public recognition, access to students as future workers and consumers). Perhaps it was an inability to deal with 'the intangible' that motivated Monarch to try and manage the partnership in a more strategic way. At a meeting held at Monarch in March 1994, with only company representatives present, Sally Long's boss suggested that the 'cost-benefit' of partnership activities should be addressed so that they focus more on 'value-added' activities. Also at the partnership review meeting, Andrew Markham raised the issue of how to make partnership activities more 'efficient.' Probably his thinking was shaped by his experience with the 'value assessment process' developed by the Corporate Council on Education for partners to use when assessing partnership activities.

It was also clear, however, that the actual investments made by Monarch were limited. In fact, Sally Long's construction of Monarch as the *active benefactor* is contradicted by her comments about a specific request made by the school:

S: They came to us to create a very new IB[9] program. They wanted to do a summer institute with [Monarch], and we couldn't do it. We just couldn't muster the resources for it. So they were kind of disappointed.

A: What was it that they had in mind?

S: Creating an entirely new IB course that would include a semester in grade eleven, a semester in grade twelve, and a two-week summer institute hosted at [Monarch] that the kids would attend and be taught by [Monarch] personnel. Big ambitious stuff. And of course, they hit just at the (pause) I mean, the other thing is when [Monarch] originally became involved with this, we had a heck of a lot more people. And they were a lot more free with their time. The reality of the 90s is that everybody's so darn busy. (Interview 19)

She added later that with the cutbacks to education funding the school may be looking more to Monarch for financial help and human resources, 'and my worry is that after years of saying the school didn't want us, the school is going to want us and we're going to have trouble getting to the mark' (9). These comments challenge the construction of the school as *passive beneficiary* and point to tensions within as well as between partners' objectives.

'New Ways of Doing Things'

Given the interest of corporations like Monarch in the cost-effectiveness of their partnership activities, one wonders to what extent they actually bring about 'new ways of doing things' in schools, and whether there is resistance to these changes. One also wonders whether change is a one-way street or whether companies also rethink their practices as a result of partnerships. Data from observations and interviews suggest that Monarch-Academic High partnership activities encouraged the school to reproduce the values and hierarchical relations of authority that existed within Monarch. There was less evidence, however, that the human resources practices at Monarch were changing as a result of its relationship with the school.

The transferral of values and authority relations occurred in a number of ways. For example, one of the partnership objectives was to encourage students to consider careers in the oil and gas industry. Monarch provided a $1,000 scholarship to the top grade twelve graduate each year and there was talk of offering the winner a summer job as part of this award. While this interest in recruiting the brightest students was argued to result in a 'win-win' situation for business and society, the tension between the values of schools as public institutions focusing on collective social goals and corporations as private institutions oriented towards maximizing profit for shareholders was made clear in the following comments by Sally Long: 'I think when somebody is getting 98 in science, we would like them to shadow a research engineer or a research chemist at our [research centre], rather than go into – I mean, for society maybe this isn't the right thing but for business it is – rather than to have them go into cancer research, you know' (Interview 19).

Long's values as a corporate employer also came through in her discussion of the types of students who participated in job shadowing opportunities. She remarks that it is 'smart kids' who come forward rather than 'the kids that don't have a clue what they want to be' (Interview 10). From Long's perspective, intelligent students were those who had career plans. Since only about sixty students from the school were involved in job shadowing Monarch employees during the 1993/4 school year, one could argue that the overall impact of this partnership activity on the school was minimal. At the same time, comments made by partnership coordinator and teacher Barbara Phillips indicate that the values of corporate representatives were being reproduced to some extent by school staff. Discussing her process of finding a student to job shadow Markham, Phillips says, '[Andrew Markham] also requested someone specifically to shadow him. So I've been looking for, you know, just the *right kind of student* [my emphasis]. Not necessarily a really good one, but someone who I think is going to make use of what [Andrew] has to tell the student. I finally found someone this morning. I had him in mind but I couldn't find him, and now I've asked his permission, and he said, "Yeah that'd be great"' (Interview 15). The 'sorting and selecting' of students apparently had shifted to emphasize career as well as academic readiness, but the result was still hierarchical ordering.

Besides job shadowing, another program that appeared to harmonize the values and reward structures for students at Academic High with those of Monarch was Junior Achievement. For some time, Monarch had supplied employee advisers to work with students on JA projects such as Basic Business and Applied Economics. Previous partnership coordinator Andy Laird describes one of these programs as follows: 'Every year [Monarch] sends tickets up and we take our Basic Business class down to [their Annual General Meeting] ... And then after, the kids usually go to the luncheon and they get introduced by the president and the advisors are introduced and they talk a little bit about the program ... And when [the students] wind up the company [they hold their AGM at Monarch]. And the president of [Monarch] is usually there, and some executives ... It gives the kids an opportunity to see the other side of the world if you will. And they get to meet some fairly high-powered people down there' (Interview 31). Students in this program were thus rewarded for their pursuit of economic literacy by teachers and company representatives.

At the partnership review in June 1994, other areas were described as potentially fruitful for partners to pursue. School representatives expressed the view that Academic High could learn from corporations like Monarch in responding to restructuring. An assistant principal thought that teachers should use business people as models. School board representatives suggested that Monarch might become more involved in developing and delivering curriculum – for example, in environmental education – given the company's interest in this area. This counters the view expressed by 71.8 per cent of ATA respondents to the 1999 survey, who felt that business partners/sponsors should not be able to supply promotional curriculum material for teacher use. The general lack of concern at the review meeting regarding the implications of increasing business control over the purpose, organization, and content of public schooling was surprising. While the partnership did not affect the majority of students at Academic High, the goal of partnership activities was, to some extent, to harmonize educational practices with those of corporations.[10] There was less evidence of change in the practices of Monarch. The next section addresses more directly the issue of who participated in the partnership and how.

Perspectives of the 'Rank and File'

While there is a tendency to talk about school and business partners as if they are homogeneous, a closer look at who is included in these categories provides a sense of how participants' different social locations affected their perceptions. The views of Monarch employees, Academic High teachers, and students are therefore addressed. Parents are not included in this discussion, since, according to Sally Long and Barbara Phillips, they were not involved to a great extent in the partnership.

Monarch employees. Partnership activities involved the volunteer efforts of different classes[11] of employees whose goals and motivations were not necessarily synonymous with those of coordinator Sally Long or executive Andrew Markham. This was obvious from the results of a March 1994 in-house survey of employees about the partnership. Of 150 employees who were surveyed, only thirty-six returned completed questionnaires, and approximately half of these had volunteered in partnership activities. While it would be inappropriate to generalize these findings to the entire employee population because of the small number of respondents, the report does provide some useful information. Employees believed that while Monarch's image in the community was enhanced by the partnership, they personally did not benefit from such involvement.

According to teacher Andy Laird, the school did not have trouble finding JA advisors because it was encouraged by Public Affairs people as something that looks 'really good on your resume' (Interview 31). However, at a partnership meeting attended only by Monarch representatives, the latter suggested that recruiting employee volunteers for the partnership posed an ongoing challenge. Employee comments taken from a survey suggest why this may have been the case:

- Before [Monarch's] massive restructuring there were positive benefits (even though I found many students lacked interest). Since the company has gone through massive layoffs, job insecurity, low morale, added workload makes it very difficult to project a positive message or image to any student.
- This is a 'nice-to-do' piece of business in times of economic plenty. Right now it is too time-consuming for [Monarch's]

program coordinator for little, if any, return. I don't believe it supports [Monarch's] current strategic or financial goals.

* Employees have had their motivation reduced significantly with restructuring and benefits loss. They also have gained a lot more work. Most people are burnt out.

Comments about worsening conditions of work and job insecurity point to internal struggles between different groups of employees within the organization, which suggests that to talk about the company partner as if it is homogeneous is somewhat misleading. Rather, key people in Public Affairs at Monarch, such as Andrew Markham and Lillian Stewart, evidently tried to offer incentives for employees to volunteer with varying degrees of success.

Teachers at Academic High. There were also incentives and disincentives for teachers to become involved in the partnership. Probably the major incentive for teachers was the fact that it was supported by school administration. One of the changes made by the incoming principal was to introduce a leadership position that focused on the partnership with Monarch. According to Andy Laird, this position included an increase in pay and a reduction in teaching load. This change in the reward structure at the school arguably provided an additional incentive for teachers to get 'onside' with partnerships.

However, not all teachers at Academic High were supportive of the partnership. In fact, at the partnership review, Andrew Markham commented that he felt a certain 'wariness' on the part of teachers. Markham's comments probably stemmed from his interaction with department heads at Monarch. The forum was a Parent Advisory Council (PAC) meeting in April 1994 where Markham spoke about the work of the Conference Board in developing the employability skills profile and a panel of four department heads was asked to respond. Within this panel, two discussed the usefulness of the CB's work for their particular subject areas, but the other two expressed concerns over the increasing involvement of business in education. The English head asked whether schools should be in the business of turning out students for the job market, while the head of the International Baccalaureate (IB) program referred to the limitations of the ESP and then spoke about 'the myths' perpetuated about education by business and others. These educators were openly resisting the discourse of educational crisis and the role of schools in training workers.

Coordinator Barbara Phillips suggested that there were practical as well as ideological disincentives to becoming involved in the partnership. It took time for teachers to make contacts at Monarch and they were discouraged by the prospect of more paperwork as partnerships became more formalized. Both Phillips and Laird acknowledged that some teachers used the partnership more than others did. Phillips noted, 'We tend to have the *Science* teachers more willing to go out and use the [Monarch] people as a resource for the classroom ... And I think that's because they know exactly what they want, they want a speaker on petrochemicals, or a field trip to [a gas plant]. I think we also have in our *Business* area, a very good link-up. Because again, the teacher there is very specific about what they want from the partner, so we have the [Monarch] people coming in to supply their expertise. I don't think we have good use in *Social*, or in *English*, and I don't think that's particularly a function of the teachers or the curriculum. It's both, it's inertia' [my emphasis] (Interview 15).

Whether teachers ignored the partnership because of inertia or because of their opposition to corporate involvement in their school is a question that Andy Laird sheds some light on when he says, '[T]here's a lot of staff who, when [the partnership] first happened, and I think still, have second thoughts. I don't think they feel that this is the place where business should be. And I think there's a certain amount of antipathy. Certainly some have referred to the Social Studies Department as the Socialist Studies Department' (Interview 31). The comments of partnership coordinators suggested that teachers were mixed in their responses with some supportive of the partnership, some indifferent, and others opposed.

Students at Academic High. Students were not active participants in planning and organizing partnership activities as Barbara Phillips states, 'We don't have any students on [the partnership committee] right now. And that has been a problem right from day one, my very first meeting, is we've got to get students involved in this. But quite honestly, none of the students that we've talked to are really keen, or can see that their input would be of great value, and so right now they're not ... Right now, it's just one more layer way above the kids, where they're functioning' (Interview 15).

When students were surveyed by Monarch, their general indifference to the partnership was confirmed. Of 137 students surveyed, only twenty-five per cent had participated in any of the activities held during a partnership week. Reported reasons for students' non-participation were that they were 'too busy' (43 per cent) and/or 'not interested' (48 per cent). Sixty-seven per cent of respondents indicated that 'they were not interested in the partnership' in general.

Furthermore, students, like many teachers, thought that the primary role of Monarch in the partnership was as school 'patron.' For example, a summary of students' comments from the survey included the following:

- The auto shop could use a wheel balancer
- [The partnership] should be used for more worthwhile causes such as scholarships
- Give us money for new [sports] uniforms
- Perhaps [Monarch] could provide opportunities for summer employment for [NHS] students
- Need new computers (please)

Interviews with two grade twelve students at Academic High confirmed some of the survey findings. Most of what Cindy Lam and Lisa Kao knew about the partnership came from school announcements about job shadowing and other activities. Neither student had participated in either the job shadowing or the partnership week, nor did they know of other students who had. Kao planned to major in science at university, but did not job shadow at Monarch because she was not interested in working in the oil and gas industry. Lam thought that Monarch's role was to provide funding to the school. Interviews with these students point to the danger in assuming that rhetoric around the need for school-business partnerships provided a focus for all groups.

Students did, however, have opinions about Monarch. When asked why she thought the company became involved with her school, Lisa Kao suggested that it might be a way for it to become involved in the community and 'bridge the gap' between themselves and schools – 'to convince people they're not just like money-hungry powerhouses' (Interview 35). Further, when asked what kind of partner she would have picked for Academic High if she could pick any organization in the city, her response was revealing: 'Maybe I'm kind of biased, but I'd pick something, like either something environmental, if we had a Greenpeace or something in our city. But the thing is with Greenpeace, lots of people don't like it, right? I don't know. An oil company is kind of the opposite of an environmental club, you know. An oil company, you think of drilling holes all over the country. And wrecking all this wildlife and stuff. And I've gotten the idea over the years that oil is kind of going downhill. Maybe, like a hospital or something. Or something with a more interesting kind of thing to it. I can't really say though, because I'm not in the front lines of this partnership or anything, so ...'

This answer indicates that Kao was acutely aware of what constituted an acceptable partner in the eyes of decision-makers, and she resisted this construction. Given the lack of student involvement in selecting the partner, her response may explain why students could not see the value of providing input regarding the partnership. Perhaps this is why many students 'voted with their feet' when it came to activities during partnership week.

Postscript to Monarch-Academic High Case and Discussion[12]

The Monarch-Academic High partnership was dissolved in 1996. Since the events leading up to the dissolution inform the earlier analysis of the case, it is useful to sketch in some of the details. Just as there were different versions of why the partnership was initiated,[13] there were also different versions of why it dissolved. School representatives were convinced that it resulted from the activities of a group of teachers who were questioning the ethics of Monarch's international activities. Company representatives, however, commented that the corporation and school were simply heading in different directions.

After interviewing the ex-principal and a number of teachers from Academic High, and talking to Sally Long and a representative of the partnership foundation, a picture of the events leading to the dissolution emerged. In November of 1995 a number of teachers signed a letter asking the leadership committee at the school to reconsider its partnership with Monarch. The letter cited international activities in which Monarch was seen to be implicated, and argued that 'being a partner of [Monarch] is no longer a source of pride for anyone with a social conscience.' In response, the principal invited Monarch representatives to provide their side of the story to a meeting of the school council. In March 1996 the council voted to continue the school's partnership with Monarch. A few months later Monarch initiated a 'divorce' from Academic High, citing its desire to work more closely with the partnership foundation to support a larger number of schools. Since the dissolution of the partnership, Academic High has not acquired another partner. Monarch, on the other hand, became very involved with a 'high needs' elementary school and became a system partner with local schools through the partnership foundation. One of its activities in this capacity involved supporting the employability skills portfolio project, which, interestingly, is the topic of the second case.

While events in the Monarch-Academic High partnership might be construed as a series of misunderstandings between partners, more broadly it represents hegemonic struggle over the directions of educational reform in Alberta and the role of business within that. Student Lisa Kao expressed concern over the motives of the corporation, and the two department heads made the connection between corporations and the reforms that were introduced through the three-year business plan. Teachers

later questioned whether the school should continue its partnership with Monarch given the ethics of the company's international activities. Within the school, there were struggles over
the dominant construction of partnerships by the board and
school as top-down, one-way, and 'monogamous.' Within the
company, employees who were surveyed questioned Monarch's
commitment to providing volunteers to the school at a time of
internal restructuring. Therefore, outside of key promoters within
the company and school, the partnership and its practices were
not unanimously supported.

Case 2: Panorama and Employability Skills

Chapter 6 introduced Gary Baldwin as a manager who worked
for Panorama [pseud.], a large company in the oil and gas sector in Calgary. As a member of the Corporate Council on Education, Baldwin's boss was involved with the employability skills
profile, and this led to his interest in developing a system-wide
partnership initiative. Baldwin explains:

> Basically, it was about eighteen months ago [spring 1993] that
> [my boss] and I sat down. And we said [about the ESP]: 'this is
> pretty good stuff. But where does it go from here?' Because basi-
> cally, the Conference Board had done their job. They put it out.
> And it was up to creative people around the country to come up
> with something. And we started thinking of things. And we in-
> vited somebody in from one of the school boards that [the VP]
> knew to do a little bit of research on this for us. And we found
> out that something along these lines had been done in Michigan.
>
> And ... we made a presentation to our corporate donations com-
> mittee, of which I'm a member. And we got them to support it
> financially in getting the project funded.[14] And we decided to
> involve three school boards ... two schools from each ... And then
> we formed a Steering Committee made up of all six of the princi-
> pals. I'm the chairman on it and we have a representative from
> Alberta Education and someone from the federal government hu-

man resource development group; there's business people on it
as well. (Interview 33)

A development team was formed to draft the final product,
which consisted of a binder with an instructor's guide, a student booklet, and computer disks. This team was composed
largely of educators but was chaired by Baldwin. A model was
provided by the Michigan portfolio project, described in a journal article by Stemmer, Brown, and Smith (1992) as a project
piloted in 1991/2 in twenty-two school districts and involving
more than 5,000 students in grades six through twelve. The
purpose of the Michigan project was to better prepare students
for the workplace. Baldwin's description of the Alberta initiative indicates close parallels with this project in terms of its
impetus, development process, and product.

While the Development Team consisted mostly of educators,
the parameters were probably set by the use of the American
model and by Panorama's management of the development process. The process did involve some compromise and negotiation, however. Teacher and Development Team member Sandra
Morin noted that members had different ideas about how students would use the portfolio because of their different schools.
The team therefore promoted flexibility in implementation, and
pilot schools in fact did tailor the use of portfolios to their individual settings. Morin also commented that educators took steps
to ensure that portfolio binders were free from gender bias.
Educators therefore appeared to have input into the process of
adapting materials to the local context.

The three school boards that piloted the project included the
Calgary public and Catholic boards and the Rockyview public
board.[15] Baldwin said that once the idea for the project was
developed, Panorama involved two schools with whom it already had partnerships: Our Lady of Lourdes in the Catholic
board and Sir John A. MacDonald in the public board. Both
schools were highlighted in a 1992 Alberta Education report as
schools which 'offer alternative programmes to challenge capable students.' The principals of these schools were each asked

to recommend another school within their board, and in this way Holy Cross and Emily Murphy were added. Holy Cross is described in a 1993 Alberta Education report as a 'magnet science school,' while Emily Murphy is a school for pregnant teens. Two schools in Rockyview district were also chosen.

Three of the six were large schools with populations of about 1,200 students each, and in total the project included schools with approximately 4,000 students and 300 teachers. Three of the four schools chosen in Calgary catered to academic and technology-oriented students – students who in fact would best meet the future labour requirements of an employer like Panorama. A teacher at Emily Murphy, the fourth school, was interviewed in part because the school did not appear to fit these criteria for inclusion in the project.

Emily Murphy teacher Sandra Morin described the group's process of reviewing different portfolios and deciding on the content and format for the materials to be produced. She notes that the committee began writing portfolio materials for junior high students, but then decided that they would be more suitable for senior high students in the Career and Life Management (CALM) course. When asked how the group envisioned students using it, Morin replied, 'Everybody has their own idea, to suit their own school. Our ultimate goal was that a whole school, every student that came in to grade ten or if they were in CALM 20, they would start with it and carry it through. We also thought that grade seven would be good, elementary would be good. That they would start to build things on it. And it would become part of them, just something that they did' (Interview 36).

Baldwin also confirmed that developers wanted portfolios to be eventually adapted and used in earlier grades. He expressed his own desire as follows: 'My vision, if you like, is if this is successful, I could see down the road a year or two, some sort of a national advertising campaign. And what caught my eye was the one two years ago, where the kid was in a telephone booth looking for a job: "Oh, you don't have a high school diploma?" Click. I could see a very short commercial being aired where, you know, maybe a kid goes into some sort of a job interview. And maybe they're in the door at the job interview. But [the employer says]: "Where's your portfolio? You don't have a portfolio?" Something like that' (Interview 33). The national advertising campaign that Baldwin referred to was sponsored by the federal government as part of its Stay-in-School initiative. In Baldwin's vision, portfolios would attain a similar level of national visibility as they became an accepted part of the job application process for students. He added that by the time they were finished with the portfolio process, students should know what is important: skills identified by the CB, such as leadership, flexibility, adaptability, and communication. The portfolio itself involved students working through a process of identifying their skills, 'ranking' themselves in terms of employability skills, and coming up with an improvement plan. Similar to Monarch's offer of providing a summer job as well as a scholarship to top graduates, Baldwin suggested that Panorama could sponsor an employability skills contest and offer a summer job to the student with the winning portfolio. Also like Monarch, Panorama displayed an interest in assessing partnership outcomes, and the campaign hired consultants to evaluate the initiative after the pilot year (Hiebert and Tanner 1995).[16]

The portfolio project encouraged students to document and 'measure' their growth in specified skill areas. But despite the fact that they were 'users' of the portfolio, no students were acknowledged in portfolio materials as participants in the project on either the Steering Committee or Development Team. Teachers were requested to act as facilitators and to make class time available for students to work on portfolios. According to the evaluation report, actual use of portfolios varied among pilot schools, with a couple making it optional for teachers and students and others making it an expectation that they be integrated into the curriculum (Hiebert and Tanner 1995). Report writers concluded that teachers would be more inclined to use the portfolio if there was a school-wide focus on career development and demonstrated support from school leaders. More critically, one could argue that in this 'ideal scenario,' teachers would begin to view students through the eyes of potential employers such as Panorama.

To some extent this was confirmed by the evaluators' report where it was noted that 'one school with primarily a high needs student population reported that it seems to be a long process to educate high needs students about employability skills' (7). In 'comments from teachers,' the need to integrate the portfolio into courses and attach marks to it was expressed. In 'student comments,' it was suggested that 'nonacademic students and unmotivated students' needed to have 'specific assignments with marks or other check-up procedures attached to them' (9). These comments suggest transferral of the values and hierarchical ordering system of potential employers to schools (as in the Monarch-Academic High partnership).

But like the Monarch partnership, there was also resistance to this *employability skills* discourse from both teachers and students. Hiebert and Tanner (1995) comment that teachers' responses to the project were 'mixed' and that they made 'only moderate use' of the instructional support materials available through the projects. When asked whether they would like more in-service training on how best to use the portfolio, 45 per cent of teacher respondents answered no and 15 per cent were uncertain. Almost all teacher respondents thought the portfolio, if required, should be part of the CALM course. Data from students also indicate a mixed response. Fifty-nine per cent of respondents described their use of portfolios as either 'uncommitted' (24 per cent) or 'half-hearted' (35 per cent). Both teachers and students challenged the presumed link between employability and employment by requesting an 'external validity check' based on employer testimonials regarding the uses of portfolios in the hiring process. These data suggest that students and teachers were not simply accepting the employability skills discourse, but rather adapted some elements, discarded others, and challenged portfolio architects to provide proof that the discourse could fulfil its promises. The following discussion of Emily Murphy School also indicates both accommodation and resistance.

Employability at Emily Murphy

Gary Baldwin discussed the launch of the Panorama employability skills project in the fall of 1994 as follows: 'So at this October 3rd event, we've got some featured guest speakers who are top people from education, superintendents, and chairmen, president of the Calgary Chamber of Commerce, and people like that ... And [there will be 120 kids], about twenty from each of the six schools, that have basically been hand-picked by the principals and faculty as being kids who, in their minds, are kind of like leaders. And really, we're going to ask them at this event: "Why bother?" We'll be presenting them with the work booklet and so on ... We know these are kids who would bother with this, but we're concerned about the general population, as to why they would bother. And so, they're really going to become kind of patrons, if you like, of this (Interview 33). Baldwin's reference to student 'patrons' recalls Monarch's similar interest in getting more student 'opinion leaders' involved in the partnership. The 'hand-picking' of students also helps to transfer corporate sorting and selecting practices to schools.

Whether these students in fact did become patrons of the project in various schools remains unanswered. The interview with Sandra Morin focused more on how the project had been implemented in her school. When asked how the launch had gone, she replied, 'It was really good. The students really enjoyed it. They felt special. They had a nice lunch and speakers and it was fast-moving ... And they were really excited to come back and start work on it ... I think the other schools have really gone in, like [Holy Cross], have really gone in big' (Interview 36).

However, Morin comments that in her school 'every student isn't ready to do a portfolio' because many do not have resumes and 'don't understand the importance of it' (4). Unlike her impressions of some of the other pilot schools, Morin had introduced the project only to students enrolled in work experience courses, who comprised about one-sixth of Emily Murphy's population of approximately 120 students. Morin's selective introduction of the portfolio project suggested that she had adapted it to the particular needs of students at her school and was not prepared simply to follow Baldwin's request that all students become involved.

Unlike other schools, Morin also found it difficult to get the whole staff at Emily Murphy involved with the project. Part of the staff response was attributed to Morin's belief that the students at Emily Murphy were a 'difficult population to do things through':

> I think a lot of times the students here are just trying to get through it and they don't really see into their future. They live day to day. And so, they can't see any importance in this. They figure, 'well, maybe some other time, I'll put it together.' Or, 'I don't have enough to put into [a portfolio]. I want to just do a resume. [A resume] doesn't tell a lot about me, but [a portfolio] does.' This says all the things, maybe, I don't want people to know. 'If I haven't got good attendance, what else is going to tell that I've got good personal management skills?' I say, 'well, just going to school and having a baby tells that.' ... So before they can do it, there's a lot of building. You have to really pull it out. Where students at a regular high school, you would say it once and their minds would start to go, and they would come up with all the ideas to put into it. In this school, it's pulling it out of them and giving them suggestions ... But I mean, at one of the other schools, before we had our student conference on it, there were about three students who had already finished theirs. And they were wonderful looking. And I'm going, 'aw, not fair.'

The fact that students at Emily Murphy did not see the importance of a portfolio and were resistant to putting one together suggests that these pregnant teens were positioned quite differently than other students with respect to the discourse of employability skills. A large majority keep their babies and more than half live on their own. According to Morin, it was rare for a student to go directly to university. While the class background of these students was not discussed, it was clear that these young, mostly single mothers who had yet to complete high school would face significant obstacles in the labour market. Therefore, while Morin worked towards building their self-confidence, for example, by attempting to reconceptualize *personal management skills* in terms of their realities, undoubtedly these young women were aware of labour market realities and the probability that potential employers would not be sympathetic to them.

Morin's comments raise the issue of what type of student the project was designed for, and indicate the tension between her view of the purpose of the portfolio and that of employer Gary Baldwin. Morin had a sense of competition between pilot schools, with her school coming out at the bottom. At the same time, when asked whether the development team intended the project to be used with less 'advantaged' students, she suggested that it did, as follows: 'When we started it we wanted to make sure that's what it was for. And a lot of [the development team] felt, yes. We feel that a student who has high academic is going to get the job and is going to succeed. They have the personal management skills, they have all those things anyway ... We all as a group agreed that it was for the, I don't like to say the slower learners, but the student that needed the extra push ... And that was why Emily Murphy got in on it. It was something that was a tool that we could use to help our students.' Morin saw the project as a tool to build self-esteem in students like those at Emily Murphy. As she said, 'everything we do is to try to build their confidence.'

Morin's vision of the purpose of portfolios as a way of building self-esteem of students at Emily Murphy challenges the vision of Gary Baldwin who viewed portfolios as a *screening device* for employers. The evaluation report reflected Baldwin's vision: 'In one school ten students went to the offices of their corporate partner for mock interviews. The business partner said that they would have hired all ten students if they had positions for them. One of the interviewers remarked, "I really felt like I got to know the students through their portfolios; it was not like hiring blind"' (Hiebert and Tanner 1995: 7). Elements of competition were apparent in Baldwin's reference to the contest planned by Panorama, as well as in the student booklet, which noted that 'the portfolio is a way to set yourself apart.' Similarly, the instructor's manual suggested that 'a portfolio recognition night might be held [at the school] where the top ten portfolios of your graduates are recognized.' At Emily Murphy, however, Morin made a concerted effort to downplay the competitive potential of the portfolio in order to help a group of young women who faced inequitable labour market opportunity structures.

The Emily Murphy context, in this sense, brings the tension between *employability* and *employment* to the surface. These are students who need help to secure employment if they are to support their families without government assistance. They are students for whom the reality of limited opportunities is probably experienced daily. They are not, for the most part, students who are university bound and who are likely to be 'snapped up' by corporate recruiters on the basis of their portfolios. Because of this tension, the topic was broached indirectly with Sandra Morin in the following exchange:

A: Have you actually had the experience of [Emily Murphy] students going to employers with the portfolio yet?

S: No, not yet.

A: That will be interesting to see. Has there been any kind of education of employers about this?

S: We have, because we did have employers on the Steering Committee, or within the whole process. But not a great amount. But they have been approached. The community does know about it, probably the bigger employers. And they're very much behind it. (Interview 36)

As mentioned, both students and teachers who responded to the evaluators' survey expressed a desire to have the portfolios validated by employers in the hiring process. There was therefore pressure on corporate sponsors and other employers to live up to the promises of employability skills discourse.

Postscript to Panorama Case

By 1998 the employability skills project had been expanded within Calgary and beyond, and was embraced provincially by Alberta Education. The partnership foundation took over the production and marketing of employability skills portfolios and coordinated the project following the pilot. Materials were made available to schools in the six districts represented by the foundation and were widely used at the grade eleven level in CALM courses, according to a coordinator from the partnership foundation (personal communication 16 July 1998). It was decided then that the project would be more effectively introduced at an earlier level, and in 1998/9 portfolios were to be completed by every grade nine student in the six districts represented by the partnership foundation. The project was to be evaluated in a four-year longitudinal study conducted by the University of Calgary to determine how effective portfolios were in helping students gain employment direction.

This widespread implementation of the employability skills portfolio project coincides with Alberta Education's *Framework for Enhancing Business Involvement in Education* (1996a). It affirmed the CB work in developing the employability skills profile and asked that over the next few years 'school systems, with Alberta Education assistance, develop employability skills portfolios and encourage and assist all students to maintain such portfolios, beginning in junior high school at the latest' (16). Portfolios ideally would be used, together with student transcripts, by employers and post-secondary institutions for screening applicants. This report suggests that the Panorama employability skills initiative provided a *demonstration project* that was later taken up by politicians and bureaucrats in educational policy.

The strategy of developing a model that could be adopted by government policy-makers is not new. In the late 1800s and early 1900s, Ontario employers interested in gaining public funding for technical education developed demonstration schools to provide the government with models (Morrison 1974). These strategies were evidently successful since the Industrial Education Act of 1911 proposed a framework for vocational education in Ontario which included differentiated schools and governance of technical schools by a school board–industry advisory committee (Taylor 1997). From its original conception by the Conference Board to its implementation as a demonstration project in Calgary to its adoption by the province as policy, the employability skills profile/portfolio has similarly been corporate-driven and strategically promoted (Taylor 1998b).

Concluding Comments

Eagleton (1991: 48) writes that it is at the level of 'operative ideology' that we are likely to find a 'process of compromise, adjustment and tradeoff between its world view and its more concrete prescriptive elements.' The preceding case studies reveal that this process is likely to involve struggle among the different players. In the Monarch-Academic High case, there were struggles over the extent to which corporate goals of profit maximization and 'enlightened self-interest' were consistent with school goals of treating students equitably and encouraging them to participate as democratic citizens. Related to this were struggles over whether businesses should have increased control over the purpose, organization, and content of public schooling.

Interviews indicate that resistance to the vision held by partnership promoters came from Monarch employees as well as from teachers and students at the school. Struggles therefore occurred not only between school and business partners but also among the various constituencies that comprised 'the company' and 'the school.' In the Panorama case there was struggle over how to reconcile the interest of employer Gary Baldwin in making hiring more efficient, with the interest of teacher Sandra Morin in increasing the self-esteem of her students. Pertinent questions underlying the struggle were How are skills related to one's position in the labour market? Who is responsible for preparing youth for the labour market? How and when should this be done?

Gary Baldwin and Andrew Markham viewed the labour market as a competitive but just distribution system where those who are appropriately skilled reap the benefits. This contrasts with the view that skills are socially constructed and obscure divisions based on gender, race/ethnicity, and class.[17] In this latter view, labour market divisions have as much to do with the 'strategic position of certain groups within the production process and the power of collective organizations,' as with the capabilities of different groups of workers (Livingstone 1987: 3). How the labour market is viewed clearly has implications concerning whether we blame students for their 'choices' or direct our efforts towards reducing the inequities that characterize schools and the labour market.

The question of who is responsible for preparing students was key in the Panorama case. The initiative had the effect of juxtaposing the concept of 'employability' (seen primarily as the responsibility of educators and students) with the guarantee of 'employment' (primarily the responsibility of employers). By shifting responsibility for future success in the labour force to schools, companies also shifted some of the risk and cost associated with hiring decisions. However, survey comments from the evaluation report indicate that educators challenged employers to ensure that their students would be *employed* and not just *employable*. This represents another site of struggle. If educators are required to prepare students, then compromise is required, as the case of Emily Murphy suggests. Sandra Morin seemed aware that the competitive model would only produce *winners* and *losers* in the school-to-work transition and therefore ran counter to other educational goals.

Despite this evidence of struggle, the 'solutions' promoted at school district and provincial levels carried weight. Provincial support for school-business partnerships and greater business involvement in education was conveyed to districts and schools through policy documents. As in the UK context, the influence of teachers unions and other education 'producer' lobbies had been replaced by an orientation towards parents and industrialists – the 'consumers' of education (Ball 1990: 8). At the board level, the construction of 'desirable' partners and the district's involvement in arranging matches undoubtedly influenced the relationships that resulted. Board practices also influenced the 'institutional ideologies and patterns of preferment' within schools (Ball 1987: 264). Declining resources resulting from cutbacks in 1994 began to increase the pressure on schools to consider other ways of accessing resources.

In sum, the preceding discussion indicates that at an institutional level, greater business involvement in education was embraced. The province, the public and separate schools boards, and school leaders were promoting partnerships. However, moving to the level of the school and inside the company – the places where ideology becomes operationalized – yields another perspective. The partnership process at this level can be seen to involve struggle, compromise, and resistance. Tensions within partnership visions are unveiled and challenged, and their effectiveness is thwarted by the indifference of employees, teachers, and students. Chapter 8 examines further challenges to the business-in-education vision from organized labour.

CHAPTER EIGHT

The Fragmentation of Labour

We're so pleased with this advantage,
Mr Klein has told us so.
Moaners and whiners in this province,
Are completely free to go.
He's already helped the folk on welfare
Get a one way ticket for free,
Now he hopes the social workers
Will move into B.C.

(Edmonton Raging Grannies, 'Alberta's Advantage')

The Raging Grannies sing the above-mentioned song to the tune of 'Working on the Railroad,' but despite this satirical treatment, the Alberta Economic Development department publishes a report that tries to sell the 'Alberta Advantage' to potential investors. Information in *Facts on Alberta* (2000)[1] includes the following:

- Alberta has a low overall tax regime, no provincial sales tax, and a highly skilled and productive workforce. The cost of doing business is about ten percent lower in Alberta than in the United States according to a 1999 study by KPMG.
- In 1997, forty-nine percent of the labour force reported holding a university degree, or post-secondary diploma or certificate (11).

- From 1993 to 1997, Alberta had the third lowest person-days lost due to labour disputes (3.9 days per 10,000 compared to the Canadian average of 7.9). In 1997, the unionization rate in the private sector was twelve percent, in the public sector was fifty-two percent, and 'overall unionization was estimated at twenty-two percent, among the lowest in Canada' (13).
- The minimum wage was $5.90 per hour in October 1999 (lower than British Columbia, Quebec, Ontario, Saskatchewan, and Manitoba).

From a labour perspective, the Alberta Advantage promoted by Premier Klein in his trade missions to Asia in 1993 was an advantage primarily for employers. But while there was opposition to the restructuring that was taking shape at that time, opponents seemed to have little impact on government. The fact that Alberta lost so few days to labour disputes during this period of intense cutbacks in the public sector is telling. This chapter explores the perspectives of various labour representatives at this time, focusing on their relationships with other labour groups, government, and business, and their visions for education and for society as a whole.

Interview Participants

Seven representatives were interviewed from the Alberta Teachers' Association (ATA), the Canadian Union of Public Employees (CUPE), the Staff Association for the CBE, the Alberta Federation of Labour (AFL) and the Calgary District Labour Council (CDLC). Table 8.1 lists participants' pseudonyms, their affiliations, and interview dates.

Murray Walsh is a facility operator in a Calgary school and a representative of CUPE local 40. He is one of 750 custodial staff who are responsible for cleaning and maintaining buildings operated by the Calgary Board of Education. Pam Conway is from the Staff Association, representing approximately 2,000 non-educational workers employed by the board. Most of these workers

TABLE 8.1
Labour Participants

Murray Walsh, Canadian Union of Public Employees (CUPE)	10 March 1994
Pam Conway, CBE Staff Association	12 September 1995
Mark Silver, Canadian Teachers' Federation (CTF)	23 June 1993
Janet Weis, Alberta Teachers' Association (ATA)	26 April 1994
Nancy Ellis, Calgary Public Teachers	12 April 1994
Marg Szabo, Alberta Federation of Labour (AFL)	26 August 1994
Joan Farrell, Quality Education Coalition (QEC)	23 February 1994
Chris MacDonald, Calgary District Labour Council	22 April 1994

are female and many work part-time. Three participants from teacher associations at national, provincial, and local levels were also interviewed: Mark Silver works for the Canadian Teachers' Federation (CTF) in Ottawa; Janet Weis is a staff person with the Alberta Teachers' Association, representing 28,000 public school teachers in the province; and Nancy Ellis is a spokesperson for the Calgary Public Teachers (ATA Local 38), representing approximately 6,200 members.

Three representatives from umbrella organizations were also interviewed. Marg Szabo is from the Alberta Federation of Labour, representing over forty unions in the province with a combined membership of over 115,000.[2] At the time of our interview in Edmonton, Szabo was also involved with a coalition of education groups and individuals that formed in December of 1993 to 'combat the Klein government's cutbacks to education funding.' Regional working groups of this Quality Education Coalition (QEC) were later established in Edmonton, Calgary, Lethbridge, and Grand Prairie. Joan Farrell from the Alberta Union of Public Employees (AUPE) spoke to me about the Calgary group. Also in Calgary, Chris MacDonald represents the CDLC.

Relationships

Compared to the business-in-education network described in Chapter 7, labour seemed more fragmented. Within education, employee groups were divided by their differing positions within the labour process and their differing interests. A lack of established information channels and resources also made it difficult to form alliances. Representatives from various unions agreed that their relationships with government had worsened over time. As a result, part of the teachers' oppositional strategy was to solicit support from business leaders and have them lobby government on behalf of educators. Relationships within the labour community, and with government and business, are explored in the sections that follow.

'Labourers' and 'Professionals'

> [I]t is wise to think of [teachers] as located simultaneously in two classes. They thus share the interests of both the petty bourgeoisie and the working class. Hence, when there is a fiscal crisis in which many teachers are faced with worsening working conditions, layoffs ... and when their labour is restructured so that they lose control, it is possible that these contradictory interests will move closer to those of other workers and people of colour who have historically been faced with the use of similar procedures by capital and the state. (Michael Apple, *Teachers and Texts*: 32)

In the Alberta context, we see evidence of this contradictory class location historically. A critical reader[3] who had been involved in the ATA for several years comments: 'By most objective criteria teachers and their representative organization should be part of the house of labour; yet within Alberta the ATA strongly resists those pressures that would lead it in that direction. Rather, the ATA attempts to continue in its historical role of support and legitimization for the existing power relationships within Alberta and seeks to build strategic alliances to allow its members to maintain their relatively privileged position within the economy.' He notes that the historical alignment between the ATA and the Social Credit government resulted in a number of gains for educators over thirty-six years, including the entrenchment of collective bargaining rights, improvements in wages and conditions, and close involvement in policy-making processes.[4]

With the switch to the Progressive Conservative government in 1971, one might have expected the ATA's relationship with government to change. However, this reader argues that the ATA was able to integrate its goals with those of the government's emerging urban power base in the 1970s and 80s. Economic expansion in the early days made it easier to work together. By the 1990s, however, the economic situation had worsened and the ATA was confronted with the Klein government's 'introduction of neoconservative and neoliberal ideology regarding privatization and the introduction of market forces into education.' In response the ATA has tried to regain its privileged position with the government's policy community, in his view.

The *ideology of professionalism* helps to explain teachers' reluctance and failure to establish links with organized labour. While teachers' associations, provincially and locally, actively opposed government restructuring in the 1990s and showed an interest in liaising with other labour groups, they carefully tried to construct themselves as professional organizations rather than unions throughout this process. The ideology of professionalism runs through ATA-sponsored reports such as *Trying to Teach* (1993b), *Trying to Teach: Necessary Conditions* (1994), and *A Framework for Educational Change in Alberta* (1995).

Trying to Teach documents teachers' concerns with a number of government-imposed reforms such as results-based curricula, increased external testing, and the integration of special needs students without adequate resources. Therefore, even before the release of the three-year business plan, teachers were concerned about the erosion of their 'professionalism, authority, and expertise' through the intensification of their work (1993b: 24). *Trying to Teach: Necessary Conditions* tries to re-establish teachers professionalism by recommending that school boards 'draw upon the expertise of teachers rather than impose solutions from above' (1994: 22), and that Alberta Education develop 'genuine consultative structures that give parents and teachers meaningful input' into provincial decisions (23). *A Framework for Educational Change* is a direct response to the three-year business plan and echoes the theme that the government and school boards need to treat teachers more as professionals. But the report also acknowledges that how teachers and governments define professionalism may differ. Governments tend to focus on holding teachers responsible for outcomes while the ATA focuses on attaining greater control for teachers over their educational practices. Authors of the framework write, 'In contrast to *accountability*, which focuses only on what can be measured and reported, professional responsibility entails commitment to a much larger mission, which, in the case of teachers, involves meeting the learning needs of students. Teachers who are acting with *professional responsibility* will, for example, use diagnostic tests rather than standardized achievement tests to assist them in developing programs that truly meet the needs of their students. Professional responsibility also means that the teaching profession accepts responsibility for the conduct and competence of its members' [my emphasis] (ATA 1995: 9).

Of course, the danger in defining professionalism in terms of 'expert knowledge' is that teachers may be held accountable for outcomes that are largely beyond their control. The ATA *Framework* addresses this by identifying areas where government and parents should also be held accountable. CTF representative Mark Silver similarly proposes a vision of schools as sites of shared responsibility rather than as insular enclaves for professionals when he says, 'There are still a number of [CTF members] who feel business has no place at all, that teachers are the professionals. We know best, and if, to use an analogy, you have to have your gall bladder removed ... you would go to a specialist who's had the training and so on. But many are beginning to realize ... it's far more complex than that ... Because once you say – even if it were true and if you could say this – that learning takes place in schools or in institutions and there are professionals who are specifically trained for that purpose ... then what you're saying is that if learning does not take place then it is "the teacher" or "the institution" that is responsible ... [My own view] is that the delivery of education has to be devel-

oped much more on a shared basis than is presently the case'
(Interview 1). Teachers' associations are therefore being forced
to redefine what it means to be a professional within the context
of reforms that place greater emphasis on outcomes as well as
which potentially intensify and de-skill teachers' work.

The notion of professionalism has been important historically
for teachers as they have tried to 'raise their class position' from
an intermediate position between the working and middle classes
to a 'middle class position' (Apple 1986: 213). It was particularly
important for women teachers in their fight to win equal treatment, pay, and control over their day-to-day work. The fight to
protect teacher autonomy represents female resistance to male
authority, since in the past and present, teachers have been predominantly female and administrators, predominantly male.

At the same time, promoting professionalism may also reproduce gender relations. For example, when the provincial ATA
decided to run a campaign that would counter the government's
restructuring agenda, they were given the following advice by
public relations people:

> And the advice was, 'you need to change the public's perception
> of you. You need to build an image of *caring professionals* who
> care about children.' That has bothered teachers a great deal.
> Many teachers have felt that if we could simply organize a one-
> day strike across the province or get a huge march or something,
> things would change. And the more *soft-sell* approach of saying,
> 'the big issue here is public education, and we care about it,' has
> not met with unqualified consent of all teachers. But at the same
> time, I really believe it is the only way that we're going to win
> this one. That we do have to persuade parents and school boards
> and business people that public education is worth paying for.
> And that qualified teachers are a necessity ... And that it's not to
> anyone's advantage to destroy the teachers' association or to break
> it up, but rather to keep it strong. But it is an association of
> professionals *rather than a union* [my emphasis].[5] (Interview 21)

The advice that teachers adopt the rather gendered image of
'caring professionals' and a 'soft-sell' approach to government

actions indicates a tension that is described by Apple (1986: 49): '[W]hile these teachers rightly fight on a cultural level against what they perceive to be the ill effects of their loss of control and both the division and intensification of their labour, they do so at the expense of reinstituting categories that partly reproduce other divisions that have historically grown out of patriarchal relations.' Struggles over the status and treatment of teachers thus highlight tensions that are rooted in classed and gendered teacher identities and the divisions between professional and worker, authority and nurturer.

These struggles have implications for the relationships between teacher associations and organized labour groups. The historic ambivalence of the ATA towards alliances with other organized labour groups is well known in the labour community. But Chris MacDonald from the Calgary District Labour Council was hopeful that teachers were beginning to recognize their common interests with other workers. He says: 'It is the intent that the ATA will be participating in [the Common Front], as will a lot of different groups who have been reluctant to participate in our activities. I have assurances that they will ... The Calgary Public Teachers, their new president is a very good friend of ours and we work with her very closely. She invited me to speak at the ATA Public Teachers meeting a month ago. And quite honestly, that was the first time in recent history, and perhaps the first time ever, that the Alberta teachers have invited a labour body such as the Calgary Labour Council to come and speak at their meetings' (Interview 24). The Common Front is a coalition of labour and social justice organizations that was initiated in the spring of 1994 to challenge government cutbacks and restructuring. Regional groups, including one in Calgary, were subsequently established.

Nancy Ellis from the Calgary Public Teachers stressed the importance of liaising with labour groups 'when your interests mesh.' She provided the example of a coalition of employee groups and parents in education called Partners in Education that began meeting in the fall of 1993. The coalition included representatives from custodial staff (CUPE Local 40), the Staff

Association, and parents from the Calgary Council of Home and Schools Association (CCHSA). However, Ellis acknowledged that the ATA was nervous about establishing closer links with labour groups outside education because it has 'always tried very hard to portray ourselves as a professional association' (Interview 21). This 'fear of falling' in terms of occupational status, is evident when she talks about the relationship between the teachers and the Calgary District Labour Council: 'We keep in touch with the Calgary Labour Council, but we haven't had a lot of interaction with them. [Chris MacDonald] came and spoke at one of our general meetings, to tell people about the rally in Banff. And there was almost this feeling that went through the general meeting (pause). There were, oh, 3,000 people there I think, and when [Chris MacDonald] stood up and said, "Brothers and sisters," it was kind of ... (laugh)' (Interview 24). A teacher acquaintance who was also present, confirmed that MacDonald's mode of address made a number of teachers uncomfortable. In addition, MacDonald's description of the 'very close' relationship between the labour council and Calgary teachers can be contrasted with Ellis's comment that 'we haven't had a lot of interaction with them.'

The provincial association was also ambivalent about formal involvement with organized labour. Janet Weis was asked whether the ATA had much historical involvement with labour groups and she replied that they had 'observer status on a coalition at the time of the Free Trade Agreement.' As with the Calgary local, it appears that coalitions develop when 'interests mesh.' Given the tenor of her response, Weis was asked directly whether she thought ATA members see themselves more as a professional group than a union, and she replied, 'Well, I do. I work for the Association, but I see the Association as far more devoted to professional concerns. Our teacher welfare area, which is the bargaining arm, takes less than 10 per cent of our total fees that are collected. Ninety per cent of the fees that are collected from members go into professional development and representation ... We also discipline our own members and spend a considerable amount of money on our discipline investigations and charges of unprofessional conduct. So that we are concerned about the profession itself' (Interview 26).

Weis's view is reflected in an ATA position paper, The Nature of the Teaching Profession, which states, '[T]he continued professionalization of teaching is one of the major objectives of the Association. In terms of minimum educational requirements, remuneration, autonomous organization and control of service and prestige in the hierarchy of occupations, teaching has been unable to equal the classical professions. Teachers are, however, leading in the development of the modern conception of a professional occupation.'[6]

Labour representatives are aware of the ATA's ambivalence towards them, as AFL representative Marg Szabo indicates: 'I think that the ATA has always held itself sort of separate. In fact, I've heard that they've had a long-standing policy, or unwritten policy, that they weren't supposed to be getting too close to the federation of labour. There's that kind of, it's not that we don't get along, it's just that *we don't see ourselves as having common approaches* I guess. But I think that's changing' [my emphasis] (Interview 32).

One of the differences between the groups involves support for political parties – the AFL formally supported the New Democratic Party, while the ATA had a policy of nonalignment. But despite differences, other labour groups wanted to strengthen their connections with this relatively large and affluent union. Joan Farrell from AUPE refers to the strength that other QEC members have drawn from the example of the provincial ATA (Interview 7). Chris MacDonald spoke approvingly about its public relations campaigns, noting that 'a lot of our organizations have no money to put into advertising, no money to put into campaigns, ourselves and a lot of our unions' (Interview 24). Chris MacDonald, Marg Szabo, and Joan Farrell all saw the need to 'build coalitions' among labour and other individuals/groups fighting for social justice.

But coalition-building is to some extent hampered by the differences among labour groups that are based on resources, gender, race/ethnicity, educational and occupational status, and workers' relationships to the labour process. Divisions are highlighted by Nancy Ellis when she talks about the relationships within the Partners in Education coalition: 'Our own CUPE locals we work with quite closely. I have a monthly meeting with them to try and keep a united front there ... And because we're the main employee group, we're the ones that are talked about the most. And they feel kind of shoved off to one side ... [And] it's much easier to contract out the CUPE jobs. Staff Association has always felt like the poor cousin, I suppose. Because it's mainly a women's group: these are the secretaries, the aides, the lunchroom aides ... They often feel like the forgotten people, and the people with no power. So we try and meet with them monthly so that we can at least keep supporting one another and that we value them. The other thing that causes a few problems there is the [school] board talks a lot about differentiated staffing' (Interview 21). One tension between the ATA and Staff Association stemmed from the school board's 1993 decision to hire ESL assistants instead of teachers as the program was cut back. As a result, certificated teachers were pitted against paraprofessional aides.

The above quotation reveals some of the tensions among employee groups because of their different relationships to the labour process in schools. It also reveals some of the obstacles involved in trying to establish egalitarian employee group relationships within hierarchical and socially divisive structures. Structural inequities enter into the coalition dynamics and cause tensions. For example, Murray Walsh comments that teachers are provided with extensive professional development opportunities, whereas building operators must upgrade on their own time and often at their own expense. He also notes that, unlike teachers, most of his employees have been affected by cuts before. Similarly, Pam Conway suggests that teacher's aides and other Staff Association employees perceive that teachers 'get it all': 'They get paid all this money and don't have to worry about income in July and August and their benefits are covered. Like, what are they bitching about? Whereas we only get paid for what we work and you don't take a minute more than what you're supposed to for your coffee break,' and that kind of mentality ... [And] when you've got these [employee] groups and they're competing for the dollar, that kind of makes it tough' (Interview 41). Thus, while groups recognize the need to work together, they also acknowledge the forces that pull them apart.

It is evident that the 'network' of labour groups is different from that between business representatives discussed in Chapter 6. First of all, one of the largest labour groups in Alberta, the ATA, does not appear entirely convinced that it should participate in this network. It is not a member of the AFL nor is its local in Calgary a member of the Labour Council. Furthermore, CUPE 40[7] and the Staff Association are also not members of these groups. Contrast this with the active involvement of business representatives in local, provincial, and national-level organizations such as the partnership and science foundations, the ACC, ACR and the Conference Board of Canada. The general impression is that labour lacks 'internal integration' compared to business groups. While local members know one another, coalition-building is hampered by a lack of established information channels, according to Joan Farrell from the QEC. Further, the lack of resources of organized labour poses a serious problem. This can be contrasted with business-sponsored organizations such as the science and partnership foundations, which are supported by government funding.

Business-sponsored foundations can be usefully compared to Partners in Education and the Quality Education Coalition since these groups represent 'coordinating' bodies. Chapter 6 argues that the partnership and science foundations represent sites where business interests can be harmonized, a coherent vision developed, particular interests obscured, and strategies developed and implemented. Foundations were supported by government as well as by corporations. In contrast, Partners in Education was a worker coalition formed to provide strength and oppose the 'divide and conquer' strategies of employers. The QEC was also formed to build worker strength, although Szabo said that a provincial coalition was not feasible because of travel and other expenses. Szabo and Farrell also note that groups have been busy fighting their own battles with little time for coalition-building. Labour's defensive position vis-à-vis government therefore is also a key difference compared to business-sponsored foundations.

Relationships with Government

Labour representatives in Alberta suggest that their ability to influence public policy decisions has decreased over time, particularly since the Klein government took office. It was commonly perceived that Alberta had become a 'corporate state' by the 1990s, where government was run more like a business and was influenced more by business (Lisac 1995). Labour people felt shut out of the government's policy community.

A labour magazine quotes an AFL representative as saying that there had been little real communication between labour ministers and unions for the past decade (Vicars 1993: 5). Marg Szabo from the AFL confirmed that the relationship between the AFL and government was poor, adding that it had worsened over time. While AFL representatives used to have annual meetings with cabinet ministers to discuss the issues of the day, the government had become less willing to listen to the labour movement since the late 1980s, according to Szabo. The government's 1993 roundtables symbolized for interview participants its new way of doing business. Chris MacDonald comments that representatives from the AFL and Calgary labour council were not invited to the health-care roundtables. Rather, five labour people were included in the 160 who were 'hand-picked by the government to attend' (Interview 24). Participants believed that the government's agenda for restructuring had already been formulated prior to 'public' consultations.

ATA participants also perceived that their influence with government representatives had declined over time. Janet Weis from the provincial association says,

> I don't think it's changed much in the last year and a half. I think that the change has been over a lengthier period of time. I think

there's been an erosion over the past twenty years of all groups, of their control of education, or their input into education. And it started maybe fifteen years ago when [Alberta Education] eliminated the curriculum review boards which they used to have, which had representation from school boards association, the ATA, Home and School, and all of the groups that were an influence, or part of the education stakeholders ... And the province started taking over control of curriculum decisions, without the same level of influence that the other groups used to have. And so, the erosion of the influence of the other people who had interests in education over time has been phenomenal. And I think this latest tax grab is the final nail in the coffin. It gives the government total control over education. (Interview 25)

By 'tax grab,' Weis is referring to the centralization of education funding that was part of its three-year business plan. Her suggestion that traditional educational stakeholders have lost influence is supported by Decore and Pannu's (1991) study of educational policies in Alberta. Authors argue that curriculum had become more tightly controlled by the department since 1980, and has increasingly emphasized basics, standardized tests, and streamed program levels. More generally, government policies focused on centralizing control, cutting spending, and diverting funds from public education to private programs. From this perspective, the cutbacks and restructuring introduced in 1994 were not a radical departure.

There was, however, the perception that the Klein government was different. For example, Nancy Ellis from the Calgary Public Teachers says, 'I think it's really changed a lot within this year, since the government changeover. In that, our people [ATA in Edmonton] express the feeling that this is not the same government that they've ever dealt with before and that they find that the rules are different. And they're finding it much more difficult to know how to play the role and how to be involved and how to work with the government ... [In the past] they knew that there were certain people that they phoned to talk to or to have a meeting with. This year, I think they felt more stonewalled in that ... And they weren't sure exactly who was in charge, perhaps. Or that they were getting the straight goods' (Interview 21).

While the governing party did not actually change, as Lisac notes, Conservative party leadership 'reinvented itself in the early 1990s' (1995: 43). As a result of the change in its relationship with the government, Ellis suggests that the ATA was forced into a reactive mode. This perception was shared by the editor of the *Calgary Herald,* who noted that 'neither trustees nor teachers have been able to push their way onto the playing field in a constructive proactive way' (26 September 1995: A10). Despite ATA attempts to promote an 'ideology of professionalism,' the government constructed its relationship with the ATA as one of *employer* and *union.* Nancy Ellis mentioned the 'teacher bashing' that allegedly took place at the Progressive Conservative convention in 1994, where delegates passed a resolution to study the feasibility of splitting the ATA into professional and bargaining associations. Comments made by the president of the ATA in an issue of the association's magazine also suggested that Alberta teachers felt besieged (Mackay 1994). By constructing education groups as 'self-interested,' the government was able to rationalize their exclusion from policy debates.

Like other labour representatives, ATA participants were convinced that the government's agenda for restructuring was written before the government held its roundtable consultations. Ellis characterized it as a 'private school agenda' that would promote inequality. ATA representatives felt that the emphasis on standardized tests – as a way to measure outcomes and differentiate between schools – would exacerbate existing inequalities based on students' socioeconomic backgrounds, race/ethnicity, special needs, and gender. Publication of test results by schools would perpetuate inequalities as test scores began to affect parents' choices of schools, the relations among schools, and the reward structures within each board. Issues around equity therefore represented a site of struggle over educational reform.

Pressures resulting from government actions and interactions at the provincial level affected relations between school boards and their employees. Ellis describes the relationship between

the Calgary Public Teachers and the CBE at the time of restructuring: 'I think that as a teachers' association, we would still like
to feel that we had a bit more support from our board in realizing that it's to everyone's advantage for everyone to be strong
in this situation ... But some of our own board seem to feel that
if they do what the government wants them to do, then perhaps
they can establish a working relationship with the government.
And so the word "compliance" has come up a lot over the last
two months.'

The issue of contracting out was of particular concern to custodians and other non-teaching staff during the late 1980s and
early 90s. Murray Walsh states that his local 'lost six buildings
to contracting out' and membership declined approximately 12
per cent between 1992 and 1994.[8] As a consequence, he says,
'morale is terrible' (Interview 14). Pam Conway from the Staff
Association referred to the board's decision to contract out 158
childcare aide positions by 1996. She later adds that the CBE
was involved in another pilot project that involved contracting
out the work of itinerant teachers to a private company that
employed non-accredited instructors. The fact that these groups
were most vulnerable to the cost-cutting actions of school boards
adversely affected their relationships with the board and with
each other.

Labour views of the relationship between their organizations
and government paint a picture of a group that felt it was 'bang-
ing its head against the wall.' ATA attempts in the early 1990s
to construct itself as a *professional association* were countered by
government depictions of it as a *self-interested and powerful union*,
despite the ATA's lack of formal affiliation with organized
labour. This depiction is symbolic of the declining influence of
this group within the government's policy community. The
ATA's strained relationship with government probably helps to
explain its relationships with business representatives.

Relationships with Business

While ATA participants perceived that their influence with government had declined over time, Chapter 6 argued that the in-

fluence of business people within educational policy-making has increased. In fact, it was widely perceived that a 'business agenda' was driving reforms in education and in other public policy areas in the province in the early 90s. Given this context, it is not surprising that the ATA should have an ambivalent relationship with business people. Participants' comments suggest that the ATA, like other labour groups, recognized that the government's policy community had changed and that their position was less secure. Policy communities are composed of groups, both inside and outside government, that have an interest in a particular policy field, and attempt to influence it (Pal 1997). Part of the ATA response was to establish formal links with business groups as a way of indirectly influencing government. However, it could be argued that the business groups with the most political clout had the least in common ideologically with the ATA.

For example, while provincial ATA and Calgary Public Teachers were members of the Alberta and Calgary Chambers of Commerce, respectively, the extent to which they could influence these groups was questionable. The past president at the ATA sat on the chamber's Education Committee along with ACC's Dan Williams and 'found it frustrating,' according to Janet Weis (Interview 25). Similarly, Nancy Ellis from the Calgary Public Teachers notes that the Calgary Chamber was not particularly receptive: 'We decided two or three years ago that it was worthwhile buying a membership in the Chamber to try to establish communication links with the Chamber. But we have never been invited to sit on their Education Committee or to speak to the Education Committee. When they have put out news releases advising the government on what to do with education, they have never called us and said, "We're going to put out a news release. Would you like to look at it?" And I have written letters to the president of the Chamber saying, "We have a membership. We would have liked to have at least been contacted." And that letter hasn't even been responded to. So that's rather frustrating ... But I think we have to keep building those alliances' (Interview 21). Ellis commented earlier that 'it seems as though this government believes that whatever the Chamber says is the gospel.' Both Weis and Ellis mention Dan Williams's influence within the ACC and the government, and express concerns about his personal interests in the privatization of education.

Attempts by the ATA to establish formal links with Chambers of Commerce can be contrasted with its more tentative involvement with other labour groups. Chris MacDonald speaks about the local ATA strategy as follows:

> The ATA is affiliated to the Chamber of Commerce; they are a member. They are not affiliated with the Calgary Labour Council, they are not affiliated with the CLC or the AFL. But let's go back to two years ago, when the Calgary public teachers walked out for a week. When that happened, the first people to contact the ATA offering them support was the Calgary Labour Council, 'Listen, if there's anything to do, we'll help.' What's the Chamber of Commerce do? The first thing they do is come out with a position against the ATA. They come out and chastise them about anything and everything they do ... The Chamber of Commerce, their own organization, comes out crucifying one of their member groups. Now if I was to come out and crucify one of my member groups, one of the unions or worker groups affiliated with me, well, they'd be gone tomorrow. (Interview 24)

While MacDonald's criticisms focus on the Calgary Chamber of Commerce, they highlight again the contradictory class location of ATA members.

In addition to its membership in the Chamber of Commerce, the Calgary Public Teachers initiated contact with business people directly through a monthly bulletin that was distributed to more than 3,000 downtown businesses. According to Ellis this publication represented an attempt to counter misleading media reports about teachers and the Calgary school system on topics such as student achievement scores and comparisons of educational spending. A look at copies of the bulletin suggests that there was also an attempt to enlist business people by speaking their language. For example, the May 1995 bulletin attempted to quantify the 'social and private returns on investment' from education, concluding: 'A ten percent plus return on capital investment compares favourably to that offered by blue-chip investments such as public utilities.'

The purpose of distributing the bulletin was to educate business people and increase their support for public education. This recalls interviews with Calgary partnership coordinators Donna Black and Tracey Borger, who both argued that partnerships programs increase the awareness and support of business people. Business partners thus were thought to be more enlightened than other business people. Nancy Ellis, who represented public teachers on the board of the partnership foundation, echoes this view. She described representatives on the board as 'by and large, business people who care about public education and realize the importance of it' (Interview 21). Unlike the Chamber of Commerce, the partnership foundation was viewed as an organization where the ATA could have impact. For example, despite their concerns about the deficit, business people associated with the foundation were also concerned about the extent of cutbacks to education. And while some of the people on the board were affiliated with the Chamber, Ellis adds, 'I don't think they're the movers and shakers with the Chamber.'

The Conference Board of Canada was also perceived to welcome teacher input. For Ellis, its employability skills initiative provided evidence that 'the more we're willing to open up to one another and actually sit down and talk, the more commonality we find.' While Ellis did not attend any business-education conferences, she had been invited to a meeting organized by a school board administrator to discuss the CB's vision statement. When asked who else had been in attendance, she replied:

> There were mostly business people, I think. Although it's interesting. Whenever I'm involved in these so-called partnership groups, it's the same with the partnership foundation, a lot of the business people on the board believe there are *too many educators* and not enough business people. I consider myself to be almost the only educator. Because there are trustees on there and super-

intendents, but there are no teachers. There are no people involved right *at the grassroots level.* And a lot of the people are ex-trustees. But the business people still consider them to be part of the education half. And I think it was the same at that meeting. There were quite a few top business people. But there were also people like [Andrea White] who now works with the Science Foundation. And I might consider her business. But other people might consider her education; she was a trustee quite a few years ago [my emphasis].

Despite her impression that the interests of business people and educators were converging, Ellis appeared to be conscious of the *eclipsing* of teachers that occurred within the consultative framework that had been developed by the CB and others.

Her admiration for the CB was therefore tinged with the sense that business groups had usurped the place of teachers within the policy community. Furthermore, even the most enlightened business people could not provide the commitment needed to make a significant difference. Referring to business representatives involved with the foundation, she said, 'A lot of their endeavours are excellent. But it's like a little drop in the pond. And I find it frustrating sometimes to sit around this big board-room table in this lush office, and listen to them patting themselves on the back about the wonderful work they're doing. And realizing how little it affects the total picture.' Ellis felt that business people needed to take more responsibility for establishing partnerships, offering apprenticeships, and communicating job opportunities to students. Weis also commented on the need for Canadian businesses to invest more in training workers.

Both Ellis and Weis were concerned that while some business people voiced support for public education, others supported the government's restructuring of education. Discussion of perspectives and practices of business representatives in Chapters 6 and 7 suggests that this assessment is probably accurate. However, the distinction that Ellis and other participants made between 'enlightened' business people who had contact with schools and 'ignorant' business people is more difficult to sustain. Chapter 7 suggests that while corporate executives Andrew Markham and Gary Baldwin worked to develop relationships with schools, their ideas for educational reform did not differ substantially from those of Dan Williams. The 'contact hypothesis' expressed by Nancy Ellis and the partnership coordinators is described by Troyna and Carrington (1990) in relation to racism. They argue that because racism is not simply 'an illogical belief system' or a 'product of ignorance' but is rooted in structures and relations that privilege or oppress, it cannot be assumed that people will become less racist as they have more contact with people of colour and are more 'educated.' Similarly, given their objective interests within capitalist structures, it cannot be assumed that business people will become more supportive of public schooling as they have more contact with teachers and students.

The distinction made by Ellis between enlightened and ignorant business groups and representatives recalls the observation from Chapter 6 that ACC representative Dan Williams adopted a *confrontational* stance with respect to teachers, while the CB and partnership foundation constructed themselves as *collaborative* and inclusive. It is not surprising therefore that the ATA should prefer to ally itself with the latter groups. Given the increasing influence of business and the decreasing influence of labour, such alliance is strategic. However, whether the goals of the ATA can be achieved by increasing its political leverage through business 'allies' is rooted in the question of whether the interests of educators and business people are, in fact, converging.

Challenging the Alberta Model

Livingstone (1983) suggests that efforts to restructure current social reality involve understanding the existing society and having both a vision of the future and strategies for getting there. Government representatives in Alberta arguably allied themselves with dissatisfied employers (and to a lesser extent, unhappy parents) in the hegemonic work involved in developing restructuring plans for education. Solutions included making schools more responsive to employers and parents through changes in governance and accountability structures, introducing more choice, and prioritizing employability skills. The promise of economic prosperity following the short-term pain of cutbacks and restructuring helped elicit consent from the broader public.

Analysis of restructuring must consider the response of labour and other participants to these efforts, bearing in mind two ideas: first, the social/political/economic analysis presented by elites, while ideological, also corresponds in certain ways to the material realities of many citizens (Hall 1988); and second, the resulting vision of elites may overlap as well as contradict those of other groups, in this case, organized labour.

A Vision for Society

Labour representatives perceive a system where government and business leaders 'call the shots' and organized labour and other marginalized groups struggle to be heard. They know also that some of their members are supportive or indifferent towards the Conservative government, which makes it more difficult to engage in counter-hegemonic work. Obstacles include the lack of political alternatives, elite control of the media, the material basis for discourses, and the extent to which reforms and discourses in Alberta are consistent with international trends.

The first obstacle to counter-hegemonic work is the lack of political alternatives. For example, Chris MacDonald of the CDLC suggests that the question in the 1993 election was whether it would be 'massive cuts by the Liberals or brutal cuts by the Tories' (Interview 24). The New Democratic Party did not win a seat in this election. A second obstacle concerns the type of perspectives presented in the media, which contributes to members' political indifference in MacDonald's view. He attributes this to the ideological 'spin' that is placed on news as a result of government and corporate control of the media, adding 'if you wake up every morning and you're told black is white, black is white, eight times a day, sooner or later the people start hearing that.'[9] A third factor, according to MacDonald, is that concerns over economic competitiveness have a material basis: 'People are very fearful for their jobs. They are scared to stand up for their workers' rights, they are doing jobs that are unsafe, and they're scared to say "boo" to the boss. Because they know – there's officially 40,000 unemployed Calgarians, but in reality, there's about 80,000 in a workforce of 400,000 looking for employment as we speak – and employers say, "if you don't want to do that unsafe job ... there's 1,000 people at the door" ... There isn't a person in our society who hasn't had a family member or a close friend lose their employment. And even more so when you start looking at the disadvantaged groups in our society, be they women, immigrants, people who need ESL.' His final comment acknowledges social divisions based on gender and race/ ethnicity, which, along with class, affect the way people relate to particular discourses. MacDonald's reference to the fear experienced by workers suggests also that hegemony can work through coercion as well as by consent.

According to labour participants, trends in several other Western industrialized countries also lend support to government actions in Alberta and influence the public response to these actions. Szabo and MacDonald agree that the 'private sector ideology' promoted by Alberta Tories was influenced by actions taken by the International Monetary Fund (IMF) and the World Bank. The increasing power of multinationals in securing and benefiting from free trade, diminished powers of elected officials, and the increasing number of decisions made in corporate boardrooms affect citizens and governments. Szabo, MacDonald, and Farrell all make connections between government reforms in Alberta and reforms in New Zealand, Britain, and the United States. Szabo compares influential reformers in Alberta and New Zealand. Chris MacDonald compares charter school legislation with changes introduced by Thatcher's government, while Joan Farrell suggests that Alberta is moving towards a U.S. model of schooling characterized by wider disparities based on socioeconomic status.

In the process of making sense of reality, labour participants critique aspects of the vision that has become hegemonic in Alberta. For example, MacDonald echoes the Canadian Centre for Policy Alternatives when he suggests that federal debt is related more to high federal interest rates and tax breaks for the wealthy than to high social spending. He adds that Alberta's spending on health, social services, and education is sustainable if we 'look at both sides of the balance sheet' (Interview 24). Both MacDonald and Marg Szabo from the AFL suggest that the discourse of fiscal crisis distracts attention from provincial reforms focused on creating a more market-driven society.

Participants also challenge the discourse of education for economic prosperity. Szabo, MacDonald, and Farrell all point to the contradiction between provincial funding cuts to education and the idea of education as investment. They reject outright the *revised human capital* assumption that education can be made more efficient and effective by restructuring the system's priorities and operations. Challenging the discourse of education for economic prosperity, MacDonald argues that there is a contradiction between human capital rhetoric and the practices of private sector employers in Canada who contribute little to the training and education of workers compared to other industrialized countries.

A second rhetorical strategy used to challenge the discourse of education for economic prosperity focuses on its assumption that economic growth will occur in highly skilled, high-tech areas. When asked about the job market in Calgary, Joan Farrell from AUPE replied that there are just not a lot of jobs. She gave the example of a friend who 'sold his house, put all his money into a computer course [at DeVry], and ended up without a job for two years' (Interview 7). Marg Szabo talked about the Alberta market more broadly and suggested that future growth may occur in the areas of science and technology as part of global changes, as well as in the skilled trades and service industries.

However, she also noted the general trend towards temporary contract employment and de-skilling.

MacDonald raised the prospect of a flight of jobs out of Calgary and Canada as a result of technological innovation and globalization rather than a growth in high-tech jobs. His comments about the exporting of work reflect those of a corporate executive in Calgary, who states, 'Right now I can hire a guy in Ukraine for eleven dollars a month, a guy with a university degree, Master's degree. Poland, a lot of these Third World countries that have got good solid universities and are marketing their expertise worldwide. And we'll seriously be facing that issue in the next few months. I have to hire a bunch of people in high-tech areas and I'll have to compare the logistics of working with somebody from another country with perhaps broken English who'll work night and day for me, versus the local guy who wants to go home at 4 o'clock' (Interview 9).[10]

The comments of Farrell, Szabo, and MacDonald reflect uncertainty about where future jobs will be created and what the impact of global changes will be on Canadian workers. However, MacDonald's comment that the labour council was working to establish labour solidarity across borders through the International Labour Organization moves discussion beyond the nationalistic frame of education for economic prosperity. It juxtaposes the image of *global cooperation* among workers against that of *global competition*, and offers prospects for an alternative vision.

There are similarities as well as differences in the understandings and visions of labour and business participants. Both Chris MacDonald and Marg Szabo see a need for more education and training, and agree that one of the purposes of education is to prepare students for a changing work world. Szabo expresses the concern that 'we're not plugging people in enough' to the labour market. By accepting the assumptions of the need for tighter links between the education system and the workplace, she may be acknowledging that, as unemployment grows, 'working-class parents are obliged to take the competitive side of education more seriously' (Hall 1988: 54).

But the understandings of labour also differ from business in several important respects. MacDonald expresses the concern that the focus on 'employability' by business and government makes false promises since it encourages students to focus on 'marketable' areas with the assurance that jobs will materialize. He is concerned that the narrowing of curricular choices will lead to a narrowing of occupational choices and job prospects. Rather than leaving education and training to the 'discipline of the market,' labour participants tend to advocate for more government involvement in labour market processes. Szabo would like to see Alberta participate in the Canadian Labour Force Development Board (CLFDB) and develop a job strategy to address unemployment. Similarly, MacDonald suggests that the role of governments is to redistribute income and 'to take care of those people who cannot take care of themselves' (Interview 24).

This contrasts with the competitive individualism expressed by business representatives. MacDonald's image of a more 'caring society' recalls Mike Popiel's reference to the 'garbage bear syndrome,' which he sees as a by-product of the welfare state. Discourses promoting smaller and more efficient governments were arguably more popular in Alberta in the early 90s, as evidenced by the high level of political support for the Reform Party. Similarly, in the 1980s the British welfare state attracted the negative connotations of a 'spendthrift, bureaucratic totalitarian machine' (Hall 1988: 189).

A second area of difference between business and labour participants concerned who should be involved in policy matters and how that participation should be organized. Not surprisingly, Marg Szabo wanted organized labour to play a more active role in education and training decisions. She talked specifically about work experience programs as follows:

> M: I think there's a fairly high degree of commonality of interest [between business and labour] on the basic program itself, the program of getting people trained so that they can be productive as soon as they step into the workforce. There's

nothing more frustrating for me than to see kids come out of high school without a clue about what going to work means, what their rights are when they go to work.

A: Where do you think the interests diverge?

M: I think they diverge at the more fundamental, *who controls the workforce*. The streaming that I talked about earlier, I think we may have some differences there. About *who makes the decision* about where kids are streamed, what occupations they're going to be streamed into, or that type of decision-making. Or this whole thing about private schools[11] and whether or not you should have a really low basic curriculum. ... So the *role of public education* might involve a difference of opinion [my emphasis]. (Interview 32)

Szabo recognizes the need for labour to form broader alliances, noting that there is a need to 'educate kids about unions, about their right to belong to a union, about environmental issues and what unions think about them, women's issues' and other labour concerns. She envisions an education system where labour has a greater voice and all students have access to high quality, publicly funded schooling.

Szabo's acceptance of the need to 'plug people in' and her concern over 'who decides' where students get plugged in, reflects a tension within social democracy that is also identified by Hall (1988: 53) in his study of Thatcherism. He writes, '[The Labour party] has always been caught between competing goals in schooling: to improve the chances of working-class children and the worse-off in education, and to harness education to the economy and efficiency needs of the productive system.' Similarly, organized labour representatives in Alberta must address to what extent they should work within the existing inequitable system and to what extent they should challenge it. The question of labour strategies is based no doubt on labour leaders' assessment of both the wishes of their members and the balance of forces at a given moment.

Participants differed in their views of whether organized labour should support political parties, but tended to agree that coalition-building was key. Through the Common Front, MacDonald, Szabo, and Farrell envisioned bringing other unions, community groups, and individuals together to educate one another and exert political pressure. Strategies mentioned by Szabo and Walsh included educating workers about the implications of government actions, educating the public about the contributions of particular employee groups, and working with the government when it was perceived to be potentially effective.

During the implementation of the 1994 restructuring, however, the AFL did not cooperate with government even when invited. For example, although Szabo noted that the AFL planned to participate in the MLA team's advisory group looking at business involvement in education,[12] it did not do so. A representative later remarked that the AFL president at the time – a member of the social workers' union which had confronted government in an illegal strike – had adopted a stance of noncooperation (personal communication 2 February 2000). The AFL also decided not to participate in the Klein government's Growth Summit in the fall of 1997 – organized to consult invited participants about government 'reinvestment.' Instead, it organized an Alternative Summit attended by people from labour, social, environmental, and community groups, and from this conference produced a report with recommendations. Labour clearly judged participation in such corporatist forums at this time to be ineffectual.

At the time of the interviews, it seemed that the strategies adopted by organized labour participants focused more on sharing their analysis of existing reality with members and the public than promoting a fully developed alternative vision. There are probably a number of reasons for this. First, the primary concern of labour groups was to protect the interests and rights of their members in the face of government attacks. Joan Farrell suggested that there was a need to establish better communication channels both within and outside of labour organizations because of previous failures to determine 'where the membership wants to go on some of these issues' (Interview 7). Second, the education of members was made more difficult by the ideological success of neoliberal discourses and the need to develop counter-hegemonic discourses. Concerns about how to ensure member participation were accentuated by the rapid pace with which government changes were introduced in 1994. This situation challenged labour representatives to articulate a vision that moved beyond members' immediate concerns. Finally, as the preceding discussion indicates, labour participants felt they were fighting an uphill battle because of the lack of political alternatives, media support, and resources.

A Vision for Public Education

Participants from teachers' associations, like other organized labour participants, challenged some aspects of the reform discourse that was promoted in Alberta and agreed with others. They agreed with the need to prepare students for an uncertain economic future by introducing greater flexibility in curriculum and involving business in students' transition from school to work. In Alberta, as in other jurisdictions, teachers have been encouraged to 'listen harder to what employers want and to look for closer links between schools and the workplace' (OECD 1992: 11). As mentioned, teachers unions were also looking to business groups as partners and political allies as they recognized their importance as stakeholders in government discussions over educational reform.

However, interests did not converge in all areas. ATA representatives expressed concerns over the promotion of a narrow view of education as preparation for work, the attack on teachers' professionalism through performance and accountability measures and differentiated staffing, and the potential impact of market-driven reforms on accessibility and equal opportunities for students. Like MacDonald, Farrell, and Szabo, participants from teachers' associations were struggling to assess reforms critically in terms of their immediate and longer-term impacts and to develop and promote a vision that was more in keeping with their interests.

Mark Silver of the Canadian Teachers' Federation (CTF) was more optimistic than other participants about the possibility of developing an educational vision that could be agreed on by the various stakeholders. While he admitted that there was a 'gulf between perceptions in the business community and what we [teachers] would consider to be reality' in terms of what's happening in schools, he attributed this to the 'lack of a common information base that's agreed upon by the major partners in education' (Interview 1). He expressed faith that one day the CTF, parents, governments, the CB, and Chambers of Commerce would be able to agree that 'this is the picture, and this is where we're at, at the moment.' Silver wanted to develop a 'shared view' before opinions 'have crystallized or become politicized within the various groups.' His view can be contrasted with a conflict perspective which assumes that we make sense of reality and our experiences with the aid of different ideological frameworks that are often tied to class and other socially divided interests. Strategically, Silver appeared to be a pragmatist. He recognized that a vision that could claim the support of multisectorial partners – a corporatist settlement, in other words – would have a much better chance of being endorsed by governments.

But while Silver was interested in working collaboratively with the CB, he challenged some of the arguments associated with this group. On the topic of dropouts, he disagreed with the CB interpretation of statistics, noting that student retention has increased dramatically since the 1960s along with the diversity of student populations. He half-jokingly referred to bankruptcy rates and corporate bailouts as being indicative of the business 'dropout rate' and concluded that a business model would not necessarily 'lead us to the promised land in education.' For example, he attended a session on total quality management (TQM) at a CB business-education conference where 'equations were being made from commodities to human beings,' and commented that 'it just didn't click.'

The reason it 'didn't click' for Silver relates to his view of public education as a 'societal institution' that was not the 'property of a single constituency.' Therefore, a model that assumes *buyers* and *sellers* or clients and service providers was not consistent with his view of education. The attempt to relate national competitiveness directly to what happens in schools was also inconsistent with his view of reality. Focusing on employment as a measure of economic health, Silver argued that even if 'we all woke up and we're suddenly the most skilled people' it would not reduce the unemployment rate by much. He went on to mention other problems that affect student outcomes, such as poverty and violence.

Silver's perspective on certain issues was quite different from that expressed by business participants. He had concerns about some of the value assumptions associated with the CB's assessment of educational problems and solutions. At the same time he emphasized the importance of dialogue. His focus on the potential offered by the Canadian Learning Forum (recommended by the Prosperity Initiative) thus made strategic sense since such a group would provide an opportunity for his organization to be at the table in national-level discussion.

In the Alberta context – where opinions had arguably crystallized – Teachers' Association representatives were more cynical about their role within the government's policy community and about the prospects of developing a shared vision. ATA representatives Janet Weis and Nancy Ellis felt that the Alberta government had listened to selected stakeholders in developing educational reforms. According to Weis, two key groups were unhappy parents and dissatisfied employers. While the parents' groups 'have specific things that they're against, like the Impressions Reading Series,' Weiss thought that business was behind the 'whole move towards privatization' (Interview 25).

Weis acknowledged the American influence on the privatization move with reference to John Chubb, co-author of *Politics, Markets and America's Schools* (1990) and a CB speaker, as noted in Chapter 3. She comments, '[John Chubb] is definitely on the side of privatization, entrepreneurial, let's run schools like a marketplace economy. He's out to lunch (laugh) ... But I'm frightened that they're all getting together and they're having tremendous influence. And where they're having influence is, especially in the States, they're getting people elected to school boards, they're getting people elected in positions of authority.

So their voice is not just a voice spitting in the wind. And they're making decisions for everyone. They're becoming more influential all the time.'

Ellis mentioned the external influences and models provided by countries like New Zealand. Making connections between reforms in Alberta and those implemented elsewhere was therefore part of the ATA's sense-making process, as it was for other labour groups. A number of articles in the *ATA News* discussed reforms in Britain and New Zealand in comparison with Alberta (Flower 1994; Gammage and Little 1994; Gariepy 1994). Since reforms had been in place in other jurisdictions longer, these cases provided a basis for predicting repercussions in Alberta.

Despite Weis's comment that John Chubb was 'out to lunch,' like other labour participants she admitted that reform ideas were based somewhat on people's lived realities. In addressing the discourse of education for economic prosperity, she began by noting that 'there's a little bit of truth in everything and in every point of view. It's how far you take that truth' (Interview 25). For example, she asked if we have to 'give up heritage and culture, our belief in protecting the rights of human beings' in order to 'fit into the global economy' (7).

The discourse of *choice* is another complex topic since it connects with some aspects of individual experience while obscuring the bigger picture. Weis discussed issues around *choice* as follows: 'Well, I think when parents say they would like to have a choice in deciding what kind of education they want for their children, I think parents should have some choice in the way their children are educated. There's nothing wrong with that. It's when they are going to impose their will or their form of education on everyone else. They shouldn't have the right to determine what's best for society. Now, are you in favour of public education or are you in favour of education only for your own children? ... Also, accessibility, equal opportunity, are not taken into consideration when these groups decide what's right for everyone. And so I'm opposed to that.' Weis's awareness of the 'little bit of truth' in the ideological construction of choice perhaps led her to conclude that charter schools were not necessarily bad in principle since they could provide a place to try out innovations in teaching. But she went on to deconstruct the concept of choice by asking who is able to access these choices. Her comments parallel the argument made by Barlow and Robertson (1994) that choice is not evenly distributed in society.

ATA representatives located charter schools within a broader reform movement away from publicly elected school boards towards a voucher system. Like Silver, Weis viewed the shift towards a system that constructed parents and teachers as clients and service providers as inconsistent with her view of education as a public institution. The centralization of school funding removed the ability of school boards to tax and introduced a model where funding followed students. This change was also seen by ATA participants as moving education in the direction of a voucher system. Increased choice and centralized funding were therefore consistent.

Charter schools and increased standardized testing were also consistent since these schools created the need for additional provincial monitoring. Weis referred to American models as follows: '[M]ost of the charter schools that have been formed in the States, anyway, have conformed to the outcomes-based education, and have promised accountability or a performance level for those students. So, it seems that the charter school movement, to be successful, has to be pinned to some kind of performance or outcome-based ... You're not going to have any portfolio assessment in charter schools. Most of them are based on taking standardized tests of one kind or another.' Increased standardized testing allows charter schools to be held accountable by the province and permits 'objective comparisons' between this new model of schooling and traditionally governed public schools. Weis and Ellis perceive that reforms move education in the direction of a market model with negative implications for student accessibility and teachers' working conditions.

Staff Association representative Pam Conway also addressed the effect of reforms on access for students. She opposed the assumption that individuals should be valued primarily in terms of their economic contributions, saying, 'Now I believe that a person deserves an education just by virtue of the fact that they're a person, and they should have that right. I think people need to have the skills in order to learn how to live their life. And the economy is part of that, but it's not everything. I think education is not just there to earn dollars for a country. It is there for a quality of life for the people in that country' (Interview 41). Earlier, Conway had criticized the Klein government's agenda, stating that it involved getting 'all the losers out of the province and just [having] the people here that make money' (8).

Ellis questioned the discourse not only because of the value assumptions that underpinned it, but also because her observations of the labour market in Calgary indicated that it was invalid. She referred to the economic crash that occurred in the early 1980s and noted that 'the people who were laid off from oil companies and so on had good education' (Interview 21). Adding that we already have the 'second highest educated workforce in Canada' in Calgary, she concluded that 'if that was the only link you needed, it would be there.'[13] Like Silver, she added that prosperity depends not only on education but also on reducing poverty levels and making sure that children are healthy, well fed, and secure. Ellis also noted that one of the responsibilities of educators was to ensure that students were aware of the 'huge variety of jobs out there,' as opposed to encouraging students to pursue specific occupations in specific companies. In juxtaposition with the focus on high-tech jobs within the discourse, Conway referred to the number of graduates from teachers' college who were working as school aides in Calgary because they were unable to find jobs as a result of cutbacks.

In sum, labour representatives from education challenged various claims and assumptions made by dissatisfied employers and the state. They saw education as a societal institution that should open up opportunities for all students, as opposed to a tool of economic elites and middle-class parents. But like other labour groups in Alberta, they were struggling to develop an alternative vision that was consistent with the interests of members and could enlist broader public support. This was not unlike struggles in other provinces. For example, Bascia (1998) uses the teachers' response to Bill 160 in Ontario to comment more generally: 'Encountering similar challenges, teachers' organizations in other parts of the country and the world are working to transform and renew themselves by articulating more proactive and grounded visions for education, identifying specific initiatives that provide a wide variety of crucial programs and services for teachers and schools, providing teachers with both real leverage and symbolic legitimacy for fuller participation in the educational system, and amassing more widespread support for public education' (39).

Concluding Comments

> Over the last six years, [teachers] have watched their salaries decline, their colleagues put out to pasture, their workloads increase tremendously and their working conditions deteriorate ... They've watched as less expensive, non-certificated staff were hired in some jurisdictions to fill the positions of certificated teachers and as some private colleges have been given the right to grant teaching degrees. They've listened as members of government caucus and groups such as the Chamber of Commerce, the Alberta Taxpayers' Association and various right-wing media have demanded that administrators be removed from the ATA, that the ATA be split into a union and a professional organization, that membership in the ATA be optional and that teachers be granted term certificates. (Bauni Mackay and David Flower, *Public Education*)

Teachers clearly felt under siege after the fall of 1993, as did other labour groups in the province. In addition to the attacks on the profession described above, class sizes had increased while resources decreased. Custodians and teacher aides were even more directly impacted by contracting out and staffing cuts. Interviews with labour participants in Alberta indicate that the fragmentation of labour opposition was related to employee groups' differing relationships to the labour process, gender divisions, lack of resources, and lack of established networks.

The contradictory class location of teachers helps to explain the ATA's ambivalent relationships with labour, government, and business. The ATA belonged to the Common Front, a coalition organized to fight government cutbacks, at the same time as it boasted memberships in the Alberta Chamber of Commerce and the Conference Board. Teacher groups used the language of business to garner support while decrying a business agenda in educational restructuring. While these may be seen as parts of a multifaceted strategy, actions were probably also related to the ambivalence of members, who identified with workers but also wanted professional status. Therefore, although threats of further de-skilling and intensification may have shifted educators' perceptions of their objective interests towards those of other workers, the fear of falling was also a factor. As the critical reader says, 'Once teachers commit themselves as part of the trade union movement, they will find it difficult to regain their professional pretensions. Such a move would probably lead to the end of the ATA's protected status under Alberta legislation – it would surely lead to the emergence of an internal opposition of conservative teachers wishing to re-establish a "professional association."'

At the same time, there were tensions between the visions of business people and those of educators. Representatives from the ATA opposed the use of the discourse of fiscal crisis as a rationale for cutting education funding. They challenged the competition and hierarchy implicit in the discourse of education for economic prosperity, and its lack of correspondence with their realities. CTF writers Robertson (1998) and Froese-Germain and Moll (1997) raised warning flags for educators about school-business partnerships. The discourse of parental choice was also seen to contradict concerns about equity and social justice. Yet labour participants acknowledged that the 'little bit of truth' and inversions within hegemonic discourses made them difficult to challenge. For example, the caring welfare state became an inefficient bureaucratic machine, and social spending became an unaffordable luxury. Labour participants seemed to recognize the need to reframe discourses based on an alternative vision. Strategies thus focused on educating members and the public and forming coalitions across diverse groups.

The ATA's response to government restructuring in 1993 and 1994 can be seen as ad hoc and somewhat reactive. Seeing the need for a longer-term strategy, it launched the Public Education Works program in 1995, 'based on the belief that successfully influencing decisions about the public education system depend upon convincing the public to speak up for public education' (Mackay and Flower 1999: 64). The Public Education Action Centre (PEAC) engaged in several activities, including a provincial survey of teachers in 1995, which asked about the impact of restructuring. Following on the heels of the 1997 Growth Summit, teachers held a rally which attracted thousands of protesters. In the late 1990s parent groups also became more vocal in demanding increased funding for education as news of budget surpluses spread. Despite this pressure, per pupil funding in real dollars for public schools in 1998 was less than it was in 1993, and Alberta had fallen to seventh position among Canadian provinces by 1996/7 (Mackay and Flower 1999). Concern was heightened in 1998 when a task force on private school funding recommended to government that grants to private schools be increased from 50 per cent of the basic pupil grant given to public schools to 60 per cent.

CHAPTER NINE

The Diversity of 'Producers'

'The orientation of policy-making [in England] is now towards the consumers of education – parents and industrialists' while the 'producer lobbies [teachers and school boards] are almost totally excluded,' wrote Stephen Ball (1990: 8). Interviews with teachers and school boards suggest that a similar shift occurred in Alberta. In the early 1990s, education groups were vying with dissatisfied parents and employers to have input into the policy process. The government's restructuring plans in 1994 reflected the shift in power. Trustees, for example, were losers. Between 1993 and 1995 the number of school boards was reduced from 141 to 63 and the number of trustees fell from 1,184 to 435 (Evans 1999). With centralized funding, trustees also lost the ability to levy education taxes at the local level. The numbers of second-tier central office positions also fell from 190 to 95 between 1993 and 1995 (Young, in press). Those administrators and trustees who remained were required to set budgets during difficult times. In addition to less funding, the government placed restrictions on the amount boards could allocate to governance and system administration, and system-based instructional support. There were also restrictions on the ability of boards to transfer funds between blocks (Bruce and Schwartz 1997). Educators also faced greater challenges because of cutbacks and restructuring. Teaching positions were eliminated, salaries rolled back, and supports reduced.

In discussion of educational reform, 'producer' groups tended to be constructed collectively as supporting the status quo. As Ellis from the Calgary Public Teachers stated in Chapter 8, in the expanded policy community, teachers, trustees, and administrators were often lumped together as 'education' representatives. As a result, there was little acknowledgement of the varying interests and perspectives of teachers, administrators, and trustees based on their different locations within existing structures. This chapter acknowledges some of the diversity within and among 'producer' groups by focusing on interviews with board-based and school-based participants in Calgary. Since this is an urban area that was not affected by amalgamation, interviews do not bring out the full range of issues associated with restructuring. However, following Chapter 8's discussion of labour participants' response to restructuring, it does explore further the relationships among players and how subjects made sense of changes announced in the three-year business plan.

Interview Participants

There are two parts to the discussion that follows. The first is based on interviews with 'board personnel,' including two trustees, an administrator, and two partnership coordinators. The second presents an analysis of interviews with 'school-based personnel,' including a high school principal, an assistant principal, one department head, two teachers, and a consultant (and ex-teacher) who had been seconded to Alberta Education to work on a curriculum project.

Bruce Reid was an administrator with the Calgary Board of Education, while Marcia Jensen and Marilyn Simmons were elected as trustees in the 1992 municipal elections. Both women had been actively involved as parents with the CBE. Donna Black and Tracey Borger (introduced in Chapter 7) were involved in partnership programs with the public and Catholic boards, respectively. At the school level, interviews with the assistant principal, department head, and teacher from Academic

TABLE 9.1
Public Education Participants

Bruce Reid, Administrator, Calgary Board of Education (CBE)	24 March 1994
Marcia Jensen, Trustee, CBE	22 June 1994
Marilyn Simmons, Trustee, CBE	27 April 1994
Donna Black, Partnership Liaison, CBE	22 February 1994
Tracey Borger, Partnership Program, Calgary Catholic Board	15 February 1994
Ron Leckie, Assistant Principal [Academic High]	22 March 1994
Andy Laird, Department Head [Academic High]	23 June 1994
Barbara Phillips, Science Teacher [Academic High]	22 March 1994
Carol Oliver, ESL Teacher, Calgary	8 March 1994
Karen Gold, CBE Consultant	25 March 1994
Carl George, Principal [Native High School]	3 March 1994

High School are revisited (see Chapter 7). In addition, Carol Oliver was a teacher at another Calgary high school and Karen Gold was a consultant who was seconded to Alberta Education to work on curriculum development. Both women had backgrounds in ESL instruction. Carl George was a principal of Native High School (NHS)[1] in Calgary, a school within the CBE that aimed to meet the needs of Aboriginal students. These latter three participants were able to address the potential effects of educational restructuring on traditionally marginalized students. Table 9.1 lists participants, their affiliations, and interview dates.

Board-based Personnel

Participants' sense-making was influenced by their relationships with other stakeholders in public education. Relationships between the CBE and government MLAs immediately following the release of the three-year business plan were confrontational and characterized by mutual distrust, whereas those between the board and local business partners appeared to be seen as collaborative and satisfying. While relations were no doubt rooted to some extent in historical practices, two factors probably contributed to the situation in 1994. First, administrator Bruce Reid was arguably instrumental in establishing board relationships with business people. Reid was a supporter of the

Conference Board and had worked to establish close relationships with local business leaders. He can therefore be described as a noncorporate *organic intellectual*[2] whose interests were perceived to coincide with those of CB affiliates. Second, Reid and other board personnel distinguished between the reform vision of business partners and that suggested by government reforms. As a result, business partners were constructed as 'experts' who could help offset the impact of cutbacks and restructuring without acknowledging that business representatives were part of the policy community that developed reforms in the first place. The effect of these constructions was to reinforce business hegemony within the board.

Board Dynamics

[Bruce Reid] is a consummate bureaucrat in the finest sense of the word. He runs that place like a fine violin. He controls the board of trustees, he controls administration, but that never becomes public. You could sit in board meetings as I did for a year, and it becomes extremely obvious who controls whom. (Dan Williams, Alberta Chamber of Commerce)

[Bruce Reid] is fabulous, he's an outstanding individual. And he has been criticized for not exercising his ability to influence us. And his ability to influence his other leaders in the system. His leadership style is not that way at all. And we've asked him as trustees, more and more, to speak out and let us know what his opinion is. Because of his experience and because he has earned my respect, when he says certain things – sometimes we have to pry it out of him – it does influence you. (Marcia Jensen, Calgary Board of Education)

Despite the difference in the above perspectives, administrator Bruce Reid was clearly an important player within the CBE. A number of factors undoubtedly enhanced his ability to influence trustees. First, several trustees, including Jensen and

Simmons, were in their first term and were therefore more likely to view administrators as 'experts' in terms of the day-to-day operations of the board. Second, while it is quite common for trustees to have been involved previously with the school board as parents, Fine (1993) suggests that this experience is often not welcomed or valued within the educational establishment. These two factors, along with the observation that in 1994 six of seven trustees were women while most school leaders were men, suggest that relationships between trustees and administrators were probably asymmetrical.

At the same time, the potential views and actions of trustees cannot be read off from their locations within existing structures. Jensen acknowledged power dynamics within the board and the irrationality of processes that led to particular board decisions. Simmons challenged the authority of other trustees and administrators in her efforts to represent more generally the interests of parents and voters in her ward. She was the only trustee to vote against the CBE budget for 1994 because she felt that too much money would be taken away from classrooms. She felt strongly that administrators as well as teachers needed to be held accountable for their actions, and as a result brought a motion to the board recommending the 'auditing of our system and different departments to make sure we're efficient and effective' (Interview 26). Simmons also disagreed with administrators over school-based budgeting and public reporting of provincial test results on a school-by-school basis. In both cases, she was supportive of these actions while board administrators were more reserved. Simmons was also more open to the concept of parental choice. Her positions were consistent with what she perceived to be parents' interests and rights. These examples suggest that while the trustee participants respected and relied on administrators within the CBE, there were also areas of tension.

Relationship with Business

One area where trustees and administrators seemed to agree concerned business involvement in education. Bruce Reid was influential in introducing trustees to the work of the CB and in fostering support for partnerships. Through Reid's involvement, he had developed relationships with corporate CEOs across Canada. As an administrator in one of Canada's largest school districts, his relationship with business leaders was probably not unlike that described by Slaughter (1990) in her analysis of the Business-Higher Education Forum in the United States. In his previous administrative positions, Reid had become committed to business-education partnerships and cooperative education and had developed strong links with the business community. He initially attended Reaching for Success conferences as a participant and after he moved to Calgary was approached by the CB to become a 'representative for Western Canada' (2). Given this history, Reid's perspective was probably influenced by his investment in the CB over time, his personal relationships with corporate members, and his increased status within the board as a result of this liaison.

Reid's interest in encouraging corporate ties, however, was seen as *pragmatic* by trustee Marcia Jensen, who said, 'He doesn't speak of [growing business involvement in education] as his choice. He thinks it's reality. And he believes that public education will be better for it' (Interview 30). Similarly, Dan Williams referred to Reid's interest in business partnerships as follows: '[Reid] wanted to bring the business community in to control them, rather than have them have their own agenda on the outside. In other words, let's get them inside the tent and have them part of the process, in that, they're inside my tent. Let's not have them establish another tent, outside my tent (laugh). And you know, that's good politics. And I think that's how [Bruce] approaches partnerships' (Interview 11).

The question of who was in whose tent in this situation is interesting to consider. Williams suggested that Reid's proactive approach to business involvement in education was based on his interest in retaining control over the education system in Calgary. However, his actions could be interpreted also as those of an educational leader who shared the institutional values of corporate elites. As mentioned, Reid's relationship with the CB was comparable in several respects to that of American university presidents who were involved with the BHEF. Slaughter (1990: 22) describes the forum as a 'self-consciously elite organization' in which both corporate and academic leaders share similar backgrounds and values. She notes that while the BHEF purported to bring these two groups together as equal partners, business concerns and interests dominated the forum's agenda. Therefore, in contrast to an image of equal exchange, Slaughter concludes that 'dependency theory' was a more apt descriptor since one partner needed the other more, power relations appeared to be unequal, and one partner was able to dominate. Chapter 3's discussion of the CB similarly argued that conferences and other forums functioned as a way for corporate leaders to bring educators into their 'tent,' and, like the BHEF, to create a climate that supported the ideological primacy of the private sector.

The two trustees were clearly impressed by the CB and Reid's involvement in it. Both Jensen and Simmons attended the 1994 Reaching for Success conference as trustees representing the CBE. Like Dan Williams, Marcia Jensen believed that through his connections, Bruce Reid could influence CB members as well as bring information back to the school system. In the local context, she viewed corporate allies as potential 'government lobbyists:' 'If we have companies involved, and if the government starts to do things and we do our best to keep things going well in school, but they start to really run down schools, and people start to notice because they've been there beforehand, I think there will be political power and will to tell the government that they're wrong. And that's *one of the strategies*, of course, in school systems. And one of our vested interests in having [business people] involved, is that we have more eyes and ears to support us if the government is to make horrible moves that are bad for kids. So in that case, their role would be, and has been I think, even through some of this, having *advocates* in corners where the government might be surprised to hear them coming from' (Interview 30) [my emphasis].

Again, the parallel with Slaughter's (1990) work is worth noting. She notes that business leaders involved in the BHEF were also seen as government lobbyists. The main difference is that in the case of the BHEF, they were expected to lobby governments primarily for research funding, while in the Alberta context they were expected to lobby against particular reforms and to help schools deal with funding cuts.

According to Simmons, allowing businesses to have a greater say in the schools through partnerships was desirable. When asked why she attended the CB event, she replied, 'Well I just went because I heard it was very good, to see that perspective. That's the first time I've been and it was excellent. A gentleman was there from Nova Scotia, speaking on entrepreneurship for students.[3] And so I invited him here to talk to the trustees yesterday. And they thought it was really good. And [his project] involved working with service groups like the Chamber, and there's seed money from the government to provide money to teach children how to be entrepreneurs. Because how do we know what jobs they're going to have in the future? And that's why being involved with business is so important. Because the job market for students is so grim' (Interview 26).

Simmons' final sentence implies that business involvement in schools will reduce the labour market uncertainty experienced by students and parents. Jensen also talked about the positive aspects of partnerships for students when she said, 'I can speak from having seen how they work at the school. And it's outstanding. It's wonderful in all kinds of different ways. First of all, to have business supporting public schools is wonderful. And the kids feel the support of *people that count in the society*, really supporting them. Coming in and being the volunteers and giving them certain kinds of money. It shows that *people who are important*, that is, people who have jobs in companies, care about them' (Interview 30) [my emphasis].

Jensen's comments about who 'counts' in society are revealing. Business people were seen therefore as resources as well as government lobbyists. They were resources who could help students learn about the professional work world. According to Jensen, they were also resources for trustees and educational administrators. She suggested that business partners had provided useful 'restructuring' advice to the CBE as follows: 'Our business partners speak to us about managing change and what to look out for, what they learned from restructuring, the mistakes they made ... They may say, "I think we can be leaner there." Those would be the kinds of critical comments, the things they're looking at saying to us. And some of them are good and some of them aren't. For example, in business when they downsized and restructured, some of it was because they had a loss of business; we still have 96,000 students.' Jensen obviously relates to business partners in this instance as a 'fellow manager.'

Bruce Reid focused on partnership benefits at the board level. He commented that 'we've established wonderful working relationships in most cases' with business, adding that Calgary has been a model for many school systems in its work with the business community. For Reid, the establishment of the partnership foundation in Calgary was 'one of the best things that I've been involved in since I've been here' (Interview 17). The commitment shown by business leaders also made him more hopeful about the effects of government cuts and restructuring: 'Well, the meeting I was at yesterday, it was hosted by [John Smith].⁴ And it was a lunch for businesses that had contributed surplus equipment over the last year or so. It leads me to believe that there's a commitment there that, as resources are dwindling and as we try to change the delivery model, that business is going to try to help us with that. So I'm encouraged. You know, there's a *silver lining* to everything and the *silver lining* to the downsizing, the fiscal reality in Alberta, is that people are going to have to realize that education's everybody's business' [my emphasis]. Reid's comments about the 'silver lining' of reforms remind us of the private sector opportunities seen by Mike Popiel of the partnership foundation. Not discussed, however, was the question of who would be able to participate in a meaningful way in the new delivery model and who would benefit from reforms.

Reid's focus on corporations as education partners, as opposed to small business, is evident when he says, 'The *small business person* is not really in a position to be able to train someone, they just don't have the resources to do that. So when they have someone coming out of a school, they want the person to step into the small business and be productive ... The *large corporation* is more willing, I think, to say, "Well you know, if the kids have the basic skills, and they have a good work ethic, and they have a good attitude, etc., we can spend a bit of time and money training them, and we're willing to do that." In other words, skills can be more generic in nature, you know? ... And most of our contact is with large corporations, *that's where I contact'* [my emphasis]. Reid saw the interests of public educators as more aligned with large corporations, despite his acknowledgement that these companies tended to hire university graduates. His perspective challenged that of labour representative Marg Szabo who expressed greater ideological affiliation with small-business people.

It can also be contrasted with the comments of the partnership coordinator for the Catholic School Board, Tracey Borger. Borger compared the types of educational involvement of large and small businesses this way:

I always feel that [co-op education] is really a form of community partnershipping, and yet it's not really viewed as being as glamorous as these one school/one business partnerships. And sometimes I think that's too bad, because I see the reality of what goes on in our co-op ed program, and I see the commitment of individual employers. You know, small-business people who will take on a student – sometimes an 'at-risk' student, a high-needs student – and really contribute in an incredible way to that one young person's future. And yet, it's not as glamorous as a large corporation partnering with a school. So sometimes it takes a back seat in people's minds and in the media ... [And] like I said, the Conference Board, in part, has really put a lot of emphasis on the one school-one business partnership, and it just became a real topical thing, where business started to say, 'We want to have some impact. We want to influence the schools.' (Interview 5)

While Borger emphasized the benefits of cooperative education programs, Bruce Reid suggested they were time-consuming and costly because of the need to tie the curriculum of the school classroom to the work site. He concluded that 'as school systems downsize, they don't have the resources to do that' (Interview 17).

Borger's differences with Reid extended to her view of the CB and its work. In speaking about its employability skills profile, she suggested that perhaps 'in their eagerness to embrace that concept,' educators did not think about it as critically as they should have (Interview 5). In general, Borger expressed more reservations about the CB's work than did representatives from the Calgary board. The fact that Catholic board administrators did not have the same amount of contact with the CB as did public board leaders,[5] and that Borger herself interacted with business people from small, medium, and large firms, may explain her more challenging approach.

While the CBE was connected to the CB through Bruce Reid, it was also connected to the local Chamber of Commerce through the chair of the Board of Trustees. Marcia Jensen commented on this relationship: '[The Chair of the CBE's] husband used to be the president of the Calgary Chamber of Commerce [CCC]. And so, she has all these kinds of connections that she just works, and it is behind the scenes on certain things. And it's part of her life. But she brings those networks to us, in a sense ... And we meet with [the Chamber's Education Committee] a little bit and they always send us copies of their press releases and I think we send them copies of ours ... A pretty close relationship' (Interview 30). Compare these comments about the school board–Chamber of Commerce relationship with the Calgary Public Teachers CCC relationship described by Nancy Ellis in Chapter 8. Despite the fact that her local was a member of the CCC, Ellis suggested that its education committee had not been particularly receptive to input from teachers.

Bruce Reid was more ambivalent than Jensen about the CBE's links with the CCC. He suggested that although his board had a 'fairly productive working relationship with the chamber,' its deficit-reduction mandate was a source of tension at times

(Interview 17). He therefore acknowledged that the chamber and government were ideologically aligned on this issue. Another source of tension for Reid concerned the willingness of some business people to believe the criticisms of provincial chamber (ACC) representative Dan Williams. He said, 'I talk to business community after business community about how well Alberta kids do, relative to other students, on our national testing.' Chapter 8 noted that ATA representatives had also spoken to Chambers of Commerce around the province to try to get business people onside and that the Calgary Public Teachers had sent out bulletins targeted towards local businesses. Again, educators' interest in 'educating' business groups to become more informed participants within the government's policy community was evident.

CBE representatives seemed to accept increasing business involvement in education. While they were critical of business representative Dan Williams, they viewed CB partners and other corporate leaders in Calgary as allies who could lobby the government in support of public education and school boards, and as experts who could help the board deal with the impact of reforms and cutbacks. Tracey Borger of the Catholic board, on the other hand, did not appear to make the same ideological distinction between CB members and ACC representative Dan Williams. In fact, she questioned the role of both groups in influencing government reforms as follows: 'I was just discussing [the impetus for reforms] with some of my colleagues the other day. And I feel kind of awkward sometimes because, like I said, I'm not a teacher. And here I am "courting business," so to speak. And there is a reaction among my colleagues that some of this restructuring has come from business, and Chambers of Commerce, maybe in part from the Conference Board, you know. I just say that in passing because they're organizations that obviously come to mind. But you know, I think there's a lot of concern. Certain teachers that I've spoken to have the view that there's a small group of business people who have the ear of the government, who have told them that this kind of restructuring is necessary. I don't know. I mean, where is it all coming from? And you can't help but wonder what role business has played' (Interview 5).

Response to Government Reforms

While school boards may not have welcomed government reforms, they anticipated them. For example, Bruce Reid says,

> I think we all knew that there were going to be some reductions. I mean, I came [to Calgary] prepared for the fact that, like most school boards right across Canada, the expectations had grown out of hand. As well, there'd been so much downloading onto education from all other agencies, like social services and health. Education was picking up all of these issues and all these pressures, while at the same time, funding was drying up because realistically we just couldn't continue to spend that amount of money. And because of my association with the Conference Board of Canada, I was aware (right across Canada) of how the public was beginning to say, particularly the business community, that what we're doing was not good enough. Anybody who had done any reading about the global economy and the need for competition knew that we were going to have to change the way in which we deliver service to students. But it all came together in a very short period of time. I think it caught a lot of us, not by surprise, but it came faster than we thought. (Interview 17)

But while he expected reforms, he was critical of the approach taken by Alberta Education. Reid bluntly suggested that government restructuring involved 'compliance, control and money.' Like ATA representatives, he noted that the government had become one of public education's 'greatest critics' over time and that educators had lost ground in the policy community to Stephen Murgatroyd,[6] Joe Freedman, Albertans for Quality Education, and an 'inner circle of informal if not formal advisors.' As a result, the government adopted elements of models from New Zealand, Britain, and the United States that did not fit the

Canadian context, in Reid's view. He felt that the workbook for government roundtables lacked vision and discouraged philosophical debate about educational practices and objectives. Reid also noted a lack of consistency between what he heard at the roundtables and subsequent government reforms. In terms of the three-year business plan, Reid was especially critical of provincial restructuring of the 'governance model of education.' Reid's criticisms may explain why the relationship between the board and government was strained throughout the implementation of reforms. Trustees and administrators were viewed as bureaucratic and resistant to change by government, while MLAs were depicted by trustees as ignorant about school board practices. These tensions were reinforced in 1997 when Education Minister Gary Mar commissioned a review of CBE operations and management after receiving complaints about overly bureaucratic board operations.

Reid supported the work of the CB but eschewed actions taken by the Alberta government. This is interesting, given that themes from the CB's business-education conferences seemed consistent with government reforms in Alberta, such as the need for more *choice* in public schooling, an emphasis on outcomes-based education and increased testing, and closer ties between business and education. Therefore, while Reid selectively focused on 'centralizing' aspects of the three-year plan, other aspects were consistent with conference themes. Ideologically, Reid's distinction allowed him to paint government representatives as power brokers who lacked vision while corporations became allies in the struggle. The effect was to equate popular interests with those of corporate leaders without recognizing the contradictions.

Board representatives also distinguished between government funding cutbacks and reforms, and focused their criticisms on the latter. Reid explained that the CBE supported 'the government's intention to reduce the deficit,' believing that it was 'necessary to downsize.' However, the CBE did not support their loss of access to the local mill rate. Again, this was an area where the board felt that business allies would support it, as Marcia Jensen suggests: 'Our board hasn't spoken of opposition to the cuts ever. What I would think businesses would question is loss of autonomy and the ability to tax. Businesses very much felt that we were right on in talking about holding our own CEO accountable, instead of the Minister interfering and controlling from there. So they were good advocates because they understood that concept ... And so it's really helpful to have people who have very sophisticated understandings of how big organizations work. Taxation – I don't know their support for that. The cuts – one of the things about business is that it's made up of individuals ...' (Interview 30).

Perhaps because of their perceptions of public sentiment, CBE representatives strategically focused on challenging restructuring rather than the discourse of fiscal crisis of the state. Funding cuts were constructed as *inevitable* and therefore *natural*.[7] Even trustee Marilyn Simmons, who opposed the CBE's proposed budget for 1994, suggested that she had to reconcile herself to the impact of cutbacks. As she says, 'I do have a few concerns with the restructuring and user fees, that the philosophy [of educating all students] might be changing drastically, which I find upsetting. I haven't come to terms with that myself. The more fees that are put down, access to education is affected, to my dismay. *But I have to come to terms with it.* I think some trustees have come to terms with it, that there is a change of philosophy about public education' [my emphasis].

The implication of accepting the discourse of fiscal crisis was therefore that trustees were required to practically implement it and to legitimize its effects. Simmons later commented that 'maybe I'm just expecting too much from public education' and 'maybe the parents are putting too many demands on public education.'

The need to *reduce expectations* was echoed by Bruce Reid when he said, '[T]he most difficult challenge [in this position has been] to try to maintain quality education through a period of fiscal downsizing and changing expectations. Because it's not just the question of fewer dollars; it has to do with expectations of parents. They're still up there, and dealing with all the different pressure groups who believe that it's necessary to cut back, but not my area in particular. That's been a real challenge for the board and for me, because every group has legitimate concerns ...' (Interview 17). In his view, the whole 'raison d'être for public education' which was 'quality education and equity of opportunity' was being reworked within the school system. The message from Toward 2000 Together, that 'individual Albertans must reduce their expectations of what services government can and should provide,' (Advisory Committee 1993: 10) had been transmitted to trustees and to citizens more generally.

Accepting the discourse of fiscal crisis of the state, trustees were forced to prioritize and make trade-offs to address the decline in resources. All board-based respondents acknowledged the potential impact of reforms on accessibility for students. Black suggested that changing fiscal realities in public education potentially would result in long-term social costs as particular groups of students were denied access to a quality education. Simmons expressed concern about the potential development of a two-tiered system, and Jensen decried what she saw as a government-sanctioned movement towards private schools. Borger shared the concerns of other board participants, adding, 'When I came on in 1990, there was a great emphasis on at-risk kids. You know, kids who have kind of fallen through the cracks, kids who maybe needed assistance to see their way clearer, even to prevent them from dropping out of school. There was a lot of talk about that ... And now it seems like it's turned all the way around, like now, there's no money. You know, that's a luxury, to worry about that percentage of kids' (Interview 5).

The view that the goal of 'equality' in education was outmoded had become part of the new common sense. This view was expressed cogently by reformers like Dan Williams, who commented on the difference between his view and that of Bruce Reid:

[Reid] is such a strong believer in total equality, and this is where he and I would see things much differently. In that I think that belief stands in the way of him accomplishing what he would like to accomplish. It's my belief on that issue that if every child has to be treated exactly alike, then we lower the common denominator, and all of society suffers ... [I]n theory it's beautiful. But it doesn't work in reality. Now he believes that it can work in reality. And I think he has spent a lifetime in education trying to make it work and my guess is that he's probably very frustrated that he has not been able to institute the kind of changes that he would like, within that belief system. And at the same time, observing this tidal wave coming at him, that may consume him. So that would be a quick view of what I think is very presumptuous on my part, but that's it. (Interview 11)

Williams' comments may be presumptuous but they perceptively point to the widely held view that the goal of *equality of opportunity* was misguided and unattainable. Several authors argue that this belief facilitated the shift toward New Right ideology in education in Canada and elsewhere (cf., CCCS 1981; Connell et al. 1982). According to David (1993: 216), New Right proponents in Britain: '[A]rgued not only that social-democratic strategies had not been effective in their own terms, not achieving economic growth as had been expected, but also that they had led to increased bureaucracy at the expense of individual freedom and choice, and that therefore they inhibited economic development.' David argued that the result was a shift in the policy context from a focus on equality of educational opportunity to the maintenance of educational standards and 'parentocracy' – a program of educational privatization that uses the slogans of parental choice, educational standards, and the free market.

Like proponents of 'parentocracy' in Britain, business representative Dan Williams supported the idea of an educational market and the rights of parents to buy the product they preferred. Similarly, business leader Andrew Markham suggested that his experience of having his child in a private school made him more supportive of 'choice' and caused him to think that public schools could learn from private school models. The two trustees that were interviewed were more mixed, and to some extent contradictory in their views of the move to a competitive model. Simmons thought that involving private educational providers in the public system might actually ensure that the system could continue to address the diverse needs of students. She suggested, for example, that the CBE should explore working with Sylvan Learning Centres in order to 'bring in more resources ... and expertise' (Interview 26). Simmons's belief that working with private companies would *reduce inequities* in schooling represents something of an inversion in traditional ways of viewing public-private relationships, although it was consistent with the melding of public and private sectors in Alberta in the 1990s.

Jensen, on the other hand, felt that the government was abandoning a meritocratic ideal by encouraging privatization. She argued that the movement towards private schools was based on the idea that 'who you're going to know is important' so 'we'd better decide where we're all going to school so we can all know the right people' (Interview 30). This parallels Brown's (1990: 66) suggestion that the latest wave of educational reform has shifted from the idea of educational meritocracy to that of parentocracy – where 'a child's education is dependent increasingly upon the wealth and wishes of parents, rather than the ability and efforts of pupils.'

Relationships with Labour

The CBE's relationships with government and business people had observable implications for its relationships with employee groups. Compare, for example, Reid's very positive comments about the board's relationships with business partners to his comments about CBE-labour relationships:

> [W]e try to involve labour groups. We can't seem to do as well with them as we'd like, although we have involved them recently. [Chris MacDonald], I don't know if you know him or not. He's very active in labour. I have invited him to a few of our forums ... So we try to reach out there, but in terms of our own working relationships with some of the groups like CUPE, we're

not doing as well. And the reason we're not doing well is because, as a school system, we're committed to doing things differently, and in more cost effective ways, and that means contracting out in some situations. And as soon as you contract out,
you run into trouble with the trades and with CUPE. So I think
it's fair to say our working relationship with our trades and CUPE
are somewhat strained ... largely in the last two or three years
when we committed ourselves to contracting out. (Interview 17)

Relationships with Staff Association representatives were also
strained, according to Pam Conway, as the board sought to
contract out non-educational services.

Jensen provided an historical interpretation of board relationships with labour as follows: 'I believe [the impetus for change]
originally came from the concept that the people who were running all kinds of publicly funded institutions realized that there
needed to be good practice, driven by good management principles ... Why did they start to think that? I think that from
within, our leaders, our superintendents and so on, started to
feel exploited by unions. And the concept that there was always
more and that you always had to give ... And that our collective
agreements were getting in the way of good management (Interview 30). Harrison and Laxer (1995) refer to the Klein
government's construction of 'the enemy within' – public servants
who, in their selfish demands, have 'produced the enormous
crisis of provincial debt and deficits' (6–7). While Jensen was
not a strong supporter of the Klein government, she accepted
this construction and adopted a similar managerial perspective.
Simmons was also somewhat lacking in sympathy for labour
unions, suggesting that the ATA might become more moderate if
it was split into a union and professional organization.

Several changes in the CBE-business and CBE-labour relationships were at least partly attributable to cutbacks and restructuring. Relationships with business partners were strengthened
as a result of government activities, whereas relationships with
employee groups worsened. Relationships with labour appeared
to have shifted from fairly collaborative bargaining relationships to more traditional adversarial relationships, as resources

became scarce and alternative methods of delivering services were sought. Under these conditions, it seemed that CBE representatives saw themselves as having more in common with business managers who could provide advice on how to handle human resources and other issues associated with downsizing and restructuring. The capacity of large employers to offer resources during this period of cutbacks was also attractive. In turn, the increasing strength of CBE relationships with business partners could be expected to further exacerbate worsening relationships with employee groups. Therefore, while strengthening relationships with corporate representatives appeared to be in the *immediate* interests of board personnel, one might question whether it was in their longer-term interests.

Board participants' constructions of their realities arguably helped to maintain educational settlement. The interest in connecting schools more closely with the workplace, the need to come to terms with fewer resources and to lower expectations, and the need for greater involvement of business people were not challenged in any significant way. CBE administrator Bruce Reid believed that change was inevitable because of the fiscal crisis of the state, inflated public expectations, and growing dissatisfaction with educational outcomes. Perhaps as a result, the board challenged its loss of local autonomy as opposed to provincial cutbacks. Trustees Jensen and Simmons were coming to terms with the need to lower public expectations regarding education. Business partners were constructed as allies, potential government lobbyists, and *advisors* on restructuring and human resource management. Reid, Jenson, and Simmons were spreading the word of the CB within the board. The CBE's open relationships with business can be juxtaposed with its more strained relationships with its employee groups. A managerialist view was pervasive.

School-based Personnel

School-based participants were more mixed in their responses to educational restructuring. Interviews included three staff from Academic High School, who were introduced in Chapter 7, the principal of Native High School (NHS), and two ESL educators. Academic High staff had direct contact with business partners, unlike other participants. They also worked with students who were mostly from middle-class professional family backgrounds, while other participants were involved more directly with so- cially disadvantaged groups of students. Related to these differ- ent locations, participants had diverse experiences of reform and attitudes towards it. While science and business teachers from Academic High were concerned about the impact of re- forms, their programs appeared to gain status in the restructur- ing of priorities within the system. Teachers who worked with socially disadvantaged students, on the other hand, had already experienced the impact of fiscal crisis and the increasing marginalization of their programs. They had firsthand knowl- edge of the fact that certain groups of students were being side- lined by cutbacks and restructuring. However, reform ideas that promised enhanced opportunities for non-college-bound stu- dents had appeal. As we see in the following section, educators were mixed in their views, and, like labour participants, faced barriers to counter-hegemonic work.

Making Sense of Reforms

> Where are these ideas coming from? Like, I sit around and say, is this a bureaucrat? Is it some Deputy Minister who decided this stuff? And people say, 'Oh no, it's so and so because he's mad about this,' or 'it's this Cabinet Minister because he ...' or 'it's so and so who now belongs to ...' Like, everybody's trying to figure it out. But it just proves that there's no ... (Tracey Borger, Calgary Catholic School District)

To finish Borger's sentence for her, it just proves that educa- tional reforms in Alberta have no single origin. While we can agree that it is not that simple, hegemonic settlement involves the coming together of various forces within a particular politi- cal terrain. One of the questions to participants therefore asked what they saw as the impetus for reforms. In response, they usually mentioned highly visible individuals such as Joe Freedman or Dan Williams, and the group Albertans for Quality Education. They also agreed that the Chambers of Commerce were influential. Participants tended to view deficit reduction as the motivation for certain changes, and, like most Albertans, accepted with resignation the discourse of the fiscal crisis of the state. The ideological effect was that the idea of change as *inevitable* continued to frame discussion.

Individuals focused on different political, ideological, and economic influences on policy debate and formation. ESL teacher Carol Oliver, for instance, suggested that government reforms may be 'an ego-driven thing' on the part of key Tory politicians who were ideologically committed to a 'zero deficit' by election time (Interview 13). More generally, Native High School Principal Carl George argued that changes related to a general 'right-wing swing' in society, and parental worries about 'their own kids,' which caused people to become more self-interested with respect to education. Consultant Karen Gold suggested that Canadian education was greatly influenced by trends in the United States. Like Bruce Reid, she felt that the result was educational reforms that did not necessarily fit the Alberta context. Taken together, comments form an image of political reforms that were fiscally and ideologically driven. Writers in Ontario discussing Bill 160 paint a similar picture of reforms there. For example, Pascal (1998: 5) suggests that educational reforms introduced by the Harris government are, at best, 'the unfortunate consequence of a government which needs cash fast for its fiscal plans' and, at worst, 'part of a plan to till the soil for vouchers and charter schools and an ideologically driven, two-tiered, have/have not system.'

In Alberta, specific groups were seen to be promoting this ideology. Gold mentioned the private school sector, Joe Freedman, and 'Parents for Quality Education'[8] as allies in the promotion of choice and centralized funding. The Calgary Chamber of Commerce was seen as advocating the view that education should be run more like a business. Academic High Assistant Principal

Ron Leckie added that the government's proposal for charter schools, the move to more testing, and the centralization of funding all fit with Albertans for Quality Education. Gold and Carl George suggested that the government's *process* was partly to blame for outcomes since some groups had influence beyond their numbers in roundtables while others, such as Native youth, had no voice.

Participants were also critical of the negative impact of reforms on teachers and students. The funding cutbacks and restructuring initiatives introduced in Alberta Education's three-year business plan were seen to take power away from teachers as well as school boards. Increased standardized testing, 'accountability' through public reporting of results, and greater parental choice effectively reduced the autonomy of teachers. In the new quasi-markets for education, teachers were assessed in terms of the commodity that the school was 'placing on the market' (Connell et al. 1982: 36). Provincial funding cutbacks reflected in school board cutbacks led to the intensification of teachers' work overall and particularly within certain program areas. In a 1996 survey of teachers by the ATA, 67.9 per cent of respondents said that their average class size had increased since 1993, 81.2 per cent said that time available for spending with students has decreased, and 78.2 per cent said assistance for special needs students had decreased (Mackay and Flower 1999: 77). Changes clearly impacted the work structure of teaching. For example, with increased standardized testing, Gitlin (1983) suggests that teachers experience 'de-skilling' as opportunities to conceptualize curriculum activities are reduced and 're-skilling' as they become more bureaucratic in their need to adhere more tightly to schedules and fulfil test administering and reporting functions. Such changes limit opportunities for critical reflection and depersonalize relationships between students and teachers. In interviews with teachers, the impact of change on their daily practices was an important topic.

While reforms in Alberta affected the way teachers work, the way schools are run, and the delivery of curriculum, the impact on different schools varied. Academic High, for example, was better positioned than Native High School to adapt to changes. The former adopted a proactive approach to reforms by restructuring its leadership team and programs while the latter struggled to stay open. Native High Principal Carl George said he was preoccupied increasingly with raising funds to keep his school running, because the province refused to fund students over the age of 19 (approximately 60 per cent of his school's population). He therefore spent a lot of time putting together grant applications to submit to various state agencies and charitable foundations.

While his school was unusual in this regard, Karen Gold suggested that all principals were expected to become more entrepreneurial:

> The role of principals has really changed in the last ten years. I think that there was a time when principals were viewed as *managers of the school plant*. They were responsible for evaluating teachers in their school, but they relied on people from outside the school to provide curriculum leadership. I don't think that was a bad thing, but that's the way it was. Then it changed so that principals were *instructional leaders* ... And they were responsible for leadership within the whole school program in addition to allocating resources. And now, in addition to all of that, has come the involvement of the community, and the necessity for schools to almost act like *independent entrepreneurs*. So, if you're looking at business partnerships, for example, those principals who are willing to go out and get those business partnerships, get government funding and so on, those schools will benefit from that [my emphasis]. (Interview 18)

To support Gold's last statement, in 1997 public schools in Alberta raised a total of $124 million through 'private donations, parents fundraising, and sales to staff and students' (not including fees for course materials) (Evans 1999: 153). Not surprisingly, there was a gap between amounts raised in rich versus poorer areas. This has implications for a school like NHS, where fundraising was a means of survival rather than a way of supplementing existing programs and resources.

The move towards *site-based management* encouraged by the three-year plan also reinforced the idea of 'principal as entrepreneur' since it gave school leaders greater responsibility for managing school budgets. While site-based management had been adopted by the Edmonton public system earlier, it was new to most other boards. Of the three main forms of school-based management described by Leithwood (1998) – administrative control (where the principal is the main decision-maker), professional control (where teachers decide), and community control (where parents and community decide) – Edmonton was said to provide the 'most mature example of administrative control SBM [school-based management]' (36).

School-based management clearly changes the role of school leaders by devolving to them responsibility for the day-to-day budget and management of their staff. Yanitski and Pysyk (1999) argue that, after funding cuts, school-based management presented the greatest challenge to Alberta's principals (outside of Edmonton). Suddenly, school leaders were required to develop education plans for their schools, which outlined every program and budget item. Principals' duties and responsibilities increased, without increase in staffing or time. In addition, media reporting of provincial test results on a school-by-school-basis meant that 'pressure has been placed on principals to have their schools and students do consistently better than other schools' (171). Open boundaries and increased choice of schools meant that this pressure potentially had real consequences for enrolment.

However, this competitive scenario was not yet reflected in Assistant Principal Ron Leckie's comments at the time of our interview in March 1994. He did note, however, that with centralized funding and increased testing, school administrators at the local level had very little freedom. Academic High responded to the direction taken by the CBE by involving more parents, community, and business people in school governance. The school developed a Leadership Council with representatives from various community 'stakeholder' groups, including parents and business people. Leckie was responsible for overseeing the partnership with Monarch.

While school leaders focused on the changing governance of schools, Business Department Head Andy Laird emphasized the impact on programs in his area. Laird was generally pleased by the attempt to increase the status of vocational programs within the school and in the province more generally. He mentioned the decline of these programs that resulted from the Review of Secondary Programs that was conducted by the government in the mid-1980s. This review resulted in the establishment of two diploma streams: regular and advanced. Since most parents encouraged their children to enrol in the advanced program, which allowed for fewer options, enrolment in these areas apparently declined while enrolment in academic programs increased. Laird suggested that while the business department and other areas were contracting in the late 1980s, the science department was expanding. The province's introduction of the Career and Technology Studies curriculum in the three-year business plan was an attempt to increase enrolment in vocational courses by introducing modules that permitted more flexibility.

But while CTS was welcomed as a way of revitalizing vocational courses, it was also viewed as a new curriculum that was imposed by the province without adequate resources and planning. Laird notes that at a meeting to discuss CTS in 1992, a number of department heads expressed dissatisfaction with the level of support offered by Alberta Education and said they would refuse to implement it even if it were mandated. He added that a number of principals were also resisting the implementation of CTS: 'I really don't know what's going to happen in 1997 when this stuff becomes compulsory. I have a feeling that what will happen in a number of cases is that numbers will be assigned to these various courses, and somebody in Edmonton will look at those and say, "Oh yeah, they're coming on line." But go down and look in the classrooms and they'll know that nothing is happening' (Interview 31).

Apple (1993) similarly argues that when faced with mandated change and a lack of resources, the accomplishment of some goals in schools will be more symbolic than real. While the government talked about business people becoming involved in CTS program delivery, this was another area where Laird predicted that the reality of implementation would not match the rhetoric. His experience suggested that business people did not want to become involved in the day-to-day operations of schools because they were too busy. There were also problems associated with coordinating such involvement even when business people are willing. As a result, Laird doubted they would take on a key role.

A more pressing issue for Laird, as a teacher of computer courses, was the lack of money for computer upgrading in his school. While the province requested greater use of computers in schools, it failed in his view to provide adequate support. At the time of the interview with Laird, he was frustrated: 'This school, technologically, is twenty years behind ... As I say, it scares me sometimes when I think of what could happen with continued budget cuts. Because we did budgeting this year, and the guy said, "Start with last year's number and take ten percent off." Well, we've done that. The public thinks this is just starting this year. I haven't had a budget increase in five years. But my prices have all gone up. My equipment's older. There's a limit to what I can do. And when some people say, "Do more with less," I say, "I already am. Be realistic. And give me a break." I'm not doing more with less; I'm going to do less with less' (Interview 31).

Laird's frustration was addressed to some extent by subsequent government actions. A provincial program to help schools purchase computers and other technology was implemented as a result of recommendations in *Framework for Technology Integration in Education* (Alberta Education 1996b). As stated in an Alberta Education news release in February 1998, the government allocated $25 million in funding for technology integration in 1996–8 and promised to commit an additional $20 million a year from 1998 to 2001 as part of its reinvestment strategy. While critics may say that this was still not enough to ensure that schools were up to date technologically, technology integration had become an area of spending priority.

This 'reinvestment' is particularly noteworthy when we turn to participants who work with ESL students. Students who were defined as ESL by the province comprised 2.5 per cent of all students in Calgary schools in September 1996[9] (Alberta Education 1998). The central issue for ESL teacher Carol Oliver involved CBE cuts to the ESL program. Consultant Karen Gold confirmed that the level of service to students with English language learning needs had been reduced by approximately 80 per cent in the previous two years, and that the CBE had reduced the amount allocated to ESL services over time to the amount paid by the province in supplemental funding for ESL students (Interview 18). According to Gold, ESL programs had been treated more harshly than other programs in the CBE's 1994 budget: '[I]f you look at the budget this year, there is an additional $12 million – which is the largest amount being taken out of any sector of programs in the Calgary board – and it's not just ESL, it's all the special education services as well. So there's a $12 million reduction in that amount.' Thus, for both Oliver and Gold, CBE cuts to funding for ESL programs represented a major issue.

The comments of Oliver and Gold, and George's comment that he had essentially become a fundraiser for Native High School, recall Chapter 4's discussion of Achieving the Vision reports (Alberta Education 1991, 1992, 1993a). In these reports, provincial goals of 'success for Native children,' and 'success for immigrant children' appeared to involve little action when compared to goals of 'excellence in science,' and 'challenging our most capable students.' That the first two goals were less pressing was confirmed by interviews with educators who worked with Native and immigrant students.

When discussing the impact of cutbacks and restructuring, Oliver (who was also a member of a feminist organization) emphasized that they were particularly hard on women. Dacks, Green, and Trimble (1995, 270) agree that 'women have borne the brunt of reductions in health care, social services, and education spending' in Alberta under the Klein government. In education, greater parental responsibility meant greater responsibility for women, who, in Oliver's experience, were primarily responsible for interactions with schools. She also observed that the cuts to ESL programs greatly affected the work of those teachers, the majority of whom were women. Further, while she observed that most school leaders were male, Janet Weis from the ATA felt that this was unlikely to change in the near future since the 'last hired, first fired' phenomenon applied to women administrators who lost positions as a result of the amalgamation of school boards. Young (in press) confirms that cutbacks and restructuring have had particularly negative effects on women's participation in second-tier superintendency roles in the province. At the same time, the number of part-time educators (90 per cent women) increased by over 40 per cent in the 1990s. Fifteen percent of teachers were part-time in 1995–6 (Young 1999). Oliver argued that female students were also adversely affected by the increased policy emphasis on technology, since they were disproportionately represented in high school technology courses. Computer teacher Andy Laird observed that the majority of students in computer programming courses were male while the majority in computer applications such as word-processing was female. Therefore, while absolute numbers may be similar, the occupational possibilities for which students were being prepared differed significantly.

Oliver was concerned about questions of *access* as well as the *content* of curriculum, which she described as 'male' and 'white.' In this respect, she differed from some of the other participants who talked about the potential for reforms to create a two-tiered system of education. Carol Oliver, Carl George, and Karen Gold were under no illusion that public education had ever been particularly 'equal.' Perhaps because they worked closely with historically marginalized groups of students they did not idealize public education in the same way as Academic High teacher Barbara Phillips, who said, 'I believe schools are the last place we have where everybody's on a common footing ... In terms of society, school is school is school' (Interview 15).

In contrast, Carl George spoke about his school's disagreements with the CBE over the distribution of extension grants for adult students. He concluded: 'What we have always claimed is that the CBE has something like 207 schools, and if we were tied for 206th place in terms of how we are treated, we would be pleased. Instead of being alone in 207th place' (Interview 10). George referred to battles with board administrators over programming during the fifteen-year history of the school, commenting that one of the school administrators threatened to fire him if he introduced a 'Native curriculum' into the school. When they eventually did develop a curriculum, the minister of education apparently told him 'it was biased because it was very pro-Indian.'

The comments of George and Oliver raise issues over *content* (what is being taught) and *control* (who decides what is important knowledge) as well as *access* or equal opportunity (cf., CCCS 1981). Karen Gold also pointed to the *context* of reforms as important when she suggested that it was important to look at the assumptions held by reformers as well as at how changes were implemented. However, even oppositional discourses may fail to acknowledge that access is not enough, and that *equality of opportunity* can become: '[A] formula expressing the reconciliation of a genuinely radical and popular demand for more, and empowering education, with a stratified and competitive social order and the interests which are dominant within it' (Connell et al. 1982: 196–7). From this perspective, the focus on access or equal opportunity fails to move beyond the assumption of meritocratic schooling to examine how social inequities are perpetuated in schools, in families, and in the labour market. For example, it discourages teachers from challenging sexist and racist curricula by encouraging accommodation to existing structures rather than transformation.

Despite these criticisms of an oppositional discourse that focused on equal opportunity to the exclusion of other factors, participants clearly felt that this was the first line of defence in the attack represented by educational reforms. Oliver, for example, commented that cuts to ESL programs have meant that many of her Asian students were 'becoming disenfranchised' and were turning to crime (Interview 11). Her comments remind us of Tracey Borger's comment that non-college-bound youth in general were slipping through the cracks. Carl George argued that social problems such as suicide and incarceration rates[10] within the Aboriginal community also resulted in part from a lack of opportunity. Karen Gold articulated the sentiments of all three participants when she said, 'When we start excluding people from the education system, and we start to say we can't afford to educate certain groups of people, who are we going to choose not to educate? And who are we going to choose not to give access to, open access to the educational system? ... I think we want a technological society where everyone is able to participate in the democratic processes. The more we exclude people from participation, the more we set ourselves up for revolution to occur' (Interview 18).

A result of the 'swing to the right' was perhaps a narrowing of debate over equity to *access*, while other aspects – such as the control of education, the broader context of education within family and labour market structures, and the content of curriculum – were pushed into the background. The emphasis on funding cuts distracted attention from the fact that educational reorganization was promoted through 'internal restructuring of priorities and operations within the education system as well as through fiscal retrenchment' (Wotherspoon 1991: 21). While programs aimed at ESL and special needs students were cut back, CTS curriculum was slated for introduction and technology integration became a priority.

Views of Business Involvement in Education

Participants who had direct involvement with a business partner – Ron Leckie, Andy Laird, and Barbara Phillips – emphasized the benefits of the relationship for students and the school. Like school board representatives, they pragmatically viewed business involvement in education as part of current reality. From this perspective, resistance to business involvement came from teachers with 'blinders on,' or from those who were suspicious of business motives. Andy Laird, on the other hand, thought educators could learn from business people who were genuinely concerned about education.

However, Academic High representatives acknowledged that not all business input was positive. For example, Barbara Phillips talked about the push for accountability as follows: 'I think that's a business thing. And unfortunately, we have this metaphor, this model for learning that approaches the computer or the business model. Where students are inputs and they come out as products, and the product has to be "efficiently made," and that's really sad. But, the bottom line is money in our society, and money is connected to business, and products, so that's the way kids are viewed. I think it's really awful' (Interview 14). Comments made by business representative Gary Baldwin reinforce this view: 'A great deal of investment is made in education through tax dollars and things like that. And I think there has to be something come out of it. You're making an investment and you want to make sure that you're getting something productive and useful that comes out at the other end. And you know, if we're not doing it, we're going to have to go and get the labour force somewhere else, or we're going to become unproductive as a country, uncompetitive' (Interview 33).

Phillips did not perceive that her school's business partner, Monarch, promoted this very utilitarian view of schools. She suggested instead that the company demonstrated a willingness to invest in training and education and concluded that 'they're a very high-minded kind of a group of people to work with' (Interview 15). Phillips's comments indicate that she did not see business people as different from other individuals in their views. They were neither homogeneous nor predictable. Karen Gold also stressed that business people were also people in the community and parents of schoolchildren. From this perspective, 'it would also be in their business interest to be part of an educational process that is preparing citizens for the society' (Interview 18). These comments serve as a reminder that identity is multifaceted and consciousness complex.

Besides the problem of assuming that business interests were uniform, challenging business involvement in education was difficult because certain aspects of the new discourse of vocationalism appealed to educators. In particular, Ball (1990) writes that 'vocational progressivism ... [H]ighlights the vocational challenge to the liberal-humanist, academic domination of the secondary school curriculum. It also indicates the basis of common cause that exists between some members of the industrial lobby [in England] and new progressives in the educational establishment on matters of curriculum structure, assessment and pedagogy' (102).

Consistent with this challenge, Oliver felt that work experience programs were extremely valuable for students who needed 'that "hands-on" experience' (Interview 13). She thought these programs were good for ESL students in terms of learning English and gaining confidence. Gold also described herself as a 'supporter' of work experience and cooperative education programs (Interview 18). She was pleased that the CTS program attempted to integrate academic and vocational studies instead of encouraging students to develop skills in one area or the other. Both Gold and Oliver were conscious that the needs of all students had not been met adequately within a system that streamed students into academic and vocational programs and placed more value on the former.

At the same time, Gold recognized a tension within 'vocational progressivism' when she said, '[E]ducation is not a job preparation process and I hope it never becomes simply that. Presumably better-educated people are better employees, but that might not always be the case. A better-educated person might question more strongly what some employers might do. I mean, if the purpose of the education system is to educate people as *critical thinkers* [my emphasis] and as people who take actions according to their beliefs – people who are articulate and can recognize justice, for example – then that might not always be in the interests of the bottom line in business ... On the other hand, a well-educated person presumably would be more flexible and would be able to learn.' Gold thus suggests that the *progressivism* within the new vocationalism may be quite superficial.

There is also a clear gender subtext to the new vocationalism with its emphasis on trades and technical skills. As Blackmore

(1997) writes, with reference to Australian education trends, the construction of skill is no less gendered in the new vocationalism since it continues to ignore relationships between the public and private, and promotes the positivist view that skill is 'a fixed and measurable attribute defined by the technical needs of the workforce' (233). Accepting that debates which focus on the vocational function of education are really about 'who is taught what curriculum, how and by whom' (226), a priority in the Alberta context seems to be on non-college-bound male youth who are perceived to best meet the needs of employers facing shortages in skilled trades. Returning to discussion in Chapter 7, it is not students from schools like Emily Murphy who appear to be targeted for vocational programs like RAP (the registered apprenticeship program).

Despite these issues, the comments of Gold and Oliver point to the genuine concern that many teachers have about how best to prepare their students for the future given an uncertain economic climate. Since educators were not well informed about current labour market opportunities, it was not surprising that they saw vocational programs as meeting a need they could not address. Carl George also argued that there had to be a connection between the workplace and education. Otherwise, he said, 'it means that for our students to come here is just a temporary absence from welfare' (Interview 10). At the same time, George recognized that strengthening school-workplace linkages for students in his school potentially meant re-establishing the damaged links between a 'working-class school and the lower end of the labour market' (Connell et al. 1982: 204). His perspective on this issue was therefore mixed.

On the topic of school-business partnerships, participants were also generally supportive, although again, they commented on outcomes in relation to the goal of promoting equity. Gold said,

> I think there was some attempt to centralize and equalize the opportunities [for CBE schools to be matched with businesses], so it wasn't just on the shoulders of the principal to do that, which is good. But it still leads to an inequitable distribution of

resources. If my school has a partnership with Joe's Autobody Shop down the road, and somebody else's school has a partnership with IBM, there are obviously going to be differential resources available from that partnership. They might be equally valuable, in some ways. Like, we might be able to send kids to work with the people at Joe's Autobody's Shop, whereas they may be able to get thousands of dollars worth of computers into the school (laugh). But it's different, you know. And, is it based on the needs of the school, or is it based on the ability of the principal to be the PR person to present the school in a positive light to do all this? (Interview 18)

Of school-based participants, Carl George was most openly critical of increasing corporate involvement in schools:

C: I also think that large corporations have pulled the wool over the eyes of the average citizen and the school boards and the governments. They have been leading the fight for no more increased taxes. And meanwhile, they're now willing to have an input into these schools through partnership programs.

A: Do you see a connection between their fight for no increased taxes and their interest in schools?

C: Yes I do. I think what they're doing is getting free advertising. They're paying the same amount of money. But one way they would be paying it through tax with no influence on the schools ... So are we going to allow all of those corporations, not just to advertise, but undoubtedly in the very near future, if they don't already, to have good influence on the curriculum. That's ridiculous, that's just pure nonsense. You know, what kind of environmental studies program is going to be at the U of C when the whole department is controlled by oil companies? Probably not too good. And I think that those corporations have deceived the public as well as the politicians, by giving them this line. And then, they are so generous because they're willing to come up with a few bucks for some of these programs. That's just a load of crap. (Interview 10)

Concluding Comments

Interviews with school and board-based personnel suggest that the educational settlement represented by the three-year plan was maintained by: the work of noncorporate organic intellectuals like Bruce Reid; the distinction between government reforms and the work of business partners, acceptance of the discourse of fiscal crisis and the inevitability of change, the fact that parts of educational reform discourses connected with the lived experiences of educators, and the lack of communication channels among teachers who were most likely to engage in counter-hegemonic work.

For example, administrator Reid helped define the CBE's relationships with the 'business community,' Alberta Education, and its employee groups. Corporations were seen as partners, restructuring experts, and potential lobbyists; the government was seen as authoritarian and power hungry; and employee groups seemed to be perceived more as 'resources to be managed' than as active participants. Reid and other board representatives distinguished clearly between government restructuring and the role of business partners, and accepted the discourse of the fiscal crisis of the state. The effects were that change was seen as inevitable, board representatives resisted restructuring rather than funding cuts, and help from business partners was welcomed. School-based participants also accepted the fiscal crisis discourse, albeit reluctantly. Academic High teachers were unsure of the impact of cuts, while educators who worked with ESL and Native students noted the further marginalization of their programs.

Interviews with Gold, George, and Oliver also indicated that greater involvement of businesses in education responded to some of their concerns. The discourse of 'vocational progressivism' had appeal for educators who were concerned about their abilities to prepare students for a changing work world. At the same time, these educators were concerned about equity and the impact of changes on the control, access, and content of schooling. However, there seemed to be few forums for expressing these concerns. Previous cuts to the ESL program meant that board-level coordination of staff development and in-service for these teachers was almost eliminated. With the removal of the designation of ESL teacher in the CBE's budget, formal networks between ESL teachers would be even more difficult to maintain. Communication between George and like-minded educators was hampered by the fact that he was in 'survival mode,' applying for funding grants and attempting to keep his school operating. It is therefore difficult to envision networks whereby educators like Gold, Oliver, and George could 'pool knowledge among themselves and develop a broader, more comprehensive analysis of the operation of the system at large' (Seccombe and Livingstone 1996: 175).

Interviews at board and school levels provide a sense of participants' responses to the release of the three-year plan before the full impact of restructuring had been felt. Still, participants indicated a strong awareness of the discourses guiding reforms and their potential effects. School-based participants tied the themes of accountability, standards, devolution, and choice to discourses of the unhappy parent and the dissatisfied employer. Educators working with historically marginalized students were particularly concerned about the further development of a tiered system of education. Their concerns were no doubt related to the awareness that funding cuts along with increased focus on outcomes and individual choice would probably exacerbate inequities. For example, the promotion of choice and markets by mostly middle-class parents legitimizes resulting outcomes, however inequitable. In addition, despite the interest in increasing enrolments of non-college-bound students in CTS and apprenticeship programs, there is a strong academic bias in schools. In the competitive context of the 1990s, requests to better meet the needs of college-bound and non-college-bound youth were in danger of being translated as improving sorting and selecting mechanisms in schools through earlier streaming. Recognizing that debates about the role of education are also about access, content, and control of schools, it becomes more difficult to see the silver lining of reforms. The next chapter suggests that parent groups were also struggling to make sense of changes, based on their different relationships with each other and with the school system.

CHAPTER TEN

Students, Parents, and Community

In discussing the forces that prompted educational change in Canada, Barlow and Robertson (1994: 137) suggest that 'the "conservative alliance" has always comprised strange bedfellows, whose pragmatic interests coincide more often than their world views.' They point to members of the religious Right and business lobbyists as two groups of unlikely allies that 'have a vested interest in destabilizing public schools.' We see this to some extent in Alberta, where educational settlement addressed concerns of both unhappy parents and dissatisfied employers. The three-year business plan supported the idea of greater parental involvement in education through greater choice, school councils, and increased accountability measures for schools.

Of the three elements, school council legislation changed most through the implementation process. While school councils had been introduced in 1988, the 1994 amendments to the School Act strengthened their role significantly. They were to be mandatory and the majority of members were to be parents. Councils were to be given responsibility for the educational and financial operations and policies of schools (Bruce and Schwartz 1997). However, as the MLA Team on Roles and Responsibilities in Education held public meetings in 1994, it became clear that most parent groups were interested in having an advisory and consultative role rather than the more substantial role outlined in the initial legislation. The School Act was therefore amended in 1995 to reflect this change. As discussed later, school councils were also the reform that could be said to have rebounded on the government since they provided a mechanism for parents to become politicized and to protest other aspects of restructuring.

Back in 1994, however, parents did not have strong organizations through which to voice opposition. The Alberta Home and School Councils' Association was the provincial body through which concerns were raised. The Calgary Council of Home and Schools Association also represented school councils in Calgary, although the majority of schools in the city were not involved in this organization. There were other groups organized around particular issues such as special needs students and ESL students, and there was the group Albertans for Quality Education (introduced in Chapter 2).

This chapter is organized around interviews with students, parents, and AQE. Since several participants recognized the AQE group as a key player in the development of educational settlement, interviews with representatives are helpful in articulating the relationship between the agendas of unhappy parents and dissatisfied employers. With reference to post-1970 reforms in Britain, Miriam David (1980: 245) argues that parents were offered the 'semblance of greater rights over their children's education, on the premise that this would encourage them to press for improvements in educational standards and hence in the conditions for the reproduction of capitalism.' In the Alberta context, it could also be argued that parents helped to promote neoliberal reforms. The three-year business plan promoted a market model for education by constructing parents and employers as 'customers,' and students as 'products.' But as in Chapter 2, we need to ask to what extent the interests of unhappy parents and dissatisfied employers were consistent, and whether unhappy parents represented the majority of parents in the province. Interviews with participants help answer these questions.

Introducing Participants

Because students were constructed by restructuring advocates as the 'products' of the school system, they tended to be ig-

TABLE 10.1
Students, Parents, and Community Participants

Wendy Smith, High School Student	23 May 1994
Cindy Ho [Academic High Student]	30 September 1994
Lisa Kao [Academic High Student]	30 September 1994
Leslie Pearce, Parent	11 February 1994
Rebecca Rees, Parent and Community Worker	31 March 1994
Don Coulter, Calgary Council of Home and Schools	8 June 1994
Katherine Hennessey, Calgary Council of Home and Schools	27 April 1994
Susan Law, ESL Parent Group	4 March 1994
Justin Hall, Stan Jones, Albertans for Quality Education (AQE)	3 February 1994
James Kozak, Journalist associated with AQE	15 April 1994
Rhonda Dixon, Save Public Education (SPE)	31 May 1995

nored as subjects. For this reason, three high school students were interviewed: Lisa Kao and Cindy Ho from Academic High (introduced in Chapter 7), and Wendy Smith, a grade ten student from another high school in Calgary. Five parent participants were also interviewed. Don Coulter and Katherine Hennessey were involved with the Calgary Council of Home and Schools Association[1] a group that included approximately fifty representatives from Parent Advisory Councils in Calgary. Susan Law belonged to a coalition of ESL parents that formed in 1992 to advocate on behalf of ESL students in Calgary schools. Two women who were not formally affiliated with a parent group are also included: Wendy's mother, Leslie Pearce, and parent/community worker Rebecca Rees. Discussion of the Albertans for Quality Education group is based on an interview with two representatives of this group (Justin Hall and Stan Jones), a journalist who was affiliated with this group (James Kozak), and a parent who was able to provide some history about previous struggles over parental choice in Calgary (Rhonda Dixon). Table 10.1 lists participants, their affiliations, and the dates of our interviews.

Students

Cindy Ho and Lisa Kao were in grade twelve at the time they were interviewed. Wendy Smith was in grade ten at a high school that was known to have a strong Fine Arts program. These students were not chosen to 'represent' all students. All three are female, two are children of immigrant parents (from Hong Kong and Vietnam), all planned to attend university, and all attended schools in northwest[2] Calgary. Therefore, issues raised by these students were likely to differ from those of 'non-college-bound' male students. The choice of participants was motivated in part by an interest in incorporating race and gender perspectives that are often excluded in order to better assess the implications of policies for different groups. Two themes emerged from interviews: first, all three students expressed concerns about educational cutbacks and uncertainty about job prospects; and second, they felt powerless in the face of government actions.

All three participants had thought about how educational cutbacks would affect their future plans. Senior students Lisa Kao and Cindy Ho talked about increases in tuition fees and stiff competition for scholarships. When asked what concerned her about public education, Lisa Kao answered, 'I'm kind of worried about how I'm going to get to university. Like, I have the grades and all. My dad is retiring in about two years, my mom can't work [because of poor health] ... Like, I don't know what's going to happen. I know if I go to university, I have to find my own finances ... So I hope to get some scholarships and work too. But you're hanging in the balance. You don't know what's going to happen' (Interview 35). Cindy Ho hoped to get a scholarship as well, but was more optimistic that her parents could also provide financial help.

For these students, it was unthinkable that they would not attend university. When Ho was asked if this was typical of most students she knew,[3] she replied, 'I think that is a general goal because right now we have, well, we're kind of short of employment, just big competition now. Almost everything, you need a university degree, so ...' (Interview 34). According to Ho, even students who were not getting good grades or who faced financial difficulty were planning to upgrade or work for a year in order to enter university at a later date. While the immediate future looked more secure for grade ten student Wendy Smith, she was concerned that potential cutbacks to Fine Arts programs at her high school would affect her future. She also noted the potential impact of cuts on the program for deaf students in her school.

Concerns about education were related to the grade twelve participants' uncertainties about their future job prospects. Lisa Kao acknowledged that her perceptions of the job market affected her decision to enrol in science at university. After noting that her two occupational choices would be in medical research or in the entertainment industry, she continued, 'The thing is, it's like a ... OK, if I was living in a different time, and say our economy was really good, there were lots of jobs. I would go into my latter choice, which is the film industry or whatever. But if you look at it, I'm limited now. There are not many jobs there. You never know if you're going to make it. And if you don't make it, you don't know where to go. Right? So I guess there are two options, and I'd have to take the first one ... It's what *you want to do*, and what *you should do*. That's the thing' [my emphasis] (Interview 35).

Kao then stated that her parents also encouraged her to take sciences: 'Well, my parents are, like, first generation immigrants. They want me to have more and be better than they ever were. I guess they're pushing for the sciences, because there's more stability. My dad and my mum want me to be a pharmacist.' Cindy Ho similarly commented that 'basically it's our parents that are worried' about their children's future job prospects. But like Lisa Kao, she added that her view of the labour market demand influenced her decision to choose environmental chemistry over architecture at university.

Wendy Smith was more resistant to the idea that students should try to match themselves to areas of projected labour shortage. When asked what she thought when she heard people say that students should go into particular fields because there were more jobs, she replied, 'I don't think anybody's going to listen to it, just because there are more jobs there. People aren't going to do it. I mean, engineering – most people don't want to go into that. And if they do, it's mostly men. Most women don't want to go into that' (Interview 28). Smith's comments convey both her awareness of the types of jobs that students were being encouraged to pursue and the extent to which the reality of a gender-divided labour market affected students' 'choices.' Appendix B, Table 4 provides statistics on the occupational breakdown by sex that confirm that gender is an issue.

The sense-making of students was no doubt related to their family situations also. Smith and her three younger brothers lived with their mother who was pursuing a master's degree in the social sciences. Kao's parents were Vietnamese immigrants and her two older sisters were studying medicine at university. Ho's parents were immigrants from Hong Kong. She commented that her father was a victim of economic downturn and that 'eventually he just got into self-employment to make sure that nobody laid him off' (Interview 34). She also referred to the experiences of her cousins as follows: 'I have two cousins who got out of university but couldn't find a job. They had to get into something else. [One] came out of school with an electrical engineering degree. But he couldn't find anything in that. And he went to Toronto for a while, came back here, still couldn't find anything. So he just went into accounting, and found something in that area. And my [other] cousin also found something in accounting; but she came out with a nutrition degree from the university.' Students' experiences and their social locations in terms of gender, race, class, and family situations therefore influenced their expectations and 'choices.'

What is interesting to note about Kao, Ho, and Smith is that all three were university-bound academic students who were concerned about how well they would be served by further education. This raises the question of how 'nonacademic' students think about the value of education. Wendy Smith's mother, Leslie Pearce, talked about Wendy's brother: 'You should interview my thirteen-year old, find out what he wants to do in his life. Because I have no idea. And he has no idea. So if that's the case, does it really matter that you get 40 per cent in science? Like it starts to make sense. You know, I look at it and I think, aren't you worried when you hear what's going on in the world and you're going to need a 75 to get into university. All this stuff, and it doesn't mean anything to him, absolutely nothing' (Interview 4).

While Pearce did not connect her son's attitude with his vision of future job prospects, Ray and Mickelson (1993: 12) suggest that the lack of motivation attributed to non-college-bound youth in the United States may be explained by their belief that 'as adults they will face jobs that are unstable; lack opportunities for advancement; pay low annual wages; and provide few, if any health benefits.' Schools and markets have therefore 'lost their credibility as fair mechanisms for distributing opportunities' (12). The effect of this, in the authors' view, is something of a performance strike by students. This is an interesting inversion of the discourse of *education for national prosperity*, which suggests that economic problems are *caused* by the fact that workers are not motivated/disciplined and lack skills.

This inversion results from the fact that Ray and Mickelson began from the experiences of students to explain their attitudes and behaviour rather than from the experiences of corporate representatives. Leslie Pearce also observed a difference in perspective and 'realities' when she asked what school-business partnerships meant to the child who was involved in them. In her view, the notion of encouraging students to gear their day-to-day activity towards a longer-term goal 'came out of an adult sense of the world, certainly not a thirteen year old's' (Interview 4). Ehrenreich (1989) would add that the push to get students thinking about their future careers was tied to a distinctively middle-class preoccupation with *discipline* and *delayed gratification*. According to Ehrenreich, middle-class parents believed that fostering these values would ensure that their children maintained or improved their socioeconomic status.

Pearce's comments raise questions about the extent to which students were objects of reform as opposed to stakeholders in their own right. Certainly the idea of starting from the experiences of students appeared to be sadly lacking in business initiatives in education as well as educational reform more generally. Chapter 7 suggested that Lisa Kao and Cindy Ho felt that they were not in the 'front lines' of their school's partnership with Monarch and saw it as having little significance for their day-to-day lives. This feeling that students had little power over their lives in school was reinforced in other comments made by Lisa, Wendy, and Cindy. Departmental exams and curricula such as the Career and Life Management course that was mandated in the 1980s were viewed as 'facts of life.' Student resistance was confined to describing CALM as a 'waste of time' or 'a joke' and questioning the relevance of certain curriculum topics for their everyday lives. Student protests to government actions in the fall of 1993, on the other hand, represented more overt resistance.

The three participants expressed mixed feelings about the events of the fall of 1993. A rally involving approximately 3,000 high school students had been held on 27 October to protest potential cuts to programs suggested in the roundtable workbook. Wendy Smith talked about her participation in this event: 'It was wonderful. I'm really glad we did it. Like, everybody said it was stupid and you shouldn't have done it, but it was really good. And Ralph Klein, he's so dumb (laugh). It was really good. It made people really listen, even though they think we're stupid. We made them listen' (Interview 28).

Lisa Kao also expressed support for the actions of fellow students, saying, 'it was really good to see the student voice for once. Rather than administrators or adults telling us, "Don't do this. Don't do that," you know?' But when I asked whether she felt students have much of a voice, she replied, 'In the school, yeah, pretty much. But in the government, no. It's like, they don't really care. That's the impression I got. Like, after all the people went down to City Hall, and there were photos in the newspaper of all these students. And they shut the doors on us, or something, in the legislature. So it's pretty futile. It was a good thing to do. But in terms of the reaction, it looks futile, you know?' (Interview 35).

Cindy Ho also recounted her personal protest attempt:

C: We found out the number to Klein's office. And [Klein] kept telling us, 'I'm willing to take in your suggestions. I'm doing this because there's no other choice.' So I called up their office, and I say, 'You know, I'm against these cuts. Because here you are looking at some of the people in the government who are getting huge pensions. And they're using government money for their own purposes. And here we are suffering in our education.' So I told [the receptionist at Klein's office] about that, and she says, 'There is no such thing going on.' And she slammed the phone on me. And I was just appalled.

A: So how did that make you feel?

C: Well, I kind of felt betrayed. Because as a citizen I felt that I had a right in what kind of education I'm getting. I don't feel that he should make whatever cuts he wanted. I mean, this is not absolute rule; we have democracy in this country. So that was how I felt. I was very angry about what happened.

A: So how do you feel about participating in democracy now?

C: It's fake (laugh). (Interview 34)

It is apparent from the above quotations that these young women enjoyed having the opportunity to collectively voice their concerns to policy-makers. At the same time, they were disappointed by the response of those in authority. They recognized that their knowledge and experiences were not considered to be relevant by policy-makers who were focused on budget cuts and reforms, and who viewed students as outputs in the schooling process. Aware that they had been relegated to the status of children by those in authority, their faith in the effectiveness of political resistance was shaken.

Interviews with students suggest that while hegemonic work did not include their perspectives, counter-hegemonic work must do so for three reasons. First, high school students represent future citizens, parents, workers, and employers; second, it cannot be assumed that stakeholders in the policy community are able to act in the best interests of students in their diversity otherwise; and third, students have demanded the legitimate right to be part of the discussion (as the rally in Calgary demonstrated).

Parents

Parent participants shared some of the cynicism of students. As a group, participants were all well educated and could be described as middle-class, which corresponds to David's (1993) comments about parents who are typically involved in school reform. Four of five interview participants were women, which is also typical, although Hennessey noted that the numbers of men involved in parent councils was increasing. Leslie Pearce was a single parent of four children aged eight to fifteen years including grade ten student Wendy Smith. Susan Law was a representative of an ESL coalition, and Rebecca Rees represented a community education centre that worked in coalition with her group. Rees's centre was involved in anti-racist and global education work with schools. She was also the mother of three teens who attended public schools. CCHSA representative Katherine Hennessey and Parent Advisory Council member Don Coulter each had two children aged eight and twelve.

Relationships with Other 'Stakeholders'

Chapter 2 refers to the potentially unifying effect that the concept of *the parent* played in discussions about education; the parent could be made to appear 'classless, without gender, and seeking a better life for the child – a generalizing focus for worries about "the nation" and its children' (CCCS 1981: 202). A number of writers, including David (1993) and Dehli (1996), critique the homogenizing use of the concept of the parent. David (1993: 6) argues that gender, legal and marital status affect parents' relationships to schools, as do social divisions around class and race. Dehli also cautions against the assumption that parents are similarly located in relation to New Right discourses around educational reform. Given these comments, it is useful to examine how some of these differences played out in educational reform discussions.

CCHSA members Katherine Hennessey and Don Coulter were 'insiders' in terms of their knowledge of the school system and interactions with key reformers, compared with Rebecca Rees and Susan Law who were associated with less 'mainstream' organizations. As an unaffiliated parent, Leslie Pearce was even more of an outsider. As with labour groups in Chapter 8, there appeared to be an implicit hierarchy of parent groups based on their positions within mainstream structures. CCHSA members worked closely with the ATA and school staff[4] whereas ESL group representative Susan Law argued that the ATA could have taken a stronger stance when the public board was replacing ESL teachers with aides. Further, while both the CCHSA and ESL group were somewhat critical of the actions of trustees and the school board,[5] the former group was invited to work with the board whereas the ESL group felt marginalized.

Perhaps because of historical patterns of preferment as well as the lack of contact between the CCHSA and her group, Law questioned the representativeness of the Home and Schools group, saying, 'I don't know if they've played a particularly strong role in getting ESL parents to become part of the Parent Councils' (Interview 12). Single parent Leslie Pearce also felt that women in her situation were not well represented. In her view, most parents who became involved with Parent Advisory Councils were in the 'classic' kind of two-parent family situation, where mothers had the energy to participate because they were not in 'survival' mode (Interview 4).

Katherine Hennessey acknowledged that Home and Schools groups needed to represent more schools and people, but added that the existing degree of diversity in terms of public/separate, rural/urban already made it difficult for the provincial body to achieve consensus on specific policy positions. Hennessey's comments recognize important differences within the category 'parents.' Although Susan Law's ESL group held forums that included speakers from other groups that were 'under siege' – adult educators, Labour Council representative Chris MacDonald, and Native High School – she added that 'we haven't amalgamated our resources enough' (Interview 12). Community worker Rebecca Rees summed up the problem of fragmented opposition as follows: 'I haven't seen [the Calgary Status of Women Action Committee] play an active role around this issue. In general, I guess that's an issue for me. I don't have a sense of a lot of community groups coming together ... It disturbs me that we haven't found a way to come together in a meaningful way around health, around education. It's like different groups seem to have different pieces of it ... So [there is a need for] more direct work around trying to fend off cuts to ESL and encouraging the coalition to get connected to other broader coalitions like the [Quality Education Coalition] out of Edmonton' (Interview 20). She later reflected on the seeming lack of impact of NGOs and church-based groups and social justice organizations like her own that were 'about alternative views on the world' in light of the relatively high level of support for the Klein government.

These comments raise questions concerning how to build alliances that can accommodate differences within existing power structures,[6] and how to develop alternatives that can be embraced by a broader public – challenges faced also by labour organizations. A further challenge, according to Hennessey, was the fact that the CCHSA was a voluntary organization staffed mainly by mothers who were focused on improving education for their children.[7] There was little time for coordination between groups or for working beyond the micro-issues. Therefore, as with labour groups, the lack of resources presented another obstacle to developing effective counter-hegemonic opposition.

The lack of alliance among parent groups such as the CCHSA and the ESL coalition is interesting to contemplate in light of the balance of power across the policy community. The lack of influence of even mainstream groups such as the CCHSA was confirmed by Dan Williams's reference to it as a 'group of stay-at-home mothers' who were politically ineffectual. This condescending assessment from a participant who clearly had access to political power, reinforced a gender dynamic whereby the

views of predominantly male business people with remote connections to schools were privileged over the predominantly female parents interacting with schools on a regular basis.
Williams's comment also pointed to the problem of fragmented
opposition in the face of seemingly unified groups like the
Alberta Chamber of Commerce.

While their relationships with each other were not as strong
as they might be, parent participants shared a critical view of
government actions. They referred to their relationships with
the province in a way that recalls comments made by ATA
participants. Katherine Hennessey stated that her group did not
have 'nearly the kind of input that we thought we would have'
in the government roundtable process. She added that this lack
of meaningful consultation continued into the implementation
of the three-year business plan by MLA teams. In early 1994,
when the CCHSA expressed specific concerns about reforms
and asked the province to establish a parent advisory board to
advise them on policy matters, it did not respond. Hennessey
was therefore sceptical about whether the government actually
wanted parents to have a meaningful role in school governance
(Interview 27).

As a representative of a group that was not invited to the
government roundtables, Law was also cynical about the way
reforms were approached in Alberta: 'I guess, to a certain extent, there can be a reluctance to accept such drastic changes to
ideas that haven't been promoted in a kind of democratic way;
it's been kind of thrust on Albertans. And I think that's one of
the difficulties with what's happening with education. There's a
great fear of creating a many-tiered system. And I think it's not
an unfounded fear, especially if it's being rammed down your
throat. And because of the way it's being done, perhaps there's
the fear at the provincial level that these kinds of ideas will not
be adopted by the general population – so let's not reveal all
that we need to reveal to the people. So they haven't bothered
to educate the people in promoting it in the way that in a general democratic society we would expect' (Interview 12). Like
Law, Pearce and Coulter also suggested that public participa-

tion was more difficult because people lacked information. However, one could also argue that access to information was asymmetrical. Dan Williams, for example, did not seem to lack information, nor did members of the AQE. However, parent participants clearly found it more difficult to gain information and provide input.

The comments of Hennessey and Law suggested that if the government process had been more democratic in terms of including more people and taking their views seriously, the results may have been more palatable. But in the following exchange, Leslie Pearce suggested that for certain groups the ability to participate, even when invited, was limited:

L: I think that even within the alternative [roundtable] situation [sponsored by the ATA and Home and Schools], we're talking about a certain kind of individual, and there's a whole range of people out there who do not fall into either category. There are a lot of voiceless people out there, people who don't understand the issues, people who are just too concerned about survival to worry about the education system. There is a large population, and that population is going to become larger because, you know, people are worried about survival. How their children are being educated cannot be as important as it should.

A: That's interesting because you hear about the need for more parental responsibility in schools.

L: Yes, but I hear that as a middle-class woman who's working on her second degree, who grew up in a family where education was somewhat valued. I can respond to that. I can go home and work with my kids ... But there are lots of people who can't do that. (Interview 4)

Participants agreed that a consequence of the lack of public participation in the policy process was reforms that would lead to greater inequality. Programs for already disadvantaged students may be sacrificed to maintain programs for the children of elites. For example, Pearce shared her experience with the gifted program that one of her children attended: 'What happened is that initially the program was started to meet a need, children who were gifted were having trouble because the classroom could not respond to them ... so they were doing very poorly or having behaviour problems. [But then] the shift went over to "we want children who are well-behaved." I don't have confidence that the people who are running this and the people on the board really understand what their program is for. This is not for the children who come out of [name of a private school], and honest to God, these are the children who are coming in, children from upper-middle class ... Now I resent paying my taxes to look after some person who probably lives in some mansion up here, so that their child can be called 'gifted' and go to a school like that.' Pearce went on to suggest that the gifted program, which in her view represented a sanctioned two-tiered system, was unlikely to be affected by funding cuts and reforms. Although Pearce was under no illusion that equal opportunity existed prior to cutbacks, she believed that inequalities would be exacerbated by reforms.

Making Sense of Discourses

Interviews reveal what participants saw as the impetus for reforms and how they located themselves in relation to the discourses of the unhappy parent and education for economic prosperity. They challenged the discourse of the unhappy parent by questioning the representativeness of AQE, and raising concerns about effects of government reforms on different groups of students. They also challenged the discourse of education for economic prosperity by questioning its labour market assumptions and highlighting the differing opportunity structures that existed for various groups of students. But while participants shared a critique of this discourse, their reform solutions differed.

The impetus for reforms was discussed both in terms of specific groups and individuals that participants thought were influential in Alberta and in terms of broader social, political, and economic trends. Coulter, Rees, and Law all mentioned the in-

fluence of 'business groups' and 'unhappy parents.' In discussing the three-year business plan, Coulter argued that while 'the
population was ignored, and professionals with years and years
of experience were ignored' by government, 'Albertans for Quality Education were not ignored – they're going to have their
shot at having Charter schools' (Interview 29). He added that
politicians listened 'to a certain Chamber of Commerce who
bought and paid just about everything they wanted. And what
they want for education is private schools.' In sum, Coulter
thought that educational reforms represented 'a full frontal as-
sault by special interest groups, extreme right-wing religious
groups, and government officials' (4). His comments parallel
the suggestion made also by Janet Weis of the ATA and by
Barlow and Robertson (1994) that the two main drivers of reform were the religious right and business groups.

Rebecca Rees also mentioned this dual thrust of reforms when
I asked her if she saw a coherent agenda for change in Alberta:
'No. I mean, I think you have this push from very conservative
elements. But Klein himself doesn't even seem to be on top of it
all. You know, you've got an agenda to cut costs, you have an
agenda to get business more involved, you have kind of a fundamentalist agenda in terms of what's being taught and resistance to global ed and multicultural ed.[8] But whether that's coherent (pause). Probably it is in some minds, but whether it's
coherent in terms of all the people and the push. Yeah, I think
there are forces that are coherent. Whether it's already present
at the government level, it feels like it, but I don't know if it
really is' (Interview 20).

The main impetus for reforms, however, came from neoliberal
policy trends in her view:

[W]hat we've heard the government talk about over and over is
greater interaction between the business community and schools;
business has to become more involved. And this isn't new for
this government. I mean, even at the national level, I think the
Board of Trade has done programming around the high drop-out
rate across Canada [the Conference Board?]. Exactly, the need for

business to become involved. There's a real paradox there, which is that the business community in Canada has been promoting economic policies in Canada such as free trade ... which in turn put us in a situation where we find governments increasingly cutting back in areas like health, education, and social services. So it's almost circular. And policies which create high unemployment. Which make it very difficult for youth, especially those who tend to drop out, to see why they should remain in school. And so I think Alberta is almost a microcosm of that general pattern. But one that's very much accelerated. I feel we're a testing ground for that attitude among business circles and some parts of government. And I find it frightening because I think we're looking at the privatization of education.

Susan Law added that there had been a clear shift in Alberta from a social welfare system to one where people were expected to be self-reliant.

Rees's comments paralleled some of the oppositional arguments presented in Chapter 2. Her emphasis on the connection between free trade policies and other reforms echoed arguments made by Barlow and Robertson (1994) and Calvert and Kuehn (1993);[9] her focus on unemployment rates as a key measure of economic health reflected the arguments contained in Canadian Centre for Policy Alternatives publications (1992, 1993); and the idea that the attitudes and actions of youth were tied to labour market realities echoes the arguments of Ray and Mickelson (1993) and Livingstone (1999).

Katherine Hennessey and Leslie Pearce discuss the impetus for reforms in terms of broader social trends. Hennessey explained parents' interest in returning to basics and discipline as their response to a rapidly changing world. The impetus for educational reforms thus came from a fearful reaction to social uncertainty, and the need for parents like Joe Freedman to feel that they could control change. Hennessey characterized it as 'a right-wing agenda' that was also shared by the AQE. Leslie Pearce placed this agenda within an historical context in the following exchange:

L: There was a vision in the 60s – if you talked to people, they could describe to you this vision, this picture of a better world, a better life, people getting along, better care, and this kind of thing ... People don't think like that any more, people don't vision like that.

A: How do you think they vision now?

L: Very practically. And that's why I think we're into this age of computers, tangible stuff that you can touch. So, more confidence put into things that are hard, solid, secure. And maybe that has come out of the last twenty or thirty years. With us kind of living with this nebulous vision of something better that never could come to be ... So what we see today has been coming, it's been growing and developing for some time. But if you ask me to pinpoint where it comes from, this fascination and this belief in the security of the computer age ... It's a wave and it's growing and gaining momentum and I think people are very, very frightened. And cynical as I am about things, I feel myself getting swept by it sometimes too. In particular, in regards to my kids. Because sometimes I get quite panicky if they don't do well in school. And my one child is doing very, very poorly in school. If I really think about his future, I can get myself feeling sick (Interview 4).

Pearce's reference to the current vision as a response to the 1960's 'nebulous vision of something better that never could come to be' reflects the idea that the success of right-wing political forces in industrialized countries was partly attributable to the failure to achieve 'social democratic' reforms in the 1960s and 70s (CCCS 1981; David 1993).

Both Katherine Hennessey and Leslie Pearce talked about the impetus for reform in terms of parental fears about social and economic changes. Pearce's comments about her son and Hennessey's more generalized comments point to the attraction of a political vision that offered the promise of security for parents and their children, given their material realities. Clearly, Hennessey and Pearce saw themselves represented in part within the discourse of education for economic prosperity. However, Pearce also recognized the danger in succumbing to a vision that was 'fear-based,' totalizing and individualizing, just as Hennessey argued that the return to more traditional forms of education failed to acknowledge 'the diversity of kids' and society's needs' (Interview 27).

The Unhappy Parent. Participants challenged whether proponents of the discourse of the unhappy parent were able to represent other parents. They disagreed that the AQE spoke for working-class parents and suggested that the reforms supported by this group would only exacerbate the positions of marginalized youth and their parents. While participants acknowledged that the discourse of the unhappy parent tapped into some of their own concerns about the inflexibility of schools and their failure to address the learning needs of all students, participants disagreed with reformers' strategies and solutions.

Although the CCHSA faced its own issues around representation, participants undoubtedly would say that Home and School groups were more representative than the AQE and its proponents. Coulter and Hennessey disagreed that unhappy parents had public opinion on their side. In the following comments, Don Coulter expressed his image of AQE members: 'Their theory of the perfect little Alberta family is a happily married husband and wife with two children, one boy, one girl. Both children get outstanding marks in school and have never been in trouble in their neighbourhood. Dad is fully employed and mom is home carrying the third child and making the evening Sunday meal. End of conversation. That's it. They pay their taxes; they all vote right wing. And everybody goes to the same church' (Interview 29).

Hennessey also mentioned AQE members' preoccupation with 'family values' and curriculum 'basics' and concluded, 'I strongly object when they say they speak on behalf of parents, because they don't speak on behalf of me or practically anyone else I know' (Interview 27). The poor turnout at the AQE conference in 1994 indicated to Coulter and Hennessey that the group not only failed to represent a range of views, but also failed to attract large numbers. The conference was held at the Stampede Corral in Calgary with approximately 150 people in attendance, a significant drop from the previous year.

CCHSA participants thus questioned whether the AQE could claim the support of middle-class parents like themselves. They also questioned whether AQE and its proponents represented disadvantaged youth and their parents as they claimed. Chapter 2 notes that parent reformers Freedman and Nikiforuk both argued that 'disadvantaged' students would do better with *direct-instruction* rather than *child-centred* approaches. Leslie Pearce differed, arguing that child-centred instruction was more likely to accommodate student differences. Freedman had pointed to the benefits of charter schools for 'working-class' and 'disadvantaged' youth. But again, Parent Council member Coulter disagreed, arguing that charter schools were motivated by the 'self-interest' of middle- and upper-class parents. He said: 'I regret to see that we are talking about charter schools, which have proven to be nothing, even in their early stages in the U.S., but private little enclaves for people who want things to be their way for their own family, and not necessarily for the general good of all. Nothing wrong with caring about your child. But when you start saying that a group of parents from a particular neighbourhood is going to decide which Johnny and which Susie get in there, why don't you just go ahead and set up the old plantation in Georgia circa 1860, because that's what you're going to end up with' (Interview 29). It is worth noting that these comments reflected a struggle between middle-class groups of parents who both claimed to speak *for* working-class parents.

Coulter's comments challenged AQE claims about representation and focused on the impact of reforms on particular groups. Ball (1990) would agree that the ideology of the market – represented, in this case, by charter schools – works as a mechanism for 'class reproduction.' He writes: '[C]hoice and the market provide a way for the middle classes to reassert their reproductive advantages in education, which had been threatened by the increasing social democratic de-differentiation of schools, the cultural reform of the curriculum ... and the diversion of resources to those with greatest learning needs and difficulties. Choice and the market reassert those privileges, which confer on the privileged "the supreme privilege of not seeing themselves as privileged."'

Brown (1990) predicted that the shift towards an 'ideology of parentocracy' and its market solutions in Britain would reduce the ability to enforce equal opportunities policies aimed at breaking down gender and racial inequality. This is consistent with Susan Law's view that the competitive model introduced by charter schools was likely to increase the segregation of students, to the detriment of ESL students and other marginalized groups (Interview 12). Rebecca Rees shared her concern that market forces were an inappropriate way of deciding 'who shall be educated.' Rees says, 'So who do we think we're sending to school and who are we sidelining? Kids from welfare families, kids from working-class families, kids from any family where things are totally stressed-out. But that's what I think is going wrong. And this argument has been used a lot around ESL cuts. There's this whole sense of a group of people who will never be employed, being created. You know, they're down here and they'll stay there and they're not going to aspire to much more, or they shouldn't' (Interview 20).

The assumption that all parents and students would benefit from greater parental 'choice,' and the somewhat contradictory assumption that teacher-directed instruction methods were more effective for all students was thus challenged by participants. Katherine Hennessey also challenged the 'outcomes-based' idea of accountability promoted by the AQE and Dan Williams, which called for more testing and reporting. Hennessey suggested that increased testing and reporting were not sufficient, and presented this alternative view of accountability: 'Accountability, for parents, may be going into the school and saying, "You're operating a multi-age program. Tell me why that works ... As a government you're changing the curriculum yet again. Why are we doing that?" [Or] going to our board and saying to them,

"You've chosen to support this budget that your administration has presented to us. Explain to me why this is in the best interests of our children"' (Interview 27). This alternative vision constructed accountability in terms of opportunities for meaningful parental input into the educational process.

But while participants challenged the discourse of the unhappy parent and the reforms proposed by people like Joe Freedman and the AQE, they also acknowledged their appeal. For example, Leslie Pearce suggested that she was becoming caught up in 'this wave of people who are becoming really afraid that what you do in grade eight is going to affect you when you're forty' (Interview 4). She therefore found herself taking seriously the emphasis placed on math and science and basic skills. Pearce also talked about the appeal of the discourse of choice: 'I'd like to be able to choose the kind of school my child goes to. I don't think I'd pick a multi-age or whatever it's called. I think I would probably pick somewhere else. And I think that we should have that choice. We shouldn't be told that we have to send our child to some new program, which we know isn't new, or to subject them to something that we don't think is going to work ... I think that if I really had the right situation, I would probably home school my kids for a while.'

However, other comments suggest that Pearce was committed to working within the public education system when she was dissatisfied. For example, when she became aware that one of her children was not responding to the teachers' approach to reading, she decided to work with him at home using a different approach. Her decision was based on the perception that her son was 'getting half a dozen other wonderful things out of that program' – 'the teachers think he's wonderful, self-esteem is great, they do all these self-directed study kind of things.' At the same time, Pearce's comments reflect concerns about the inflexibility of the school system.

Katherine Hennessey and Rebecca Rees agreed with Pearce that there was room for improvement in the school system. Hennessey observed that the idea of charter schools appealed to parents who were frustrated with the school system and who wanted to 'have some control back' (Interview 27). Rees argued that there was a need for alternatives that would better accommodate the learning styles of 'hands-on, practical' learners. Her comments echo the views of educators Karen Gold and Carol Oliver that schools reproduce a manual/mental hierarchy in their programs. But like Pearce, Rees believes that parents should work in consultation with teachers to change things. These participants indirectly critiqued the confrontational approach adopted by the AQE and Joe Freedman, and emphasized the importance of working with public schools in a democratic process to develop solutions.

The idea that the discourse of the unhappy parent responds to participants' lived experiences recalls ATA representative Janet Weis's suggestion that there is a 'little bit of truth in everything.' However, this discourse also obscured aspects of participants' realities by narrowing the basis for discussion about equity in schools. For example, when asked what concerned her about public education, Rees spoke about the lack of attention to infusing global education, environmental education, and multicultural/anti-racist education into school programs. Questions concerning 'what you do in the classroom, who's teaching in the classroom in the first place, what's the curriculum, what are the texts, what's the ethos of the school' were important for Rees but were becoming more difficult to address (Interview 20). Her comments echoed those of Carl George, Carol Oliver, and Karen Gold in Chapter 9, where it was suggested that discussions around reform tended to focus on *access* while other aspects of equity were obscured.

This narrowing was confirmed by the fact that issues raised by Susan Law were not part of the discourse of the unhappy parent, such as the marginalization of ESL teachers and students within the school system, the replacement of professional teachers with aides, the systemic discrimination faced by aides who were immigrant parents and whose teaching qualifications were not recognized in Canada, the disproportionately high dropout rates for ESL students, and so on. These issues were not prominent in discourses around educational reform in

Alberta although they were clearly impacted by restructuring. Both Rees and Pearce made reference to contraction, or narrowing. When asked about possibilities for resistance, Rees replied, 'It's terrible. For the first time in my life, you know, after both those elections, I have personally felt much more powerless than I ever have before. And I find that the scope of what I can address seems to be shrinking. And part of it has to do with living in a province where obviously one's ideas are in juxtaposition with most people's.' Similarly, Leslie Pearce commented that 'my place in the world, I'm afraid, is getting smaller and smaller' (Interview 4). Parent participants also recognized that they must do much more work than, for example, members of AQE, in order to be heard by government.

Education for Economic Prosperity. Participants located themselves in different ways in relation to the discourse of education for economic prosperity. They observed that social divisions based on gender, language, and race were obscured by the discourse and argued that there was more to education than job preparation. However, parents' concerns about their children's futures made it difficult for them to dismiss the appeal of rhetoric around the need to improve the match between graduates and labour market needs. Perhaps as a result, most participants welcomed the resources that businesses could bring to a beleaguered education system.

They tended to accept the idea that there was a connection between education and national economic prosperity, or, at the individual level, between one's educational background and one's earnings. Leslie Pearce commented that the better educated a person is, the more likely he or she will find a well-paying job. However, she also observed that the relationship of women to the paid labour force differed significantly from that of men, and she therefore believed that the 'prosperity discourse' was more important for women to take seriously. She was upset when her daughter did not do well in math and science, because she wanted her to be more confident than she was in these subjects (13). Appendix B, Table 5 provides statistics on employment income by sex and work activity that supports her focus on gender differences.

But while Pearce wanted her daughter to be well positioned in the changing economy, she resented the fact that the discourse of education for economic prosperity valued certain occupations over others. Referring to government roundtable attempts to define a basic education, she says:

> [G]etting back to the composition of these people who are going to get the basic education. I mean, conceivably this could be me. I don't know if I have a proclivity for certain things. I never did very well in science and math. But what would have happened to me if we had a basic education. You don't go into the next tier here, there isn't a place for you out there in the industrial world because your science and math are not up to snuff. So where am I? I'm either flipping hamburgers, or I'm a social worker. But I'm a social worker who has no respect in the system that's being created by industry. You know, we already deal with some of that. There are tiers of professions in Alberta. You know, if you're involved with oil and gas, you're up there. And if you're a lowly social worker, dealing with the social tragedies, you're way, way down there on the rung. And my concern is, that could be exacerbated by making it very clear that some people or some professions are more valuable than others. (Interview 4)

Pearce's comments reinforce the feminist view that skills are socially constructed and that how they are judged depends on how they are acquired, who possesses them, and in what context they are used (Blackmore 1997). As Pearce acknowledges, the skills typically possessed by women (social and operational) have been valued less than those possessed by men (manual, strength-related, and technical) in terms of labour market remuneration and status.

From this perspective, educational reforms aimed at tightening the links between education and the workplace become a way to more effectively sort and select workers (cf., Curtis,

Livingstone, and Smaller 1992; Shor 1986). Census data from 1991 (Appendix B, Table 4) suggest that gender is likely to be an important factor in this sorting, since women made up only 18.6 per cent of engineering and math occupations in Calgary and 17.6 per cent in Alberta overall. Katherine Hennessey similarly noted that the emphasis on high-tech jobs excluded people who were writers and artists, social activists, and caring professionals.

Participants acknowledged that the education for economic prosperity discourse also obscured differences in opportunity structures for different groups of students. Susan Law noted that the dropout rate for ESL students was significantly higher than rates overall. Watt and Roessingh (1994) confirm that the dropout rate for ESL students in Alberta was nearly three times that of the provincial average. In discussing the experiences of Black/African-Canadian students, Dei (1993) suggested that they encounter streaming, poverty, Eurocentrism, white male privilege, and discrimination, and concluded that there was a need to look at the structural conditions that make dropping out an alternative for students. Ignoring such factors leads to unrealistic expectations of schools. Hennessey provided the example of the statement within the Conference Board vision that 'all Canadian children shall graduate from high school with a high level of competency and a zest for learning.'

Comments about the type of people who were excluded from the discourse raise the question of who was represented within the discourse. Susan Law suggested that the values reflected within the discourse of education for economic prosperity were those of its corporate proponents: 'It's a bit frightening, I think. Because, you know, it's fine to say, let's compete at a global level. But there are specific business interests involved, and that can get a little bit muddled. Because I think there is an opportunity for us to lose sight of interests that are not our own. And if business interests have only a specific focus on products and production (pause). Yeah, there can be a lot of room for whole-scale manipulation of where we should be, what's valuable and what's not valuable ... Anyway, it's not in the public interest any more; that's what you're going to lose' (Interview 12).

Law went on to specify that reform-minded business leaders were probably interested in controlling the kind of people they get into their workforce from an early age. Echoing Native High School principal Carl George, she added that 'it sounds like you're taking over some of the state's responsibilities, but with your own interests in mind'. From this perspective, the discourse of education for economic prosperity offered employers the sense of regaining or increasing their control over the labour force, just as the discourse of the dissatisfied parent gave certain parents the sense of regaining control of their children in uncertain social and economic times.

Despite their critical comments regarding how different groups were situated in relation to the discourse of education for economic prosperity, participants believed that tightening the links between schools and the workplace could have positive effects. When asked what she thought of Alberta Education's plan to involve business people in defining learning requirements and providing work experience opportunities, Susan Law replied that as long as they were not focused only on specialized skills it would be 'an excellent opportunity for kids to get out into the so-called real world and get hands-on experience.' Similarly, Katherine Hennessey commented that business-education partnerships were 'really positive and really healthy' because they broadened input and allowed business people to learn how schools work (Interview 27). Hennessey's support for business involvement in education stemmed also from her belief that students would be better served by an infusion of money, opportunity, and personnel into a beleaguered educational system.[10] Therefore, while Hennessey and Pearce expressed concerns about corporate 'sponsorships' such as pop machines in schools, partnerships were viewed as benign interventions.

In contrast, Rebecca Rees expressed concern about increasing business involvement through partnerships. Coincidentally,[11] she referred to the Monarch-Academic High School partnership as follows:

I do know that there was a school here which had a partnership with [Monarch]; doesn't that sound nice? And out of that, all of a

sudden, the kids were being involved in some [Monarch] environmental campaign. When you know, most kids at the school
who had their heads screwed on straight knew what [Monarch]
was doing in different parts of Alberta. It created a lot of hard
and hot feelings there. You know, and some of those kids were
anti-apartheid activists at a time when there was a big [Monarch]
boycott going on, because of [Monarch's] role in South Africa.
This was a few years ago ... And I have a lot of respect for the
teachers in the social department [at Academic High]. They're
down here using resources that promote global education, so
(pause). You know, it just reveals some of the contradictions that
exist. (Interview 20)

Of parent participants, Rees was the most critical of the discourse of education for economic prosperity and its underlying
assumptions. Like Chris MacDonald of the Labour Council, she
questioned the idea of global competition and presented an alternative view based on the ideas of global cooperation and
building sustainable communities. She also challenged the idea
that there was a need for highly skilled workers in technical areas:

[I] think it's a bit of a myth. Because, how many of those highly
skilled technical jobs are we really going to need here? ... What's
out there? One of the fastest growing sectors is actually the service sector, right? Right across the country, and in the States. So
what are we talking about ... part-time, low paid. Women, people
of colour, are slotted into these jobs. And that's grown. And at
the same time, one has this sense of other jobs, very much hooked
up to computers, computer technology, communications. And
I'm thinking, how many people do I know who work in those
areas: two (laugh). No, I'm sure there are a lot of people down
there. We do know people who work in the oil sector and companies downtown and consulting firms. But those jobs haven't been
expanding, they've been narrowing. As part of an overall downturn and restructuring. I mean, they're saying, 'all of that will
increase.' And maybe it will, but I don't have a sense of it yet
here. I don't know where the graduates from DeVry and all those
places are going. Are they getting jobs?

Like labour participants, Rees juxtaposed the image of low skill, low paying service work and the 'reserve army' that occupies these positions within class structures against the idea of growth in the high-tech sector. This army is made up of the unemployed, those working in on-standard or contingent jobs who desire full-time employment, and those who possess credentials that exceed what is required for the job and/or whose skills are underutilized in their jobs (Livingstone 1999).

Don Coulter also questioned whether reality matched the image presented by proponents of the prosperity discourse, saying, 'how do you convince a kid in high school to keep studying when their older brother and sister who both have diplomas are unemployed?' (Interview 29). In the following anecdote, he adds that the mobility of capital resulting from free trade agreements contradicts the idea that skills are the determining factor in competitiveness: 'Two years ago, I was in San Antonio, Texas, and I was talking to some friends who are Mexican businessmen. And laughingly, one guy said, "Tell me, what is it in Canada that you make, do, provide or whatever, that even if we don't do it now, in five years we won't be able to do at one tenth of the price?" ... And for anyone who's walked that "miracle twenty miles" as we call it, just across the river from Texas where all these American: Birds-Eye Foods, Heinz, and a lot of the other ones that used to be on the other side of the river paying $13 an hour, now paying $1.50 in a swill of filth on the other side. That's free trade at its best.'

Coulter clearly was critical of the false promises inherent in the discourse of education for economic prosperity. However, his response was to argue that business groups and individuals must be forced to live up to their promises and act more responsibly. He therefore constructed business as simultaneously part of the *problem* and the *solution*. The Chamber of Commerce was part of the problem because it pushed for educational restructuring without sharing responsibility. Employers in general were part of the problem because they were contradictory. While they complained that 'our kids aren't learning to write,' they were so focused on making a profit that they did little to provide workplace supports that would help working parents. He concluded, 'I will look these $1,000 suit guys right in the eye and say, "You are 60 to 70 per cent of the problem, buster, and you don't even realize it." Life is not bottom line, contrary to popular belief.'

The idea that business people were part of the problem because they were often critical without offering actual support parallels Elizabeth Useem's (1986: 12) suggestion that relations between public schools and businesses in the United States typically have been 'fragmentary, weak, and of short duration.' She goes on to argue that despite the dangers that accompany some collaborative efforts, the greater peril lies in 'continuing corporate indifference to the needs of American education' (14). Coulter similarly believed that partnerships in education did not go far enough in supporting students, and recommended that businesses work with schools to address students' transition from school to work. In short, businesses needed to 'put their money where their mouth is': 'I want businesses to sponsor kids by name. When the parents aren't there at the high school reception, they're not there at some form of a recital, whatever the case is, somebody from Shell or somebody from Gulf Oil or somebody from Air Canada is sitting in the audience. And the kid knows it because that's like their big brother or big sister ... I believe that with all the tax breaks that so many of these businesses have gotten, that it's time to give back' (Interview 29).

Coulter reiterates the idea also expressed by ATA person Nancy Ellis, trustee Marcia Jensen, CBE employee Donna Black, and Catherine Hennessey, that business leaders who engage constructively with education potentially became champions of the system and political allies. Elizabeth Useem (1986: 230) similarly suggests that companies could play a key role in schooling by 'providing a new constituency in support of public education.' However, this 'contact hypothesis' tends to ignore the material interests that work against such cooperation. For example, in her discussion of barriers to business-education partnerships in the United States, Useem also comments that industry representatives commonly believe that the education system is bureaucratic and intransigent, and that teacher unions are obstacles to good management. Whether this view is a result of ignorance or the differing interests of stakeholders is a key question.

Coulter adopted two strategies to turn business *critics* into *supporters*. First, through his volunteer efforts, he approached several business leaders to become more involved with public schools. And second, in the spring of 1994 he launched a community education newspaper that was to share information and help facilitate communication between families and community, business, and education groups. The public school board helped to distribute 91,000 copies of this publication to schools, homes, and businesses.

In his lead article, Coulter noted that the 'goal is to promote equity and equal access to public education at all levels,' but added, 'caring for children does not necessarily mean that a person is against a free market society.' Perhaps this was a response to the reception Coulter received when he printed a business card, which stated that 'no child shall be denied access to public education due to race, colour, creed, religion, place of origin, disability or income.' A local MLA apparently said, 'that was about as socialistic and communistic as you could get' (Interview 29).

Coulter's strategies take for granted inequitable capitalist social relations and seek to 'humanize' them. Stuart Hall (1988: 182–3) suggests that such strategies are usually linked to political calculations whereby individuals decide that 'it is better to take advantage of whatever advance you can make rather than cutting off the head of the goose that sometimes – occasionally – lays a golden egg.' In Coulter's calculations, while it may not be possible to ask corporations to pay more taxes in times of fiscal constraint, they can be asked to provide more resources. However, his solutions assume that the interests of corporations are synonymous with the public interest, and ignore the long-term implications of substituting corporate 'charity' for publicly funded services.

Katherine Hennessey, who attended a meeting to discuss the CB's vision statement, highlighted this issue of interest congruence. At this meeting, she expressed concern that part of the vision statement promoted a notion of learning that was rooted in competitive individualism and implied that education was about turning out people to enter the workforce. In response, a business leader from AMOCO oil and gas corporation apparently said, 'If it's not about that, then we might as well shut it down right now, because that's what it should be about' (Interview 27). Rees and Pearce who both talked about education as 'freedom' echoed Hennessey's concern that education should be more than preparation for work. Rees agreed that education involved practical skills, but added that it should also encourage young people to understand and potentially change the world. Pearce, too, critiqued the utilitarian approach to education that was promoted by the education for economic prosperity discourse.

In sum, participants responded to educational restructuring in different ways. Like the three students, parents were cynical about the government's discourse of consultation, noting that groups like the AQE and the Chambers of Commerce had disproportionate political influence. They challenged the discourse of the unhappy parent in terms of the representativeness of the AQE and the implications of this discourse for students in their diversity. They also challenged the discourse of education for economic prosperity in terms of its underlying human capital/knowledge economy assumptions and implications. At the same time, participants were not unquestioning supporters of the current education system. They saw the little bit of truth in terms of problems and solutions, and were ambivalent about business involvement in education. Parents, like labour participants, also faced obstacles to engaging in counter-hegemonic work. Groups lacked resources, were embedded in hierarchical structures that made alliances across groups more difficult, and were confronted with the challenging task of encouraging and respecting diversity while presenting a unified position to politicians.

Albertans for Quality Education

Every day we hear that schoo–ools
Ain't what they used to be.
They don't turn out no scholars
Or good folk like you and me.
What we should do is go back to
The cane and spelling bee
That turned us out so good.

Chorus:
It's all the fault of education
Drugs and crime and copulation
Strikes and women's liberation
We blame it on the schools.

(Edmonton Raging Grannies, 'Education Song')

The Raging Grannies sing their 'Education Song' to the tune of 'John Brown's Body.' But while the words are tongue in cheek, they reflect an awareness of the impact of certain groups of conservative parents concerning educational reforms in Alberta. For example, most interview participants referred to the AQE as an influential group despite the fact that it was only formed in early 1993. A number portrayed it as dominated by fundamentalist Christians. Observations at the AQE conference in 1994 indicated that members of the private school sector (including religious-based private schools) were supporters of the group and that topics of interest included family values, discipline, and sex education.[12] On the other hand, the AQE position paper submitted to the government around the time of its roundtables emphasized fiscal conservatism and the rhetoric of educational choice. The interview with Stan Jones and Justin Hall confirmed the impression that the group was business-oriented as well as values-oriented.

The group's focus on values is reminiscent of a parent group that approached the CBE in Calgary in the early 1980s with a proposal for an alternative nondenominational Christian school within the public system. Rhonda Dixon was part of a group called Save Public Education (SPE),[13] spearheaded by members of the Calgary Civil Liberties Association, which formed in opposition to religious alternatives within the public system. SPE endorsed a slate of candidates in the 1983 school board election that opposed religious alternatives, and since a majority was elected, the contracts of religious schools were not renewed. However, parental concerns around values and beliefs within the public school system did not disappear. Dixon observed that the proponents of charter schools reminded her of this earlier group. However, the AQE in the 1990s appeared able to bring a wider range of stakeholders within its umbrella because of its focus on *choice*.

AQE leaders seemed to be trying to reconcile the interests of four groups that allied around the notion of choice: middle-class parents who had concerns about values in education, parents with concerns about particular pedagogical approaches and programs, private education providers who wanted to expand their market share within education, and employers with concerns about the discipline and skills of their future workforce. Apple (1993: 30) similarly talks about a 'new hegemonic accord' in the United States that 'combines dominant economic and political elites intent on "modernizing" the economy, with working-class and middle-class groups concerned with security, the family, and traditional knowledge and values, and economic and cultural conservatives.' AQE participants Stan Jones and Justin Hall appeared to represent two of the groups that the AQE tried to encompass. Middle manager and private school parent Jones would fit in well with business representatives from Chapter 6, while Hall was more closely aligned with parents who were concerned about multi-aging, whole language, and the perceived erosion of standards within schools.

The extent of business involvement in the AQE was surprising. The interview with representatives took place at AQE office space that was donated by Jones's corporate employer. Jones stated that 'some of our members sit on [Chamber] committees regularly' and the Chamber helped the AQE by enclosing 15,000 of its conference posters with its mailing (Interview 9). He added that he received a call from the Manufacturers' Association in Ontario, expressing interest in AQE activities. The AQE membership included a number of representatives from private schools and tutorial services. Stan Jones named four people from these types of organizations who were members.[14] When asked how they would characterize members overall in terms of background or occupation, Jones and Hall replied:

J: There's a good cross-section: doctors, psychologists, lawyers now, accountants, engineers, teachers. It's a good ...

S: ... administration. We've got two former ministers of Education ... Though parents are still the major group ... there's a number of businessmen ... At our May [1993] conference ... it seemed like probably 80, 90 per cent of the people were involved in their schools. These tend to be people that are on Parent Advisory Committees. (Interview 9)

The concept of choice therefore appeared to allow for the development of a broad coalition. This was evident from interviews where Stan Jones seemed to be working to strengthen the business part of the alliance, while Justin Hall represented the concerns of conservative parents. However, an interview with journalist James Kozak, who was loosely affiliated with the AQE, indicated an area of tension in the group. Kozak suggested that the AQE was made up of populist, action-oriented reformers. His specific description of members differed notably from that provided by Stan Jones and Justin Hall: '[They come] from all walks of life, actually. It's quite a diverse group. I mean, for the most part they are not professionals. This is not a group made up of lawyers and doctors and stuff like that – but small businessmen, people who are self-employed, concerned moms. And most of them have had some really bad experiences in the system, with one or two of their kids, and have become extremely pissed off as a result. As are, you know, most parent groups in the country – all are the same kind of people. What makes, I think, Albertans for Quality Education distinct is that, unlike a lot of other parent groups, they just get things done' (Interview 22). Kozak's comment raises the by now familiar issue of representation. If AQE was known as a group of middle-class professionals, it would be less credible when it suggested that charter schools would better meet the needs of economically disadvantaged children.

Other comments made by Kozak indicate a tension between unhappy parents and dissatisfied employers. He argued that the idea of education for national prosperity represented 'capitalism extending its hand ever more into public enterprise, in this case the school ... [in] an attempt to retool the school to be purely a function of economic need.' He contrasted the goal of education for work with the conservative goal of passing on cultural traditions valued by the community when he said, '[T]he great conflict I think you're seeing in North America right now is, what is valuable and true to a great many of the *working-class and middle-class parents* is not valuable and true to *the elites*, whether they be in education or whether they be corporate executives. They want individuals to change, to constantly put on a new set of values and skills as the technological economy changes. And all the parents are saying, "Well, that's bullshit. That's not what I think the school's about, and that's not the kind of community I want to live in." Where you're trying to produce economic chameleons. And of course, if you're producing economic chameleons they'll be social and political chameleons as well' [my emphasis].

Kozak thus articulated the tension between 'vocational progressives' and 'cultural restorationists' like himself. In the British context, Ball (1990) suggests that such tensions were 'refractions of broader tensions embedded in Thatcherism and the ideological constitution of the Conservative party: 'The neo-liberal influence emphasizes an orientation to the future, constant adaptation to new circumstances and an absence of state controls; the neo-conservative influence stresses an orientation to the past, traditional values and collective loyalties. Education is thus contested in terms of its role in both restoring authority

and responding to the contemporary logic of capitalist development.' Recall that this *traditional conservative/liberal modernizing*
tension was also apparent in the Toward 2000 Together documents in Alberta as the government tried to balance the interests of different economic players.

Within education, Kozak's juxtaposition of the interests of
elite educators and business people with those of ordinary work-
ing- and middle-class parents reflected concerns over the attempt to harmonize these interests within the AQE: 'I think
some of the people in Albertans for Quality Education take a
much more corporate view of schools and talk about customers,
you know. And I usually say, "Well this is not a corporate
institution, this is a public enterprise. And we're participants in
it; it's not composed of 'buyers,' and 'sellers,' and 'customers.'"
And I suppose there is a tendency by some of the members to
favour more extreme sort of right-wing solutions to things. Although I'll give the group credit for the fact that it has an open
mind about a great many issues. And it is also very conciliatory
towards people in the public school system.'

Kozak's concerns were not unfounded, since the AQE position paper strongly promoted a market model for education.
Jones acknowledged the apparent convergence in the views of
politicians, business people, and his group when he said, 'Well,
you know, it's true that when you look at some of their stuff
[for example, the three-year business plan], it's like [the govern-
ment] took it right out of our document here. However, when
we talk to people like [Dan Williams], or others with the Chamber, we don't know whether it's because we've all arrived at the
same conclusions' (Interview 9). Jones's comments recall Dan
Williams's suggestion in Chapter 6 that he and other Chamber
of Commerce members all reached the same conclusions about
educational reform. This ideological strategy renders reforms
natural.

A number of recommendations made in the AQE position
paper were consistent with the perspective of private school
operator Dan Williams. For example, the position paper suggested that 'a careful review be done by Alberta Education of

the public schools' commitment to satisfy their customers as a precondition to their virtual monopoly over education in our society' (AQE 1993: 11). It then recommended that 'any delivery of education, whether private, public or homeschooling, if proven to meet acceptable standards, should be properly funded by Alberta Education.' Levels of funding would be determined by a market-based approach. Given this orientation, it was not surprising that the private school sector willingly cooperated with the AQE while the public board was reticent. Jones concluded, 'And that's where we've come to the practical conclusion that you cannot [educate students] very effectively with a cookie-cutter approach where you have the same product for everybody. It's like going to McDonald's and you're told, "We sell Big Macs and Coke, and if you want anything else ..." You know, you would not sell much product. And you would not have a very satisfied customer base, so you create choices' (Interview 9). He went on to suggest that it is not until 'you bring in the private sector, included in the whole system in some way, that you're going to get the really powerful results.'

Jones mentioned other influences on the position paper as follows: '[A] lot of thinking has come from our reading and study of this issue in educational research across North America particularly, and we rely fairly heavily on one resource ... Chubb and Moe ... I found that to be extremely useful. Of all the materials that I've read, I find that to be one of the better ones; I recommend it to anybody.' Jones, of course, is referring to the book *Politics, Markets, and America's Schools* (Chubb and Moe 1990), promoted by keynote speaker John Chubb at the CB's Reaching-for-Success conference in 1991 and disparaged by ATA representative Janet Weis.

But despite critics, the free market approach to schooling represents a point of overlap between the AQE and business groups like the Chambers of Commerce. Other recommendations in the AQE position paper that paralleled the positions of business representatives discussed in Chapter 6 included performance pay for teachers, publishing test results school by school, differentiated staffing, more choice in the system through charter schools, international comparisons of results, 'assessment of learning standards by a broad cross section of commercial and industrial businesses,' and determining the cost-effectiveness of various programs (AQE 1993: 17). The AQE argument for teacher-directed instruction argued that it allowed higher pupil-teacher ratios and therefore lowers costs (20).

While performance pay for teachers had not yet been implemented in the late 1990s, newspapers in Calgary and Edmonton began reporting provincial test results in grades three, six, and nine for each school within the public and Catholic boards in 1996. Differentiated staffing occurred to some extent due to cutbacks that resulted in the replacement of full-time teachers with paraprofessionals, and there had been an increase in initiatives involving business people in the delivery of work experience and other vocational programs. As of November 1999, ten charter schools had been established across Alberta.[15] Finally, Alberta Education published annual business plans and reports on outcomes based on assessments by various stakeholders and provincial test results. The direction taken by Alberta Education was therefore quite consistent with that promoted by the AQE.

But again, tensions within the interests that the AQE attempted to represent were suggested by the comments of businessman and parent Stan Jones when he spoke about where the public school system went wrong:

> I think that where we got derailed was when we turned our public schools into instruments of social change and we started to view them as a tool of the society, i.e., of the government, to mould. I think the original idea was, 'We've got enough wealth as a society that we can afford the opportunity for every child to have at least a basic education.' And I think that's an admirable goal that they had at that time. But never at any time was the purpose of public education to reshape the thinking of the kids, you know, to become hostile to their parents' values, to create 50,000 environmentalists – and don't take that as denigrating environmentalists or anything. But you know, we get an oversupply of environmentalists because there's a continuous message

that this is a wonderful thing to pursue. So you have more people in that.

And, as a corporation, I've sat on committees where we're plotting how we can use the public schools to get our message across that favours our industry. And that's just widespread right now, that every public school is a tool. Everybody knows if you can get the kids and educate them, you've got them. And I think that's got to come to an end. You know, parents have to take back that control and say, 'We want to know who's speaking in our schools. We want to know what their agenda is.' (Interview 9)

In trying to incorporate all of the AQE constituencies in his comments, Jones ended up pointing to tensions between the objectives of parents who were concerned about values education and those of corporations that were concerned primarily about future profits. His comments also indicate the extent to which schools formed a site where adults struggled over the hearts and minds of children.

Concluding Comments

Comments made by AQE representatives can be contrasted with those of student and parent participants. The latter were frustrated and disillusioned by the process and outcomes of educational restructuring in Alberta. They challenged aspects of the discourses of the unhappy parent and education for economic prosperity in terms of who and what was included and excluded. At the same time, parent participants did not appear to have built coalitions around their overlapping interests and a common vision. Rather, like educators and labour participants, they seemed to be dealing with pieces of a puzzle. Parents tended to separate the discourse of the unhappy parent (associated with AQE) from that of education for economic prosperity (associated with business groups).

For example, AQE was characterized as a group of fundamentalist Christians. However, in addition to parents concerned about morality and values, AQE tried to bring two other groups within its umbrella – namely, parents who had heartfelt concerns about particular pedagogical approaches, and representatives of the private sector (within and outside education). Focusing only on the religious component of the AQE, as was the tendency for most interview participants, underestimates the appeal of this discourse for parents who were not necessarily affiliated with the religious Right or big business. It also misses the *connections* between the discourses of the unhappy parent and education for economic prosperity, and the ideological function of the concept of 'the parent' in the interface between the two. Once we recognize the 'conservative alliance' represented by the AQE, we better understand why the state found it so appealing. The AQE position paper provided exactly what politicians needed: a network of 'ordinary Albertans' who were devoted middle-class parents and free market supporters.

At the same time, this alliance was tenuous because of the different interests of coalition members. Ball (1990) and Apple (1993) suggest that such 'fragile compromises' may come apart because of the contradictory beliefs held by many of the partners in the new accord. The comments of Kozak indicated areas of tension between 'traditional' parents and 'liberal modernizers' within the AQE. Hennessey attributed the much lower than expected attendance at the 1994 AQE conference to the dilution of the religious component of the alliance in an attempt to broaden support. At that time, the ability of the AQE to represent all of its members satisfactorily over the longer term was in question.

By the year 2000, the influence of the AQE was much less evident and a number of other parent groups had sprung up and become a political force. At the time of interviews in 1994, the key groups representing parents were the AHSCA and the CCHSA. However, as the impact of restructuring began to be felt, several groups formed in Edmonton, Calgary, and other jurisdictions to express parents' concerns. In Calgary, the group Save Public Education – Act for Kids (SPEAK) formed in 1996 in response to funding cutbacks. Three members of SPEAK were subsequently elected as trustees in the 1999 election.[16] The earlier group, called Save Public Education (SPE), was also resurrected as Friends of Public Education in 1999. Edmonton School Councils (a counterpart to the CCHSA) formed around 1993 to provide a mechanism for parents to participate in government restructuring. This group was active, along with other school council organizations, in the work of the MLA team on roles and responsibilities as it determined the functions and powers of school councils.

In 1994 a group called Save Our Schools (SOS) formed to protest the government's cuts to Kindergarten funding. Led by three mothers with children in Edmonton schools, this group later led a protest against increased school fundraising by parents as a result of funding cutbacks. They circulated province-wide petitions and in 1999 presented 23,000 signatures in the legislature, protesting cuts and demanding government action. Representatives from this group also made presentations to school councils across the province. Another group, Parents Advocating for Children and Teachers (PACT) was started in early 1999 by an Edmonton mother who was angered by the extent of cuts in her child's school. She organized a rally and continued to raise awareness of problems tied to government restructuring, such as large class sizes and inadequate resources.

PACT organizer Dianne Williamson suggested in a telephone conversation, in February 2000, that increased parental involvement towards the end of the 1990s in Alberta resulted from two main factors. First, school council legislation politicized parents. Councils provided a mechanism for parents to become informed about the operation of their children's schools and potentially to play a larger role in decision-making. Second, schools' increased need for parent volunteers because of funding cuts brought parents into schools in greater numbers, and in more essential functions,[17] which led parents to view themselves more as 'partners.' In addition to SOS and PACT, at least three or four other parent groups were active in the Edmonton area and groups were springing up in other jurisdictions by 2000. Therefore, while parental choice advocates were still active, the discourse of the unhappy parent had largely shifted from those who promoted government restructuring in the early 1990s to those who opposed its effects.

CHAPTER ELEVEN

Alberta and Beyond

The remaking of Alberta appeared to rest on certain principles. It was getting difficult to sort out principles from clichés – living within our means; balancing the budget to avoid hitting the wall; deregulation; realizing that we have a spending problem rather than a revenue problem; reforming public life by streamlining government and trimming administration; competitive taxation; getting government out of the business of business; cutting out layers of fat ... The political and business leaders of Alberta were scrambling to gain admission to the global metropolis, to plug in to the international circuit of power and never mind if many other Albertans might be left behind.   (Mark Lisac, *The Klein Revolution*)

Lisac's account nicely captures the 'spirit of the times' in Alberta between the election of Ralph Klein as premier in 1993 and the initial implementation of the government's three-year business plans. His comments also remind us that reforms to education were part of a broader agenda for change in the province. As an author from the Fraser Institute noted in a 1995 report, the Alberta government's restructuring embraced 'a new philosophy of market-driven delivery of services – and an emphasis on the private sector to ensure economic growth.'[1] Previous chapters explore the educational settlement represented by the three-year business plan for education. The focus has been twofold: first, on promoters of this settlement – their alliances, vision, and strategies for promoting this vision more widely; and second, on other stakeholders – their relationships, responses to government restructuring, and counter-hegemonic strategies. This chapter highlights some key findings from this analysis, draws connections to other sites, and considers the implications for the development of a counter-hegemonic vision for education.

The three-year plan had several notable features. Business people were called upon to take greater responsibility for working with schools and the province to develop expectations and standards and to assist in students' transition from school to work. Parents were promised greater involvement in their children's education through school councils and greater choice through charter schools. School boards became, as a *Calgary Herald* journalist suggests in an article on 19 January 1994 entitled 'Education Revolution Doesn't Add Up,' 'the caretaker, bus driver and middle money manager' of local jurisdictions. This redefinition of roles and responsibilities undoubtedly was tied to the shift in the government's policy community towards certain business and parent groups. But despite the government's emphasis on decentralization, its control over the system was enhanced by the centralization of funding, control over incentives, and expanded management information systems. The three-year plan's emphasis on *efficiency, accountability*, and *choice* resulted in reforms that included the amalgamation of school boards, centralization of funding, school-based management, caps on boards' administrative funding, review of programs and standards, increased provincial testing, charter schools, and open boundaries.

The educational settlement represented by the three-year plan was developed through the efforts of highly visible reformers such as Joe Freedman in alliance with Albertans for Quality Education and the Alberta Chamber of Resources, Dan Williams from the Alberta Chamber of Commerce, Stephen Murgatroyd from Athabasca University, and treasurer and former education minister Jim Dinning. It was assisted by the efforts of less visible reformers and coordinating bodies such as the Conference Board of Canada and its Corporate and National Council members, the Steering Group on Prosperity, the Canada West Foundation, and the partnership and science foundations. Although this study has not focused on groups like the Business Council on National Issues and the Fraser Institute,[2] it recognizes that they also helped promote consensus around neoliberal reforms. Business groups, conservative think-tanks, and partnership foundations helped governments lay the ideological groundwork for the restructuring of education. That is not to say that the three-year business plan was fully endorsed by all of these individuals and groups. For example, private school supporters Dan Williams and AQE representatives did not feel that the plan went far enough in the direction of opening up education to the market.

The Canada West Foundation was a strong proponent of free trade in the 1980s, and a vocal supporter of deficit reduction and the 'reinvention' of government in the early 90s. Its position was also reflected in the Toward 2000 Together reports endorsed by the Alberta government. The Conference Board of Canada has promoted the discourse of education for economic prosperity since 1990 by developing a national vision for education, participating in government consultations, sponsoring annual business-education conferences, promoting school-business partnerships, and providing forums for members to become more involved in education at local and national levels. Themes[3] from Reaching-for-Success conferences recurred in federal and provincial economic visioning reports. Relationships between the Conference Board and partnership and science foundations reveal connections between national, provincial, and local levels. Therefore, while reformers like Joe Freedman, Albertans for Quality Education, and the Alberta Chamber of Commerce were politically influential, the cutbacks and restructuring of the Klein government and its three-year business plan for education also can be related to the activities of these other groups. In the *Framework for Enhancing Business Involvement in Education* (Alberta Education 1996a), policy-makers embrace the models provided by the Conference Board and partnership and science foundations.

The three-year plan draws primarily on three discourses: the fiscal crisis of the state, education for economic prosperity, and the unhappy parent. While these three discourses echo and enlist one another, there are also tensions within and among them that result in part from trying to forge a vision across difference. Chapters 2 and 6 suggested that the fiscal crisis of the state was a favourite discourse of business representatives and business-sponsored groups. Business representatives Andrew Markham, Gary Baldwin, and Dan Williams all emphasized the need for the government to eliminate the deficit in Alberta through restructuring and spending cuts. Based on their corporate experience, public sector downsizing was seen as inevitable. Their fiscal conservatism was rooted in the recognition of a crisis in capital accumulation that could only be resolved through accommodation to new global realities, or gaining admission to the 'global metropolis.' In this construction, a prosperous economy depended on the state creating the conditions that maximize the ability of private sector companies to compete in the global economy by producing/securing a highly skilled workforce (in particular, science and technology skills), and by offering investment incentives (low tax rates, a simplified regulatory environment, and contracting out or privatizing government services). The role of public education was therefore to serve the economy by developing students' skills.

However, the need for government restraint contradicts the human capital argument that the state must educate a highly skilled workforce to ensure economic competitiveness. The ideological solution to this seeming contradiction between the discourse of fiscal crisis of the state and the discourse of education for economic prosperity involved the adoption of reinvented human capital theory, expressed by interview subjects Andrew Markham, Gary Baldwin, Dan Williams, and Mike Popiel, and reflected in the vision reports of federal and provincial governments. These participants stressed that individuals were responsible for investing in themselves. This represents a shift away from the argument that the state should fund vocational education because society benefits, and towards the argument that individuals benefit and therefore should contribute financially. Reinvented human capital theory also suggested that it was necessary for the state to make *wiser* investments in education, for example, by exploring alternative methods of delivery (through user fees, contracting out, increased technology, privatization) and reducing the 'inefficiencies' within current systems (through better facility utilization and school-based management) – that is, through restructuring and cutbacks. Educational restructuring has also involved a shift in spending priorities, as indicated by increased investments in technology compared to programs directed more specifically towards the needs of marginalized groups of students.

The Conference Board and other corporate representatives reconciled the discourse of education for economic prosperity with their demands for public sector constraint and tax cuts through reinvented human capital theory. However, the ATA (in its Alternative Roundtable workbook) and several interview participants point to the contradiction between cutbacks and the discourse of investing in people in order to compete in the global economy. The attempt to reconcile contradictions between 'fiscal conservative' and 'economic modernizer' positions was therefore challenged by some stakeholders. Other participants, for example, school board representatives, appeared to accept pragmatically that the political climate had changed and that they must 'tighten their belts.' They focused on challenging restructuring changes that limited school board autonomy rather than challenging the discourses of fiscal crisis and reinvented human capital theory. While business representatives were strong proponents of a decreased role for government in education, school board personnel could be described as pragmatists.

The discourse of the unhappy parent was closely aligned with that of education for economic prosperity in the Alberta context. The position taken in Joe Freedman's *Failing Grades* (1993) was not significantly different from that taken in the *International Comparisons* report produced by the Alberta Chamber of Resources (1991) in cooperation with Freedman and Alberta Education. Attacks on progressive education, calls for higher standards, greater teacher and system accountability, and parental choice came through in both documents. Unhappy parents' desire for greater control over their children's education were consistent with employers' desire for greater control over their future workforce. This can be seen in the interview with Stan Jones and Justin Hall where they adopted both discourses. But James Kozak, indicating again that traditional and modernizing tendencies produce tension within the alliance represented by the AQE, highlighted the contradiction between the goal of promoting 'traditional values' and 'market values.'

Nevertheless, allies were instrumental in the development of educational settlement, for various reasons. First, corporate representatives in Calgary – one of the key groups within the hegemonic alliance – revealed a high degree of internal integration, despite differences in the size of firm and industry sector. Representatives of a business-in-education network worked together through the science and partnership foundations. These 'broker' organizations also provided a vehicle for the corporate community to draw educators into its hegemonic vision. Partnerships between business and schools were constructed as win-win situations. The fact that former educators staffed partnership and science foundations lent further legitimacy to these groups.

A second reason for the success of educational settlement was the distinction made by several board and school-based participants between business initiatives in education and government restructuring and cutbacks. Corporate executives Andrew Markham and Gary Baldwin were seen as *supporters* of the education system, in comparison with *critics* Joe Freedman and Chamber of Commerce representative Dan Williams, despite their ideological similarities. Visible reformers distracted attention from the efforts of less visible reformers. Further, interview participants tended to see the discourse of the unhappy parent and the discourse of education for economic prosperity as separate. For example, the AQE was seen as a group of fundamentalist parents, without recognizing that it actually brought together an alliance of reform-minded groups in public education, including predominantly middle-class unhappy parents and dissatisfied employers.

Third, the success of educational settlement rested on gaining popular support for the hegemonic vision of reformers. On one hand, economic uncertainty made people susceptible to visions that promised economic prosperity, however hollow. In addition, there was a 'little bit of truth' in discourses. For example, school systems do tend to be bureaucratic and rigid, and have not always responded well to the needs of all students. They have had a tendency to keep parents out. Further, the discourse of vocational progressivism helped to allay the concerns of educators and parents who were concerned about equity, despite its contradictions. On the other hand, interview participants challenged restructuring discourses by expressing concerns over both the process of reform and the limitations of the educational settlement. They expressed frustration over government 'consultations' and the anti-democratic nature of the educational reform process. With the exception of business participants, most others challenged the representativeness of key reformers and pointed to their narrow interests. Parents lamented the narrowing of the parameters of debate that had occurred in Alberta. Participants working with historically marginalized groups of students were concerned about the implications of changes for ESL, Native, working class, female, and special-needs students. Their comments also indicated an awareness that debates were becoming restricted to a narrow definition of equity as access, as compared to issues around who controls the production of knowledge, what gets produced, and how schools relate to other social institutions such as the family and workplace. Some participants therefore demonstrated a critical awareness of reform discourse/practices.

However, certain factors worked against effective resistance by groups wishing to translate their critical awareness into an action-oriented ideology. Chapters 8 and 10 note that labour and parent groups with seemingly overlapping interests appeared to be divided by historical patterns of political preferment as well as by social hierarchies based on gender, race, and class. More specifically, the *ideology of professionalism* adopted by teachers worked against labour solidarity, just as the marginalization of ESL parents worked against the building of alliances among parent groups. And unlike the business-in-education network, there was little evidence of coordinating agencies that fulfilled the functions of organizations like the partnership and science foundations. While employee groups in Calgary established Partners in Education, this alliance developed as a result of government changes and therefore focused primarily on fighting cutbacks and protecting the immediate interests of members. More generally, organized labour representatives did not appear to have worked out a comprehensive alternative vision that moved outside of a corporatist frame to challenge inequitable workplace structures.[4]

Aside from the ATA, counter-hegemonic groups also lacked resources that would facilitate the development and communication of a broad-based vision. Quality Education Coalition representative Marg Szabo spoke about the difficulty in building a provincial coalition because of the lack of travel funding available to interested groups. CUPE representative Murray Walsh noted that primarily volunteers staffed his local. Groups such as the Home and School Councils involved volunteers and had high turnover rates. Groups with a majority of female members such as certain parent groups and the staff association also confronted the reality of gendered power relations. The organizational constraints expressed by these interview participants can be contrasted with the resources available to the Conference Board, Chambers of Commerce, and partnership and science foundations.

Postscript to 1994 Settlement

The fact that this study focuses primarily on the period between 1993 and 1995 may leave the mistaken impression that the educational settlement represented by the three-year business plan was fixed and unchanging. While previous chapters attempt to provide a sense of what has happened since 1995, a summary of key events provides a useful supplement to the analysis. Both continuities and discontinuities with the plan are apparent.

The effectiveness of resistance is indicated in part by changes that the government made to its restructuring plans after they were released. For example, in response to public pressure, Alberta Education reinstated funding for early childhood education a year after the three-year business plan announced cutbacks. The government also backed down on its intention to appoint superintendents. Changes to the plan occurred during consultations conducted by the five MLA teams as well. The role of school councils was modified as parents and other groups told politicians that the forms and extent of input that they desired differed from that outlined by the government. Most parents did not want significant control over the operation of schools. Charter school guidelines released in 1995 placed restrictions on their numbers and operations, and therefore altered the vision of charter school proponents. Therefore, plans for educational reform were modified to some extent in their implementation through the MLA task force process.

Another example of negotiation over educational policy occurred when Education Minister Gary Mar proposed a School Performance Incentive Program in the 1999 budget. Modelled after programs in the United States, funding was to be allocated among school boards based in part on their performance on provincial achievement tests and diploma exams. Following protests from parents, teachers, administrators, and trustees, the minister of the newly amalgamated Alberta Learning department put the program on hold, pending consultations with education 'partners.' The result was the announcement of the Alberta Initiative for School Improvement Program in December 1999, a program that was more palatable to education groups. The amalgamation of Alberta Education and Advanced Education and Career Development and the appointment of a new minister and deputy minister in mid-1999 seemed to herald more positive working relationships between education groups and the government.

Education groups continued to be active in the latter part of the 1990s strengthening links, working to generate an alternative vision, and generating public support. The ATA maintained its Public Education Action Centre, and joined with parent groups to pressure the government to increase education funding. As mentioned in Chapter 10, the unhappy parent represented by the AQE was overshadowed to a large extent by unhappy parents concerned about the impacts of restructuring in the late 1990s. Education partners at the provincial level, representing teachers, trustees, and administrators, collaborated on a vision and agenda for public education that was released to the public in early 2000. The ATA also worked to develop ties with organized labour groups.

But despite some shift in the balance of forces, continuities in the policy direction of the government are also apparent. For example, Mackay and Flower (1999) refer to discussions about the future of education that took place at the Progressive Conservative Association of Alberta's policy conference in 1998. Statements referred to customer-driven education, partnerships with the private sector, increased provincial testing, focus on core competencies (with specific mention of technology skills), and alternative methods of delivery. This rhetoric is clearly consistent with the direction of the three-year business plan in 1994. It is also consistent with discussion in Alberta Education's 1996 *Framework for Enhancing Business Involvement in Education*, released by one of the five MLA teams established to implement the business plan. The framework recommended establishing a provincial Career Education Foundation (modelled on partnership and science foundations), involving business more in educational policy development at all levels, promoting entrepreneurship, and encouraging the use of employability skills portfolios in all schools. The document reinforces the discourse of vocationalism, while ignoring the complexity of factors that influence individuals' occupational decisions.

Although the discourse of fiscal crisis subsided as large budget surpluses replaced deficits in Alberta in the second half of the 1990s, spending on education did not reflect this renewed prosperity. Per student funding for education, accounting for inflation and enrolment increases, fell by approximately $600 between 1994 and 1999 (Neu 1999). At the same time, the provincial government increased the amount of per pupil funding for private schools in 1998. The task force on the private school funding process that preceded this announcement demonstrated that promoters of 'choice' continued to be a significant force in the province. Government's interest in privatizing other areas of the public sector also continued in the late 1990s.[5] These factors suggest that examinations of the influences on government policy and how settlements are achieved continue to be important topics.

Comparisons with Other Sites

In his discussion of international education reform, Levin (1997) suggests that programs in many countries have been shaped by concerns over economic competitiveness, a distrust in the ability of public institutions to change, and political unwillingness to spend more on education. In particular, reforms in Canada, the United States, England, and New Zealand shared an emphasis on the local management of schools, markets and choice programs, and increased use of large-scale student assessments.

Within Canada, the Progressive Conservative government in Ontario has embraced elements of the Alberta model for educational reform. Between 1995 and 1997, the government cut the number of school boards by about two-thirds, capped trustees' salaries, and instituted centralized funding. In addition, every school was required to have an advisory school council, requirements for school board reporting were increased, and comprehensive student testing was introduced. Bill 160 increased provincial control over education by allowing the minister and cabinet to set regulations related to education funding, class size, teacher preparation time, and so on. The bill also removed millions of dollars from the system as part of the Harris government's deficit-elimination program. The bill was passed despite massive protest from teachers and their organizations.

The government also created the Ontario College of Teachers (OCT) in 1996 to make the profession more accountable to the public. This regulatory body became responsible for developing standards of teacher practice, regulating teacher certification and professional development, and accrediting teacher education programs. When Premier Harris announced the idea of having teachers undergo competency testing every three to five years as part of his 1999 Charter of Education Rights and Responsibilities, the OCT was charged with the task of carrying this out. The Ontario Secondary School Teachers' Federation (OSSTF)[6] notes that the idea of implementing alternative methods of training and certifying teachers is consistent with the position of the Organization for Quality Education (OQE), a lobby group that has been influential in policy circles.[7] This brief description suggests that although the specifics may vary, the themes of accountability, efficiency, and marketization of education are present in both sites.

There are also parallels with other countries. While all provinces in Canada require schools to have parent or school councils that fulfil advisory functions, some areas of the United States (e.g., Kentucky and Chicago) have granted these councils greater power in staffing and planning (Levin 1997). In both countries, school administrators have gained more authority over staffing and budgets in recent years. Alberta also followed U.S. models in introducing charter school legislation. Although Alberta was still the only Canadian province with such legislation in 2000, campaigns were underway to encourage governments to allow charter schools in British Columbia and Ontario.[8] Another area of North American harmonization in education policy was in the area of standardized testing. Testing programs were commonplace in U.S. schools, and in many systems the results were publicized. In Alberta, too, reports on provincial tests were reported on a school-by-school basis in local newspapers, while across Canada most provinces were expanding their testing programs. Efforts were also focusing on integrating curriculum across as well as within provinces.

In England, the 1988 Education Reform Act introduced the local management of schools and the possibility for schools to opt out of the local education authority and become grant-maintained schools, funded directly by the central government. By the late 1990s, approximately 10 per cent of the school-age population in England was educated in such schools (Whitty, Power, and Halpin 1998). The 1988 act also introduced a national curriculum and system of assessment. In a more radical step than in the other countries, New Zealand completely removed education boards. Each school is essentially a charter school, since it is run by a locally elected committee but receives its mandate and is responsible to the Ministry of Education. Curriculum is also more centralized there than it was before the reforms in the late 1980s.

As Levin (1997: 253) suggests, governments in Canada, the United States, England, and New Zealand appear to have 'drawn from the same well of ideas' for their educational reforms. He adds, however, that there are differences in the practical implementation of these reforms because of differing social, economic, and political contexts. It is therefore important to undertake more in-depth comparisons between systems.

Political and educational reforms in Britain, Canada, New Zealand, and the United States can be related to the capitalist crisis experienced by several Western industrialized countries since the 1970s. Economic crisis led to political crisis in terms of the social-democratic accord that was in place in the latter part of this century. Dale and Ozga (1993) suggest that the economic situation was more intense in New Zealand than in the UK. Perhaps because of the failure of neo-Keynesian approaches in the early 1980s, the ground there was prepared for a radical approach. The problem was defined as the state playing too great a role in the economy and the solution was 'both to reduce the role of the state and to reform the public administration' (80). Educational reforms in New Zealand were therefore but one part of major reforms to public administration. The Klein revolution can also be attributed to economic crisis. While the question of whether crisis in Alberta was real or manufactured is open to interpretation, the discourse of fiscal crisis played an important role in educational reforms there as in other jurisdictions.

In Britain, ideological struggles in the 1970s and 80s centred on the transition from one stage of industrial development to

another. The Thatcher government was able to provide hegemonic political leadership into this transition by presenting a
vision for prosperity: 'Britain as an open playground or permanent "green site" for international capital,' based on the opening up of new financial markets and harnessed to new information technologies (Hall 1988: 87). This image hid the fact that
those who were to bear the costs were those who were most
vulnerable to technological change, namely, working class and
historically marginalized groups within the society.

The Thatcherist project, however, was not confined to a set of
political or economic policies. Rather, Hall describes it as a 'radi-
cally novel political formation,' with its success connected to its
organization in a number of social and cultural as well as political and economic sites. Reminiscent of the Toward 2000 Together reports and the 'garbage bear' metaphor invoked by Mike
Popiel, Hall (1988: 47) writes, 'The essence of the British people
was identified with self-reliance and personal responsibility, as
against the image of the over-taxed individual, enervated by
welfare-state "coddling," his or her moral fibre irrevocably
sapped by "state handouts"' (47). The Thatcherist project was
therefore described as one of 'regressive modernization' in which
liberal-modernizing discourses and traditional-conservative discourses coalesced.

The ERA was introduced during Thatcher's second term of
office. Chitty (1992: 32) suggests that it was promoted by the
most influential of 'an extraordinary array of right-wing organizations and education study groups which sprang up in the
1970s and 1980s boasting impressive titles and interlocking memberships.' It was described as the culmination of debates and
struggles over education that began with the Great Debate over
education initiated by the Labour government in 1976. Like more
general reforms, the ERA contained conservative and neoliberal
elements as well as a modernizing vocationalist tendency (Ball
1990). It was described as an attempt to 're-establish the key
structural and ideological elements of earlier education systems,
that had been undone or undermined by decades of social democratic "interference"' (Dale and Ozga 1993: 70). Chitty (1992: 36)

agreed that the act 'was intended to erect (or, perhaps more accurately, reinforce) a hierarchical system of schooling (particularly at the secondary level) subject both to market forces and to greater control by central government.' It was apparently introduced in Parliament quickly and with little consultation.

Dale and Ozga (1993) provide a thoughtful comparison of ERA reforms with Tomorrow's Schools reforms introduced in the late 1980s in New Zealand. They suggest that unlike England and Wales, education reforms in New Zealand were intended to create something new and radical, rather than hearkening back to earlier systems. In New Zealand, 'a much more important priority was getting the state off the legitimation hook (with its costly and inefficient consequences) by effectively taking education out of the arena of national public debate' (75). Therefore, compared to England and Wales, education was one strand in the reform of public administration. Also, while increased stratification was a consequence of neoliberal reforms initially introduced by the Labour government in New Zealand, reforms in England and Wales seemed to promote it more consciously.

Discussion of the history and motivation for reforms in England and Wales and New Zealand raise questions around which New Right ideas were adopted and how they were translated in the Alberta context. As in New Zealand, reforms to education in Alberta were related directly to the perceived need to cut costs and reinvent government, and to political faith in the free market. Ideas from New Zealand were readily available to Alberta politicians.[9] Visioning reports in the early 1990s indicated the government's intention to investigate privatization and the restructuring of the public sector in order to improve efficiency and competitiveness. Toward 2000 Together promoted the image of a competitive economy based on technological innovation and the ability to provide an attractive investment climate. The goal of restructuring education to do more with less formed the basis for the 1993 roundtables on education and were key parts of the three-year business plan in 1994. And like New Zealand, the Alberta government seemed intent on increasing accountability at the local level and removing education from the sphere of provincial debate.

But despite the seeming neoliberal emphasis of reforms in Alberta, there were also parallels with the conservative strand of English reforms. There have been tensions between liberal modernizers and moral conservatives within the Klein government. The premier appears to have diffused these tensions by sidestepping overtly moral issues while focusing on areas of agreement between neoliberals and neoconservatives such as legislation for charter schools. Nevertheless, there are neoconservative elements in Alberta. Until challenged by the Supreme Court of Canada, the Alberta government refused to provide protection for gays and lesbians within Human Rights legislation. Newman (1998: 443) writes that 'former treasurer Stockwell Day was the premier's link to the social-conservative movement in central Alberta.' In the summer of 2000 he became leader of the Canadian Alliance Party, formerly the Reform Party. Also like Britain, a myriad of right-wing groups are based in Alberta, including the Alberta Federation of Women United for Families,[10] the Canadian Taxpayers' Federation, and the Reform Party of Canada. Prominent education reformers like Joe Freedman advocate for a return to order and traditional conservative values.

The strands of liberal modernization and traditional conservatism found in England and Alberta were also mentioned by Apple (1993), who writes, 'The Right [in the United States] has blended together themes of nationalism and patriotism, "pro-family" issues, standards, sexuality, drugs, and so on under its own leadership and has used them for its purpose of taking an economic ideology of "free enterprise" and spreading it into every sector of society ... [But] you cannot have industrialization and unleash these market forces and at the same time defend traditional positions on the family and sacred knowledge of the past. They are mutually exclusive. So my sense is that this coalition must fracture in the long run' (175). In Alberta, the contradiction between these positions was represented by the views of AQE participants. It was not clear that this coalition had fractured by 2000, but certainly AQE activities were less prominent in the media compared to those of parents unhappy about the impacts of restructuring and funding cuts.

Hall's analysis suggests that the Thatcherist project in Britain was quite resilient, largely as a result of the ideological groundwork that was laid in the late 1970s. The project involved convincing people that 'expectations are out of control and must be lowered,' and disconnecting 'the word *public* from its association with anything that is good or positive' (Hall 1988: 206). This strategy encouraged people to view change in the direction of a free market as inevitable and to blame the victims of changes rather than governments, transnational corporations and other institutions associated with global restructuring.

Failing to adequately analyse the reasons for the success of Thatcherism, the Left became 'adept at telling the electorate "what is wrong" with Thatcherism ... but not what might be right about socialism,' according to Hall (1988: 92). The effect was an unreflective defence of the welfare state that ignored changing economic realities, and a politics that failed to reconcile the interests and demands of different groups within a larger program. This critique of the Left in Britain informs the Alberta context where organized labour faced the reality that the New Democratic Party was a weak political force in the province, with no MLAs represented in the legislature during the Klein government's first term and only two in its second. Therefore, the institutional support for developing an alternative popular politics was limited.

According to Hall and Apple, the Left in Britain and the United States failed to appreciate the appeal of ideologies promoted by Thatcher and Reagan. For example, the discourse of education for economic prosperity promises employability if not employment for students – a notion that has greater appeal during times of economic insecurity. Hall (1988, 54) discusses how this discourse addressed lived experiences in the British context: 'As unemployment grows, working-class parents are obliged to take the competitive side of education more seriously: being skilled – even if it is only for particular places in dead-end, low-skill, routine labour – is better than being on the dole. If comprehensivization in the form in which it was offered is not going to deliver the goods, then working-class children may have to be content to be "skilled" and "classed" in any way they can. This is what Marx meant by the "dull compulsion" of economic existence.' The discourse of vocationalism, particularly when targeted at disadvantaged groups, therefore had appeal.

In Alberta, several interview participants also acknowledged the appeal of discourses concerning choice and parent power. Parents noted the 'little bit of truth' in the construction of public schooling as bureaucratic and nonresponsive to the needs of students/parents. In this context, the discourse of choice and the promise of greater power for parents were appealing. In the United States, the concept of choice also generated quite wide political support. As Dougherty and Sostre (1992: 28) state, 'By the mid-1980s, school choice began to enjoy unprecedented support by such unlikely groups as liberal policy scholars, urban educators, black parents, and state governors.' Furthermore, while teachers, school administrators, and the Democratic party opposed private school choice, they generally supported choice within public schools. Discussion of the historical development of choice in the United States makes it evident that the attempt to broaden support for choice by removing its elitist connotations contributed both to its success in policy terms and to the fragility of the movement.

Choice reforms were not introduced overnight. While Milton Friedman suggested the idea of vouchers for U.S. schools in the 1950s, support for choice did not become mobilized until liberal policy scholars like Chubb and Moe (1990) and local educators lent legitimacy to the concept. It helped that the Reagan administration introduced a bill to provide vouchers to help low income youth gain remedial education. In Britain, too, the voucher idea was discussed in the early 1980s but failed for financial and administrative reasons. Chitty (1992) suggests that early resistance made the government aware that it had to move more slowly. Within this context, the ERA's introduction of per capita funding along with grant-maintained schools and city technology colleges could be said to represent phases towards the introduction of a more comprehensive voucher system.

Movements for choice within Canada have undoubtedly borrowed arguments, models, and advocates from the U.S. experience. For example, a video on charter schools released by Joe Freedman's Society for Advancing Educational Research (SAER) in 1995 contained interviews with nine American advocates and only two Canadians (Dobbin 1997). Although Joe Freedman and Albertans for Quality Education appeared to represent mostly white middle-class parents, they adopt American rhetoric around the benefits of choice for disadvantaged groups. At the same time, disadvantaged groups themselves are not promoting choice to the same extent as in the United States. Religious private school supporters, and private school supporters more generally, appeared to be advocates in Alberta as in the United States. Also, established academics such as Mark Holmes at the Ontario Institute for Studies in Education, who appeared in Joe Freedman's *Failing Grades* video and was an advisor to the Organization for Quality Education, lent legitimacy to the concept. Finally, the fact that charter schools were proposed in the 1993 government's roundtable workbook and were legislated in 1994 indicates that there was political support within Alberta Education. Probably, like their American counterparts, choice was seen by provincial politicians as a way to change education without requiring significant financial commitment.[11]

Ideologically, the 'gospel of free market school choice' promotes the idea of individual consumer choice as against ideas of collective democratic participation. But in his critique of the market alternative in education, Ball (1993) argues that the rhetoric of consumer choice within a free market was illusory in England, since the government constructed the market (in terms of defining available educational providers) and fixed performance indicators (through national testing programs). He adds that research evidence indicated a 'distinct mismatch between the Government's imposed indicators and the assumption of market theorists, and parents' actual preferences' (9). Ball's argument is supported by an empirical study of parental choice in Britain by David, West, and Ribbens (1994), which found that while examination results were a 'significant issue for "choice" as a rational matter,' it could not be concluded that they were 'the critical or vital element in the process' (144). Rather, major factors in parents' decisions about what schools their children would attend also included the 'pleasant feel of the school and the proximity of the school' (145). The mismatch between government-defined criteria for parental involvement in education and actual parental preferences was indicated also in Alberta. Parent representatives expressed a vision of involvement that was based on notions of democratic rights and social citizenship as opposed to individual consumer sovereignty.

Discourses of education for economic prosperity and greater parental choice are not specific to the Alberta context. Rather, studies by writers in Britain and New Zealand point to similar proponents, strategies, and ideological constructions. There are also institutional connections between Canada and the United States, such as the Higher Education Forums and Conference Boards. Models abound from the United States in terms of corporate involvement in education. Some of the proponents of reforms in Alberta parallel those described by Apple (1993: 30) as 'dominant economic and political elites intent on "modernizing" the economy, white working class and middle-class groups concerned with security, the family, and traditional knowledge and values, and economic and cultural conservatives. It also includes a fraction of the new middle class whose own advancement depends on the expanded use of the accountability, efficiency, and management processes, which are their own cultural capital.' The U.S. comparison is particularly important in the context of free trade agreements that critics argue may lead to the Americanization of Canadian education through the privatization of some public services and failure to protect others (Calvert and Kuehn 1993).

While the preceding discussion has focused on similarities in political contexts, stakeholders, and ideological projects between Alberta and other sites, there were also differences related to the political/economic history of Alberta and the relationships among stakeholders, discussed in the analysis of interviews. Alberta is best characterized as having a resource-based boom/ bust economy, and attempts at economic diversification have long been a preoccupation for provincial governments given the non-renewable nature of these resources. In the past, political consensus has revolved around Albertans' shared feelings of alienation towards national political institutions, and their shared interest in a single dominant sector (oil and gas) (Dacks 1986). The dominance of the oil and gas sector explains the influence of business leaders from this sector in government policy discussions and within local communities. The instability of the resource sector due to fluctuations in world prices legitimized concerns over the province's ability to respond to future economic change, and reinforced the view that Albertans must be adaptable, self-reliant, and entrepreneurial. Furthermore, for decades Alberta politics have been characterized by the dominance of a single party and a right-wing populism. This single party dominance and the relative lack of class consciousness represent key differences from the British context.

Another difference between this study and those in other sites is the focus on provincial and local levels as opposed to the national level. Moving to the local level, issues around community power structures and the informal as well as formal roles of individuals in policy-making are more evident and therefore play a greater role in the analysis. For example, among Alberta cities and towns, Calgary is distinctive in terms of its corporate culture and staunch political conservatism. Since most interviews were based in Calgary, this background is relevant to understanding the balance of forces there. It is in the relations among groups and the ways in which different groups make sense of changes that we see 'how different forces come together, conjuncturally, to create the new terrain on which a different politics must form up' (Hall 1988: 163). Several factors helped to form the ideological terrain upon which the restructuring of public education rests, as follows:

- Calgary has a very well educated population (over fifty percent of adults had some post-secondary training), and the city had more than double the national average of employees in sciences, engineering and mathematics areas.

- In 1993, eight of the Conference Board's 25 Corporate Council members were located in Calgary. The CBE administration had strong links with the Conference Board.
- The Calgary Board of Education was very supportive of business-education partnerships through its partnership program, begun in 1985. At the high school level, such initiatives commonly involved a large oil/gas corporation as the business partner.
- A strong 'business-in-education' network was facilitated through institutions like the partnership and science foundations, which were also involved in Conference Board activities.
- Several key participants in education reform initiatives at the provincial level were located in Calgary, for example, Dan Williams (ACC), John Smith (science foundation), and the majority of AQE members.
- Alliance among oppositional groups in public education tended to be tenuous and narrowly defined. They had not developed a coherent alternative popular politics, an alternative economic strategy, or a 'cultural politics capable of mobilizing alternative social identities.' (Hall 1998: 92)

Tales around educational reform clearly travel. In comparing Alberta with other sites, we can point to shared structural features such as capitalist crisis and the breakdown of the social-democratic accord. Struggles over education can be seen to be related to broader struggles over the appropriate role of the state in society and who will bear the cost of economic changes. However, reform tales are also translated differently in different sites (Dehli 1996). The historical background of reforms, relationships among key players, and the directions of reforms may differ. For example, the historical development of an anti-elitist choice discourse in the United States differs from other countries. The extent to which neoconservative and neoliberal strands of New Right thinking are apparent and whether they are reconciled within educational reforms also differs. Finally, the extent and forms of resistance from teachers and other groups will vary. Because of these differences, case studies that focus on how reforms are taken up in particular sites are critical.

Implications of the Study

This study assumes that policy research can highlight new questions and problems and help to frame political discussion through an exploration that begins with the policy community, broadly defined. If we accept that restructuring social reality involves understanding existing society, articulating alternative visions, and developing strategies for achieving these visions, then this critical work has focused primarily on the first stage. However, the intention throughout the analysis has been to raise questions and issues that may be useful in the process of developing a counter-hegemonic vision for education. The focus on 'who is saying what' encourages giving attention to how discourses are rooted in material practices and how they relate to the interests of different groups. It also acknowledges that identity is complex and multifaceted and that individuals' positions are not predetermined. For example, teachers and corporate executives are also parents in many cases. The focus on relationships among stakeholders provides an understanding of how hegemonic and oppositional discourses have been constructed by different social actors in different sites. We see that hegemonic discourses are not necessarily consistent and unified, but rather contain elements that may be contradictory. Counter-hegemonic work involves highlighting these contradictions and attempting to decouple/rearticulate discursive elements in the process of developing alternative visions. Wars of position therefore continue.

The Alberta Teachers' Association can be seen as a key player in counter-hegemonic work. This group has access to greater resources than many other labour groups. In addition, the provincial association is well positioned to articulate reality at the provincial, national, and international levels while members are well positioned to assess critically the impact of educational reforms at the local level. In the Ontario context, Martell (1995) confirms the importance of teacher organizations within the policy community when he says, 'OSSTF [Ontario Secondary School Teachers' Federation] is gradually concluding that teachers and their allies must finally take hold of the educational reform agenda. A knee-jerk defence of the public schools doesn't work anymore, even though the public school system must be strongly defended. Teachers not only have to say what's right with the education they provide, they also have to say what's wrong and spell out what to do about it (3–4).

The ATA has begun some of this work. It challenged the top-down policy approach of government (Alberta Education 1993b) in *Trying to Teach* and in follow-up reports that included an alternative education plan. During the roundtable process, it sponsored alternative roundtables and attempted to mobilize public support through its half-million-dollar information campaign and public opinion polls. Recognizing that ad hoc responses to educational reforms were not effective, it established a Public Education Centre in 1995 to liaise with teacher locals and parent groups, and to disseminate information about the impact of cutbacks and restructuring. It worked with other education partners to produce a vision and agenda for public education that was released in early 2000. The goal has been to provide an alternative understanding of reality that opens up debate over educational reforms.

Mackay and Flower (1999: 57) write that the ATA realized early on 'that it would need to find allies in its fight to broaden the based of support for public education.' This study confirms that developing alliances across social divisions is critical. This includes alliances with mainstream and marginalized groups of parents and students as well as with organized labour groups. In articulating an understanding of existing reality, there is a need to make visible the assumptions, alliances, and implications of discourses around fiscal crisis, education for economic prosperity, and the unhappy parent. The purpose is to reveal the basis of populist politics around education and to uncover the social divisions that have been obscured by the 'undifferentiated, unclassed, unsexed, unraced unity of "the people"' (Hall 1988: 192).

In addition to critiquing hegemonic discourses, there is also a need to acknowledge their appeal and the ways they correspond to the lived realities of students, parents, and teachers. For example, the discourse of vocationalism is appealing to families confronting unemployment and underemployment, particularly when it acknowledges the need to redress inequities in educational provision. There is, however, a need to highlight contradictions within the concepts of skills and vocationalism in theory and practice. To date, criticism has tended to focus on challenging the shift in educational goals from educating students for citizenship towards an instrumental view of education as serving the economy, and this is valid. However, as Hall (1988) notes, in times of high unemployment, these concerns carry less weight. A more fruitful approach might involve challenging the contradiction between the Fordist approaches to pedagogy assumed by talk of skills acquisition and competency testing and the supposed requirements of multi-skilled post-Fordist workers (Brown and Lauder 1992). Reformers therefore must be accountable to 'stakeholders' in terms of the progressive aspects of vocationalism.

A second criticism of vocational discourse is that human capital ideas about investing in workers are contradicted by the practice of government cutbacks. However, given the hegemony of the discourse of fiscal crisis in the 1990s and its continuing influence in 2000, this argument is also unlikely to generate broad-based support. A more fruitful approach might involve challenging the supply-side focus of human capital theory that is assumed by the discourse of education for economic prosperity – that is, the difference between employability and employment. Livingstone (1999) argues that the problem confronting Canadian society is less a lack of skilled workers than a lack of jobs that utilize these skills.

A third avenue might involve questioning the positivist notion of skill that underlies vocational discourse. The case of Panorama and the employability skills portfolios demonstrates that there is a need to examine how the concept of skill is socially constructed and how discourses that seek to produce equity may be translated differentially or subverted at the level of practice (Blackmore 1997). This requires further case study research to explores work-school-family relationships. The gendered aspect of the discourse of vocational progressivism is an area that has not been addressed adequately in the Alberta context. For example, the *Framework for Enhancing Business Involvement in Education* (Alberta Education 1996a) emphasizes apprenticeships and technical training for non-college-bound youth without acknowledging the gender bias inherent in this approach. Vocational programs sponsored by government can be critiqued usefully in terms of who acquires what skills and who benefits.

The discourse of choice also has appeal for parents who have legitimate concerns about the bureaucracy and nonresponsiveness of public schools. Therefore, instead of constructing choice as inherently conservative, it is more useful to point out contradictions within the discourse. For example, the marketization of schooling promotes a form of 'possessive individualism' that contradicts other goals around community building within education (Whitty, Power, and Halpin 1998). Markets are also not a neutral mechanism for distributing social goods but rather tend to reproduce and in some cases exacerbate inequities. Watson (1999) notes that 'parents' choices are shaped by their social class and ethnic backgrounds, their wider social context and the dynamics of the education market itself.' In short, white middle-class parents are more able to access schools of their choice. Further, the market model leads to consumer participation as opposed to democratic participation. Therefore, opposition must be articulated within a project that redefines and takes seriously demands for democratic participation in schooling.

Curtis, Livingstone, and Smaller (1992) suggest that alternative visions should be based on the values at the core of a democratic and egalitarian society, values such as cooperation and the all-round development of each person. This suggests a focus on who is bearing the costs of educational change, in terms not only of access, but also of the control of schooling practices, the content of curricula, and the relationship of education to other social institutions. As Martell suggests, this may involve opening up discussion to include what has been wrong with public education historically and why it has been unable to achieve certain goals, as well as pointing out how reforms are likely to promote further inequity. The development of an alternative vision thus requires us to ask what kind of society we want to live in, as well as what the role of education will be. It must be part of a larger social/political/economic vision.

But while educators and other allies must take account of the broader social and economic context, their vision does not have to be bound by that of employers who have been constructed as *labour market experts*. We might ask why the perspectives of business people have been privileged over those of workers or community groups. An alliance that includes the latter perspectives may prevent the tunnel vision that has characterized recent educational reforms. Of course, such an alliance would raise questions within the ATA about the meaning of professionalism and how teachers wish to position themselves within the occupational hierarchy. This may involve rearticulating what it means to be a 'public servant.' Connell et al. (1982) suggest that there is a need to valorize the fact that most teachers entered the profession because they thought they could contribute to the common good. Therefore, constructions of the public sector as 'inefficient, wasteful and bureaucratic' need to be rearticulated through educators' perceptions of what it means to be a public servant.

In general, groups engaged in counter-hegemonic work in Alberta have focused on the anti-democratic character of government processes and have developed their own mechanisms for achieving a greater voice at the provincial level. Like Thatcherism in Britain (Hall 1988: 83), they have argued that the Klein government represents an 'elective dictatorship.' A key strategy may involve de-coupling and rearticulating discursive elements. For example, democratic participation can mean more than voting every four years. Parent power can mean more than consumer power. Partnerships can involve more than profitable corporations. Effectiveness can mean more than aggregate scores on standardized tests. And preparing students for the new millennium can mean more than introducing better systems to sort and select them for occupations.

It is hoped that this study will provoke dialogue and suggest alternative directions for groups within and outside of Alberta who are trying to make sense of educational reforms and develop a stronger public education system. Further research in the Alberta context might move usefully beyond this overview of the responses of a number of stakeholder groups to consider in greater depth the diversity and complexity of relations within each of these groups. Research that details state processes during the 1990s, for example, through interviews with key politicians and bureaucrats, would also be an important complement (cf., Ball 1990). Finally, comparative research that critically examines educational restructuring and resistance to that restructuring within different social, political, and economic contexts will further our understanding of the conditions, actors, and ideas that give rise to educational settlement and crisis.

Chronological List of Interviews and Participants

Pseudonyms were used for all participants and for some organizations. Where pseudonyms are used for organizations, the pseudonym is followed by an asterisk.

Interview	Date	Pseudonyms and Affiliations
1.	23-06-93	Mark Silver, Canadian Teachers' Federation
2.	06-07-93	participant withdrew, Conference Board of Canada
3.	15-07-93	Lawrence Grant, Conference Board of Canada
4.	11-02-94	Leslie Pearce, parent
5.	16-02-94	Tracey Borger, Calgary Catholic School Board
6.	22-02-94	Donna Black, Calgary Board of Education (CBE)
7.	23-02-94	Joan Farrell, AUPE, Quality Education Coalition
8.	25-02-94	Mike Popiel, Partnership Foundation*
9.	02-03-94	Justin Hall, Stan Jones, Albertans for Quality Education
10.	03-03-94	Carl George, Native High School*
11.	04-03-94	Dan Williams, Alberta Chamber of Commerce
12.	04-03-94	Susan Law, ESL Parent Group*
13.	08-03-94	Carol Oliver, ESL teacher

14.	10-03-94	Murray Walsh, Canadian Union of Public Employees
15.	22-03-94	Barbara Phillips, Academic High School*
16.	22-03-94	Ron Leckie, Academic High School*
17.´	24-03-94	Bruce Reid, CBE
18.	25-03-94	Karen Gold, CBE/Alberta Education
19.	30-03-94	Sally Long, Monarch Corporation*
20.	31-03-94	Rebecca Rees, parent
21.	12-04-94	Nancy Ellis, Calgary Public Teachers (ATA local)
22.	15-04-94	James Kozak, newspaper journalist
23.	19-04-94	Andrew Markham, Monarch Corporation*
24.	22-04-94	Chris MacDonald, Calgary District Labour Council
25.	26-04-94	Janet Weis, Alberta Teachers' Association
26.	27-04-94	Marilyn Simmons, CBE
27.	27-04-94	Katherine Hennessey, CCHSA (Home and Schools)
28.	23-05-94	Wendy Smith, student
29.	08-06-94	Don Coulter, Parent Advisory Council member
30.	22-06-94	Marcia Jensen, CBE
31.	23-06-94	Andy Laird, Academic High School*
32.	26-08-94	Margaret Szabo, Alberta Federation of Labour
33.	28-09-94	Gary Baldwin, Panorama Corporation*
34.	30-09-94	Cindy Ho, student
35.	30-09-94	Lisa Kao, student
36.	13-01-95	Sandra Morin, Emily Murphy High School*
37.	25-01-95	Cliff Dumont, Advisory Committee, T2T
38.	12-05-95	Jennie Thompson small-business person
39.	15-04-95	Andrea White, Science Foundation*
40.	31-05-95	Rhonda Dixon, Save Public Education
41.	12-09-95	Pam Conway, Staff Association

Total Labour Force by Demographic Characteristics

TABLE B:1
Total Labour Force by Industry Division

Industry	Calgary	Alberta	Canada
Primary industries	33,650	180,440	868,010
Manufacturing industries	34,350	106,905	2,084,115
Construction industries	29,170	102,090	933,425
Transportation and storage	19,865	65,150	581,810
Communication and other utilities	14,625	46,145	479,185
Trade industries	72,300	237,270	2,445,690
Finance, insurance and real estate	27,370	70,640	810,565
Government service	22,010	102,470	1,111,385
Educational service	26,475	96,715	972,515
Health and social services	34,785	125,780	1,277,340
Other industries	98,400	271,235	2,656,180
All industries	413,005	1,404,835	14,220,235

Source: Statistics Canada, Cat. no. 95-373, Table 1. Selected Characteristics for Census Divisions and Census Subdivisions, 1991 Census.

TABLE B:2
Calgary's Major Private Sector Employers

Name	Industry Sector	Number of Employees	CBE Partnership Involvement
Calgary Cooperative Association	Retail grocery	3,500	No
AGT Limited	Telecommunications	2,600	No
Nova Corporation	Energy	2,400	Yes
Northern Telecom	Telecommunications	2,200	Yes
Amoco Canada	Energy	2,000	Yes
PWA Corporation	Transportation	1,800	No
Canada Safeway	Retail grocery	1,800	Yes
Transalta Utilities	Energy	1,700	No
Real Canadian Superstores	Retail grocery	1,500	No
Petro Canada	Energy	1,500	No
Shell Canada	Energy	1,400	Yes
Forzani Group	Retail merchandise	1,350	No
Walmart	Retail merchandise	1,300	No
The Bay	Retail merchandise	1,200	No
Imperial Oil	Energy	1,200	Yes
Bank of Montreal	Financial services	1,100	No
Norcen	Energy	1,100	Yes
Sears	Retail merchandise	1,100	No
Canadian Western Natural Gas	Energy	1,100	Yes
Pan Canadian Petroleum	Energy	1,000	No

Source: Calgary Economic Development Authority, October 1994; and CBE documents, January 1993.

TABLE B:3
Calgary's Major Public Sector Employers

Name	Industry Sector	Number of Employees	CBE Partnership Involvement
City of Calgary	Government	12,000	No
Calgary Board of Education	Education	10,300	N/A
Government of Canada	Government	5,000	No
Foothills Hospital	Healthcare	4,400	No
University of Calgary	Education	4,000	No
Calgary District Hospital Group	Healthcare	3,500	No
Calgary General Hospital	Healthcare	3,500	No
Calgary Catholic Board of Education	Education	3,000	N/A
Government of Alberta	Government	2,000	No
Mount Royal College	Education	1,500	No
Alberta Children's Hospital	Healthcare	1,350	No
SAIT	Education	1,300	Yes

Source: Calgary Economic Development Authority, October 1994; and CBE documents, January 1993.

TABLE B:4
Occupation by Sex in Calgary, Alberta, and Canada

Occupation	Calgary Male	Female	Alberta Male	Female	Canada Male	Female
Managerial and administrative	34,945	20,245	102,615	57,155	1,086,150	653,015
Teaching and related occupations	5,330	10,330	19,885	37,890	224,730	401,790
Occupations in medicine and health	3,565	15,260	13,110	54,550	151,490	575,845
Occupations in engineering and math	25,505	5,845	53,290	11,460	458,325	114,190
Social sciences, religious, artistic and related occupations	8,165	8,785	25,175	28,930	285,310	310,250
Clerical and related occupations	16,670	66,505	44,655	201,430	556,395	2,016,665
Sales occupations	26,695	20,390	75,075	64,415	707,085	601,625
Service occupations	25,155	30,470	76,005	113,515	795,030	1,023,345
Primary occupations	5,680	1,195	79,755	26,185	523,200	147,115
Processing occupations	4,740	1,060	20,720	4,870	304,495	106,170
Machining, product fabricating, assembling and repairing	20,520	2,965	80,595	8,555	939,485	215,685
Construction trades	23,490	725	91,010	2,710	820,525	22,815
Transport equipment operating occupations	11,480	1,170	45,655	5,620	461,760	46,805
Other occupations	13,060	3,040	50,315	9,675	525,250	145,675
All occupations	225,005	188,000	777,865	626,970	7,839,245	6,380,990

Source: Statistics Canada, Cat. no. 95-373, Table 1. Selected Characteristics for Census Divisions and Subdivisions, 1991 Census

TABLE B:5
Employment Income by Sex and Work Activity

	Calgary Male	Female	Alberta Male	Female	Canada Male	Female
Worked full year, full time	138,980	92,155	471,950	288,395	4,699,890	3,018,885
Full year, full time average employment income	42,860	27,248	38,389	25,037	38,648	26,033
Worked part-year or part-time	87,940	102,890	307,835	358,360	3,207,005	3,545,250
Part year or part-time average employment income	17,952	12,139	17,720	11,045	17,952	11,244

Source: Statistics Canada, Cat. no. 95-373, Table 1. Selected Characteristics for Census Divisions and Subdivisions, 1991 Census.

Notes

1: Introduction

1 In May 1999 the Klein government amalgamated the Departments of Education and Advanced Education and Career Development into a new entity called Alberta Learning, with a new minister, Lyle Oberg. The former minister of education was Gary Mar, who replaced Halvar Jonson in mid-1996. Jonson had been minister through the period of restructuring in 1993/4.
2 While dictionary definitions of the word *reform* refer to 'improvement' and 'change for the better,' it is used in this work simply to connote change.
3 An article published in the *Globe and Mail*, 18 January 2000, reported the newly elected Labour prime minister's reflections on the 'New Zealand experiment': 'After all these years of so-called economic reform, we've got an appalling current-account deficit, we've got unemployment locked at about six percent,' [Helen Clark] said. 'We've got very low productivity. We've had an utterly indifferent record on economic growth, utterly indifferent. So where's the success?' This contrasts with the seeming good news story in Alberta where cutbacks and restructuring in the early 1990s were followed by the elimination of the deficit and government surpluses (based on improved resource prices and economic growth) by the end of the decade.
4 This information, from an article in *Business Week*, 7 February 2000, asks whether 'private companies do a better job of educating America's kids.' See also website http://www.businessweek.com/2000/00_06/ b3667001.htm.

2: The Crisis in Public Education

1 Seccareccia (1995: 45) disputes the idea that policies pursued by the postwar state were Keynesian. Rather, he suggests that it was the inconsis-

tencies of the ad hoc Keynesianism of the early postwar period that provided an 'easy target for the monetarist and the new classical attacks that were to emerge in the seventies and eighties.'

2 Drugge (1995) challenges politicians' claims that the current low tax regime is part of the 'Alberta advantage,' arguing instead that the province's deficit problems were revenue-generated and that spending cuts will have serious consequences for future economic competitiveness.

3 Lisac (1995: 147) writes that Ted Gaebler (in Osborne and Gaebler 1993) made more than a dozen trips to Alberta to 'talk to business groups or civil servants' about ways to reinvent government and cut costs.

4 Freedman's Society for Advancing Educational Research produced a video entitled *Failing Grades*, in which evidence is provided for the view that Canadian schools are failing students and their parents. A booklet accompanies the video (Freedman 1993).

3: The Hegemonic Work of the Conference Board

1 I attended conferences in 1991, 1992, and 1993 as a delegate. Conferences are usually two and one-half days in length, are held at a large hotel or conference centre, and involve 500 to 600 delegates from across the country, primarily from the private sector and education.

2 Appendix 1 lists pseudonyms of interview participants, affiliations, and dates of interviews.

3 While non-business NCE members included mostly education leaders, there were a handful of representatives from government, labour, and non-governmental organizations.

4 The nine characteristics of a successful school system listed by Kennedy: (1) curriculum content must reflect high expectations; (2) the system should be performance- or outcome-based; (3) results should be compared with international standards; (4) the system must reward schools that succeed and change the ones that fail; (5) school staff must have more freedom to act in order to be more accountable; (6) there needs to be greater emphasis on staff development and teacher training; (7) a quality prekindergarten program is crucial, especially for disadvantaged children; (8) technology must be used to increase student and teacher productivity; and (9) health and other social services must enable children to come to school willing and able to learn (Bloom 1991: 11).

5 I was provided with evidence of the 'market penetration' of the CB employability skills profile when attending an orientation meeting at a Calgary school as the parent of a child entering grade one. The assistant

principal referred to the ESP as a catalogue of the type of skills that teachers would try to develop in youngsters.

6 Livingstone (1999) refers to the credential gap as the gap between educational attainment and credentials required at entry, and the performance gap as the gap between workers' skills and the opportunities to apply these skills in their jobs. He suggests that approximately 20 per cent of the employed workforce have higher credentials than were required for entry to their job, according to Canadian surveys, while Ontario and U.S. surveys suggest that between 40 and 60 per cent of workers experienced performance underemployment (75, 82).

7 Criteria for selecting winning partnerships included the promotion of the importance of science, technology, and math; the promotion of teacher development and enhancement; encouragement of students to stay in school; expansion of vocational and/or apprenticeship training; and the acquisition of foundation skills for employability. Awards were also based on the degree to which there were clearly defined goals and objectives, and the rigour with which the partnership measured outcomes.

8 Some of the Alberta members of the CB's Employability Skills Forum include Alberta Learning, Alberta Human Resources and Employment, the partnership foundation in Calgary, Careers: The Next Generation Foundation (a partnership led by the Alberta Chamber of Resources), and Syncrude Canada. Education departments from two other provinces – Ontario and New Brunswick – are also represented.

4: The Hegemonic Work of Governments

1 The action plan list of groups that submitted a brief to the Steering Group includes the CB and affiliates AGT, CP Rail, TELUS, and Stentor, as well as the BCNI, the Canadian Manufacturers' Association, and the Canadian Chamber of Commerce.

2 The Economic Council of Canada was a federally funded research agency whose members were drawn primarily from the business community.

3 The federal government provided $50,000 in seed funding for the Canadian Forum on Learning, a group that would provide a forum for education and business organizations to develop national learning expectations. As of 1995, this group had not been established, but the Canadian Education Association was reportedly bringing groups together annually for similar purposes (personal communication with a representative from the Canadian Teachers Federation, November 1995).

4 'Innovators in the Schools' brings scientists, engineers, technicians, and technologists into the classroom.

5 Don Simpson co-authored a study (Simpson and Sissons 1989) called Entrepreneurs in Education for the International Development Research Centre, in which the authors argue that international development is constrained by the lack of an entrepreneurial ethic. It recommends the establishment of more joint ventures and networks among public and private sector organizations to capitalize on growing 'third world' demand for human resources development skills (Kachur 1994).

6 The Alberta Chamber of Resources continues to be a key player in educational policy development. It was the driving force behind Careers: the Next Generation (CNG), a public-private partnership that aims to attract more students into the trades and ease the transition of non-college bound students into the workplace. The CNG foundation was established in 1998 and receives partial funding from the province.

7 McMillan (1996) writes that the Alberta government has spent less per capita than the average province since 1991–2. The fact that Alberta was already spending less than average before the Klein government came into office suggests that the discourse of fiscal crisis had already taken hold.

8 In 1997 the structure of Alberta's economy (in terms of share of GDP) was as follows: energy 21 per cent, business and commercial services 19 per cent, transportation and utilities 12 per cent, finance 11 per cent, whole-sale and retail trade 11 per cent, manufacturing 10 per cent, construction 8 per cent, government services 5 per cent, and agriculture 3 per cent. For facts on Alberta see website <http://www.gov.ab.ca/edt>.

9 In his book *Slumming It at the Rodeo*, Gordon Laird (1998) suggests that 'cost-cutting cowboys' Ralph Klein and Preston Manning owe much to the right-wing populist tradition of the west, and to images of prosperity, freedom, and rugged individualism. Drawing also on the cowboy metaphor, Newman (1998: 427) refers to Ralph Klein's 'lasso-faire capitalism.'

10 The Worth Report was initiated by the Social Credit government and released by the incoming Conservative government in Alberta in 1972. Wagner (1998) suggests that the Tories were not satisfied with some of the 'progressive' ideas expressed in the Worth Report (Alberta 1972), and that this led in part to the development of the 'back-to-basics' Harder Report (Alberta Education 1977). Economic decline may have also played a role in changing views about education. The Harder Report recommended 'an emphasis upon knowledge and skills relevant for employment; more

instruction time in the core curriculum; a curriculum highly specified in content and skill levels by grade; a reduction of electives; criterion-referenced standardized tests; accountability through monitoring; and citizenship training' (Mazurek 1999: 14–15). Mazurek argues that educational reforms under the Klein government continue the direction of the Harder report.

11 The sixth action for Native students proposes that they be surveyed to find out how satisfied they are with their education. In other words, more information is needed before government can act.

12 Dinning worked for Dome Petroleum before moving into politics, and in 1997 he left his position in the Klein government to join TransAlta Utilities as vice-president of corporate development. He is seen as a possible successor to Ralph Klein (Newman 1998: 440).

5: Restructuring Education, 1993–1995

1 The ATA sponsored a number of campaigns between 1993 and 1995, including a four-week ($210,000) media campaign in the fall 1993, the 1994 Know More campaign, and a two-week radio and billboard blitz in early 1995. The Public Education Action Centre was established in 1994 to implement 'an ongoing, proactive information and action program' (Mackay and Flower 1999: 65).

2 Although the issue of splitting the ATA was raised by a Tory MLA in early February 1994, the actual private members' bill was not introduced until a year later. This followed a previous members' bill in September 1993, which proposed that membership in the ATA be made voluntary. Another perceived attack on labour occurred when Alberta Education proposed introducing five-year renewable licenses for teachers in 1995 (Mackay and Flower 1999).

3 An interesting addendum to the friction between the Calgary Public School Board and the province was the decision by Alberta Learning Minister Lyle Oberg to dismiss the entire board in August 1999 after complaints from the chair of the board about dysfunction resulting from serious divisions among trustees. This was the first time in the province's history that a board in a major centre was dismissed. One trustee was reported in the *Calgary Herald*, 20 August 1999, as saying that it was the minister's 'way of silencing the Tory government's biggest critics of underfunded education.'

4 Freedman later became one of the founders and directors of Webber Academy, a private school that was soliciting student applications in

Calgary in 1997. A number of the other fourteen founders/directors were business executives or professionals. The chairman, Neil Webber, was past chair of TELUS corporation, an ex-MLA and minister of education for Alberta, and a member of the Conference Board's National Council on Education. The school's objectives included becoming a 'nationally and internationally pre-eminent university preparatory school' focusing on academic basics.

5 Research for this book was provided by the Donner Canada Foundation, which is described by Murray Dobbin (1997: 78) as 'an organization committed to promoting free market approaches to public policy issues.' He notes that the Donner Foundation also funded Joe Freedman's Society for Advancing Educational Research as well as Teachers for Excellence in Education, a B.C. group leading the campaign for charter schools in that province.

6 While there was majority support among respondents for stronger parent councils, less school board administration, and fewer school boards, there was far less support for cuts to kindergarten funding – 39.8 per cent support – and the creation of charter schools – 39.4 per cent support (Archer and Gibbins 1997: 467).

7 Mackay and Flower (1999: 55) write that the ATA was invited to join the 'common front' in the spring of 1994 but withdrew in February 1995 because the 'program did not really develop as intended.'

8 Prior to this, approximately 50 per cent of school funding was derived from local taxes and 50 per cent came from the provincial government.

9 Provincial restrictions on spending particularly affected large urban districts. As Bruce and Schwartz (1997: 398) note, 'Faced with the needs of large and increasingly diverse urban populations, and with the economy-of-scale advantages their student numbers provide, these boards have developed centrally based ancillary and support staff who provide services to schools in areas such as curriculum development, diagnostic and classroom support services for children with special needs, and central library services.'

10 Boards were allowed to hold plebiscites on local tax increases to fund special programs, but money raised in this manner could not exceed 3 per cent of the board's budget.

11 Klein's actions can be compared with those of Premier Mike Harris in Ontario, who eliminated 1,400 civil servants and cut his cabinet from twenty-eight positions to nineteen (Laird 1998: 72). Ontario pursued an even more aggressive fiscal agenda than Alberta, with 20 per cent minimal spending cuts and a 30 per cent provincial income tax cut.

12 The government introduced a Deficit Elimination Act which required that the deficit be reduced to zero by 1996/7, a Balanced Budget and Debt Retirement Act which required elimination of the province's debt by the year 2021/2, and the Alberta Taxpayer Protection Act which required the government to hold a referendum to approve the introduction of a sales tax in the province.

13 A 1998 issue of *Orbit* includes a number of articles that analyse Bill 160 in Ontario. In particular, see articles by Pascall, Hargreaves, and Dehli.

14 Stockwell Day has been known for his outspoken conservative views on topics such as homosexuality and abortion.

6: The Corporate Alliance

1 Pseudonyms are used for the companies represented by Andrew Markham and Gary Baldwin, Monarch and Panorama, respectively. They are also used for Baldwin's boss (Joseph Sanders) and for the executive who spearheaded the science foundation (John Smith). The full names of the partnership and sciences foundations are not provided, in an effort to protect anonymity. Also, pseudonyms are used when participants refer to each other in interview quotations: pseudonyms appear in square brackets.

2 Markham notes that Monarch hired approximately twenty-five new graduates in 1994 and fewer than ten in 1992 and 1993, compared with almost 100 a year in the mid- to late 80s (Interview 23). More generally, an article in the *Calgary Herald*, spring 1995, notes that Monarch cut its workforce by about 10 per cent in 1994 and expected to cut it by another 10 per cent by the end of 1995.

3 An article in the *Calgary Herald* on 4 May 1995 indicated that 25 to 35 per cent of employees in major and intermediate oil and gas companies are no longer in permanent full-time positions. The trend in the Canadian labour market as a whole is also towards 'nonstandard' forms of work including part-time, short-term contract jobs, certain types of self-employment, and work within the temporary help industry (Economic Council of Canada 1991: 71). In 1990 such work accounted for approximately 30 per cent of employment, and between 1980 and 1990 it accounted for almost half of net job growth.

4 While Williams emphasizes the grassroots, broad-based character of ACC membership, in a survey of Calgary employers, *Future Jobs Calgary*, one respondent argued that while the Calgary Chamber professed to represent small businesses 'in fact, they represent medium to large businesses' (Moore 1994: 26–7).

5 The participant who raised the most concerns about educational restructuring is former teacher and small business representative Jennie Thompson. Thompson suggests that certain groups of children may 'slip through the cracks' as a result of program cuts and that equality of access may be negatively affected. At the same time, Thompson seems able to reconcile these ideas with her view that stronger links between businesses and schools will be beneficial and that a business model for education may be appropriate.

6 The CNG newsletter *The Next* (vol. 8, fall 1999) states that in 1998–9, CNG worked with 107 schools and 395 employers in forty-two communities to develop partnerships.

7: Partnerships as Sites of Struggle

1 Newman (1998) writes that Calgary has more head offices than Montreal and Vancouver combined.

2 Almost half of Calgary's top twenty private sector employers were involved in CBE partnerships in 1993 (see Appendix B, Table 2). In the United States, partnerships have also been promoted by governments as a way to improve public education. A 1986 survey indicated that 73 per cent of Forbes 500 corporations were participating in school-business collaborations (Galvin 1996).

3 Comparing the CBE and the CCSD for the school year 1995/6, the CBE had a projected enrolment of 95,898 compared to 36,902 for the CCSD. In an article entitled 'Kindergarten Fees Chopped,' the *Calgary Herald*, 12 April 1995, it was reported that the CBE budget was approximately $470 million compared to $183 million for the CCSD. Public education in Alberta refers to both public and separate schools; therefore separate school districts (almost exclusively Catholic) receive funding based on the same formula as public schools.

4 The partnerships discourse of *matchmaking* has a clear gender subtext with the female-dominated teaching occupation reaping the benefits of liaisons with male corporate leaders.

5 Black's comment that a construction workers' union would make a great partner with 'one of our non-academically inclined schools' suggests the potential for partnerships to become part of the reproductive process of schooling, and sorting and selecting students to fill class-appropriate places in the workplace (cf., Curtis, Livingstone, and Smaller 1992; Shor 1986).

6 In contrast to the view that good partners are successful private corporations, the Ontario Federation of Labour supports the idea of broader

linkages that involve schools and a variety of community organizations rather than schools and individual businesses (OFL 1990).

7 Pseudonyms are used for the school as well as the company. The Monarch–Academic High partnership is discussed also in Taylor (1998a).

8 Career and Life Management (CALM) is a compulsory grade eleven course that was mandated by Alberta Education in its Review of Secondary Programs. Curriculum content included topics such as career planning, personal finance, skills and attitudes required in the workplace, and interpersonal relationships (Bosetti 1990).

9 The International Baccalaureate program was designed as an internationally recognized high school program for advanced students. The program is only offered in eleven high schools in Alberta (Alberta Education 1993a: 46).

10 In his discussion of the partnership between a high school in Ontario and Goodyear corporation, Palmer (1995: 36) similarly notes that the school became 'something of a company' through this relationship. As in the Monarch case, the use of student opinion leaders was considered key to the success of the program. Also, curriculum (e.g., industrial physics) became tied to the company's perceived technical needs.

11 Clement and Myles (1994: 14) related the notion of 'class' to one's ability to affect the purposes of the organization and its assets through strategic decision-making, and one's ability to command the labour power of others.

12 The dissolution of the Monarch–Academic High partnership is discussed further in 'Spitting in the Wind' (Taylor 2000).

13 School representatives suggested that the partnership was formed because of the relationship between the former CEO of Monarch and a former principal at Academic High, while Monarch representatives said it resulted in a more 'arms length' way compared to the matching process undertaken by the school board.

14 A teacher who was on the development team said that Panorama had contributed $32,000 to the project.

15 While actual names of school boards are used, pseudonyms are used for the schools involved in the project.

16 The evaluation report was prepared by two professors from the Faculty of Education at the University of Calgary, and included survey data from fifty-nine teachers and 885 students. For reasons not given, Emily Murphy was the only pilot school not represented by survey data.

17 Feminist writers Gaskell (1987, 1992), Cockburn (1985), Steinberg (1990), and Wajcman (1991) contend that the labour market skills women have are not recognized and rewarded in the same way that men's are. Henry

and Ginzberg (1988) and Winn (1988) provide empirical evidence to suggest that visible minority students and immigrants face discrimination in the job market. Finally, Curtis, Livingstone, and Smaller (1992) discuss how working-class and visible minority students are often streamed into less challenging programs in schools (which lead to poorer job prospects).

8: The Fragmentation of Labour

1 *Facts on Alberta* was found at the website <http://www.alberta-canada.com/statpub/pdf/fcts0899.pdf>.
2 This information about the Alberta Federation of Labour is contained in an October 1997 submission by the AFL to the Private Schools Funding Task Force. In this submission, the AFL voiced its opposition to increased funding for private schools in the province.
3 This teacher's comments formed part of his written response in 1995 to the chapter from my dissertation. For each chapter I had requested feedback from a 'critical reader' who was affiliated with one of the groups discussed in the chapter.
4 A useful comparison to this discussion is provided by Harp and Betcherman (1980), who studied teachers' organizations in Ontario and Quebec in the 1960s and 70s as examples of 'contrasting organizational responses to the contradictory class location of their members' (159). While the Ontario Secondary School Teachers' Federation (OSSTF) in Ontario was not affiliated with the labour movement and focused demands on offsetting the imbalance in market power in its relationship with the state, the Centrale de l'Enseignement de Quebec (CEQ) in Quebec aligned itself with the labour movement and focused on issues of control in its struggles with the state. The authors seek to determine historically what 'political and ideological relations can account for differences in the organizations' class-based actions' (149).
5 The provincial strategy parallels that recommended to the CTF a year earlier by King and Peart (1992), who suggest that the 'confrontational approach' adopted by teachers' associations in their responses to government proposals for reform may 'effectively exclude them from full participation in the design of educational change' (186). The authors go on to recommend that teachers be portrayed to the public as 'caring, well-prepared professionals' (187).
6 This position paper (revised 1992) appeared on the ATA website: <http://www.teachers.ab.ca/policy/ppers/paper09.htn> accessed March 1999.
7 Murray Walsh notes that 'we had a bit of a fall-out' with the AFL, and adds that CUPE 40 would like to reaffiliate but has been deterred by the

fact that the AFL would charge them 'back dues' (Interview 14). Walsh also says that while he liaises with the Labour Council, his organization is not affiliated.

8 This trend towards contracting out is also apparent in Edmonton. CUPE 474 custodial workers there produced a report in November entitled *Privatizing Schools: In the Public Interest?* (CUPE 474 1994) as a response to the decision of Edmonton public school trustees to study contracting out the complete operation of one or more schools, and the provision of custodial and support staff services in up to one-third of district schools.

9 In his case studies of the media, Winter (1992) similarly concludes that 'media portrayals are highly consistent with corporate interests' (xiv), and that the 'common sense' view presented by the media is often reflected in popular opinion (xviii).

10 This executive was also a representative of Albertans for Quality Education and it was in this capacity that he was interviewed.

11 The AFL's position on private school funding was made clear in its submission to the Private Schools Funding Task Force in October 1997 (see website <http://www.afl.org/presentations/privateSch.html>). In this submission, the AFL reiterates its support for public schooling and argues that the 'choice to forego free public education is one which should carry a financial cost.' The federation opposed any increase in funding to private schools, arguing that it would come at the expense of the public system.

12 The Business Involvement Advisory Group (BIAG) included representatives from business and industry groups, government, and education (including the ATA).

13 The suggestion that Calgary has a higher level of education than the Canadian average is supported by Statistics Canada 1991 census data, which indicates that the percentage of Calgarians with a university degree was 16.5 per cent compared to 11.3 per cent of all Canadians.

9: The Diversity of 'Producers'

1 Native High School is a pseudonym.

2 Eagleton (1991: 119) defines an organic intellectual as an 'organizer, constructor, "permanent persuader" who actively participates in social life and helps bring to theoretical articulation those positive political currents already contained within it.'

3 Marcia Jensen also mentioned this program from Nova Scotia called 'I Want to be a Millionaire.' It was apparently designed to teach children how to start a business and have them 'thinking in management ways

about learning all of those kinds of skills, of cost-control and profit, and financial reporting, and all kinds of things.' Jensen described the program as 'very sweet' (Interview 30).

4 John Smith was an oil executive who had been a key player in the partnership and science foundations (see Chapter 6).

5 Just as only the largest business organizations could afford to be members of the Conference Board, we can expect that only the largest school boards would be affiliated. It is therefore not surprising that the much larger public board had closer ties to the CB than the Catholic Board in Calgary.

6 At the time, Stephen Murgatroyd was an Athabasca University management professor who was known for his work on total quality management and the need for government restructuring along the lines of Osborne and Gaebler (1993).

7 Eagleton (1991) suggests that strategies for the legitimation of a dominant power include naturalizing such beliefs so as to render them self-evident or inevitable.

8 Gold is probably referring to the Calgary-based group Albertans for Quality Education (AQE).

9 There were 2,498 ESL students and a total of 99,626 students within the CBE in 1996. However, the province's definition of ESL students (for funding purposes) had been challenged by educators and parents of these children as inadequate since it under-represented the numbers of students who needed additional help because English was their second language. For example, the definition did not include Canadian-born children who needed such help and set a limit on the number of years students would be eligible for provincial funding.

10 According to George, Corrections Canada statistics indicated that males born on Indian reserves in Saskatchewan had an 87 per cent chance of being incarcerated in a penitentiary before the age of twenty-three (Interview 10). In the late 1980s, the Assembly of First Nations noted that 'Twenty percent of Aboriginal students complete grade 12, compared to 75 percent for other Canadians' (Advanced Education 1991).

10: Students, Parents, and Community

1 The Calgary Council of Home and Schools Association represents approximately one-quarter of Calgary public schools. There were no representatives from the Catholic system at the time of our interview.

2 As in any city, there are differences between areas of town, partly based on housing costs, etc. Trustee Marcia Jensen notes that the northwest is 'a

very active, educational part of the city ... because of the university and the hospital and [two colleges]' (Interview 30).

3 Chapter 7 notes that Ron Leckie, Andy Laird, and Barbara Phillips all mentioned the above average proportion of students from Academic High School who went on to post-secondary education, as well as the high level of parental support for education.

4 The CCHSA was involved in the Partners in Education coalition (with ATA, CUPE, and CBE Staff Association representatives) described in Chapter 8.

5 Hennessey commented that she sometime felt that the CCHSA acted as a 'Ralph Nader' within the board (Interview 27). She implied that trustees were very influenced by administrators as shown by their 'lack of leadership' in the 1994 budget process undertaken by the board.

6 In her discussion of politics in Britain under Prime Minister John Major, McRobbie (1994: 16) discusses the importance for 'Left' groups to stop seeking 'some central organizing body, some point of unity,' and instead to learn how to live with difference. In the Alberta context, perhaps this represents the main challenge for groups opposed to educational restructuring: to try to accommodate differences in the process of working towards a coherent alternative social vision.

7 Although the CCHSA was a voluntary group, it did receive some funding from the CBE. The AHSCA was funded primarily by the government. Observers from other parent groups note that this has affected the latter group's relationship with government, not surprisingly.

8 David's (1993: 62) description of British educational reforms in the late 1980s parallels part of Rees's comments. She says, '[T]he 1986 Education Act signalled the beginnings of a new, more coherent approach. It set limits to the kind of subjects taught in schools, such as political and peace studies, aspects of multicultural and sex education. In other words, attempts were made to distinguish between education and indoctrination, on lines similar to those set out by a new group of right-wing pamphleteers.'

9 Calvert and Kuehn (1993) explore possible implications of free trade agreements for public education in Canada. The authors suggest that trade agreements encourage the further commercialization of society, and specifically the trend towards privatization of public services such as education.

10 Neither Katherine Hennessey nor Susan Law nor Leslie Pearce had direct experience with partnerships in their children's schools. Therefore, information about initiatives probably came from education staff and publications.

11 It was a coincidence because the case study of the Monarch–Academic High partnership had already been started at the time of Rebecca Rees's interview, and she mentioned it without prompting.

12 Of twenty-six booths set up at the conference, seven advertised private schools four of which were religious-focused, six advertised tutorial services, one was set up by a company selling Christian products, and two provided information on Christian associations. Themes in AQE newsletters focused on consistency between school and family values, discipline, and sex education. Speakers at the conference included a representative from the Association of Independent Schools and Colleges in Alberta.

13 As a postscript, SPE re-emerged in Calgary in 1999 under the name Friends of Public Education, and organized forums during the school board election to raise awareness of issues around education within the context of restructuring. The notion of religious alternative programs in schools also had re-emerged. Several public school boards in Alberta had approved nondenominational Christian programs and others were discussing possibilities with interested parent groups and private Christian schools.

14 Names provided by Jones are not used for ethical reasons, and the AQE membership list was not part of available data. However, it may be predicted that private school operators and service providers were well represented since several booths advertised these organizations and representatives were included as panellists at the AQE's 1994 conference.

15 Of ten charter schools, four were in Calgary, four in the Edmonton area, one in Medicine Hat, and one in Fort McMurray. Program orientations were as follows: gifted and talented (2), traditional/back-to-basics (2), math and science/excellence (2), students at risk (1), ESL (1), learning styles (1), and music (1). See the Alberta Learning website <http://ednet.edc.gov.ab.ca/search/>.

16 As noted in Chapter 5, Alberta Learning Minister Lyle Oberg dismissed the entire CBE board after complaints about dysfunction resulting from serious divisions among trustees. A new board was therefore elected in the fall of 1999. The fact that three of the elected trustees had been active SPEAK members suggests that this group was seen as a legitimate voice for parents.

17 The mother who began PACT notes that parents were coming into schools and doing the work of teachers and aides. As a result, they became more aware of what the work involved and more politicized about the effect of cuts.

11: Alberta and Beyond

1 In 1995 the B.C.-based Fraser Institute released a critical issues bulletin entitled *Alberta Mid-term Report: The Klein Government*, which applauded the government's approach, suggesting that it was a model for other provinces and the federal government to emulate. See website <www.fraserinstitute.ca/publications/critical_issues/1995/alberta/>.

2 The Fraser Institute also promoted the discourse of fiscal restraint by releasing several reports on this topic in the mid-1990s. In September 1999 the Institute released a report promoting school choice through charter schools and voucher programs. See the report at website <www.fraserinstitute.ca/publications/critical_issues/1999/school_choice/>.

3 It will be recalled that Conference Board themes included a focus on educational crisis (based on skills shortage), the need for greater public awareness of the link between education and the economy, the need to develop highly skilled workers particularly in science and technology areas, and the need for partnerships with the private sector.

4 The Alberta Federation of Labour did attempt to develop such a vision, however, in 1997 when it boycotted the government's Growth Summit and organized an alternative summit that included a broader range of labour and community organizations.

5 The government passed legislation allowing for-profit corporations to contract with regional health authorities to provide surgical services in 2000. Talk of the potential privatization of Alberta Treasury branches was also in the news.

6 See OSSTF website <osstf.on.ca/www.issues/tchrtesting/report.htm>.

7 The OQE has argued for charter schools and funding for private schools in Ontario, and appears very similar in orientation to the AQE in Alberta. See OQE website <www.oqe.org/index.html>.

8 Charter schools were promoted by Teachers for Excellence in Education in British Columbia and the Organization for Quality Education in Ontario. In 1996 Joe Freedman prepared a paper on charter schools for an Ontario conference. It argued that the time was right for the introduction of charter school legislation in Ontario.

9 In her presentation to the Alberta Federation of Labour on 30 April 1994, Joanna Beresford of the New Zealand Educational Institute suggested that New Zealand's former finance minister Roger Douglas had been a recent visitor to the province at the invitation of Tory politicians.

10 Dacks, Green, and Trimble (1995: 279) write that the Alberta Federation of Women United for Families is 'an interest group that promotes the

patriarchal division of labour within the family and actively lobbies against childcare, employment equity, and pay equity policies.'

11 If charter schools are seen as part of a move towards a voucher system, the idea that such schools do not require additional funding is interesting to contemplate in light of a voucher feasibility study in the late 1970s in Britain which indicated that the administrative costs would be enormous. According to Chitty (1992), this was a key reason why the idea of vouchers was dropped by the government at that time.

References

Advanced Education. 1991. *The Secondary and Post-Secondary Transition Needs of Native Students*. Report summary. Edmonton: Advanced Education/ Education Interdepartmental Committee on the Transition Needs of Native Students.

Advisory Committee. 1993. *Toward 2000 Together: An Economic Strategy by Albertans for Alberta*. Edmonton: Government of Alberta.

Alberta. 1959. *Report of the Royal Commission on Education in Alberta*. Edmonton.

– 1972. *A Future of Choices, a Choice of Futures: Report of the Commission on Educational Planning*. Edmonton.

– 1991. *Toward 2000 Together*. Edmonton.

– 1995. *Public Accounts 1993–94*. Edmonton: Alberta Treasury.

Alberta Chamber of Resources (ACR) and Alberta Education. 1991. *International Comparisons in Education: Curriculum, Values and Lessons*. Edmonton: Alberta Chamber of Resources.

Alberta Economic Development. March 2000. *Facts on Alberta*. Edmonton.

Alberta Education. 1977. *Alberta Education and Diploma Requirements: A Discussion Paper Prepared for the Curriculum Policies Board*. Edmonton.

– 1991. *Vision for the Nineties: A Plan of Action*. Edmonton.

– 1992. *Achieving the Vision: 1991 Report*. Edmonton.

– 1993a. *Achieving the Vision: 1992 Report*. Edmonton.

– 1993b. *Tough Choices: A Progress Report*. Edmonton.

– 1993c. *Meeting the Challenge: An Education Roundtable*. Edmonton.

– 1993d. *Meeting the Challenge: What We Heard*. Edmonton.

– 1994. *Meeting the Challenge: Three-Year Business Plan*. Edmonton.

– 1995. *Accountability in Education*. A discussion paper prepared by the MLA team on education accountability. Edmonton.

– 1996a. *Framework for Enhancing Business Involvement in Education*. Edmonton.

– 1996b. *Framework for Technology Integration in Education*. Edmonton.

– 1998. *A Collaborative Learning Community: CBE Review*. Edmonton.

Alberta Teachers Association. 1993a. *Challenging the View: A Public Roundtable Workbook*. Edmonton.

– 1993b. *Trying to Teach*. Edmonton.

– 1994. *Trying to Teach: Necessary Conditions*. Edmonton.

– 1995. *A Framework for Educational Change in Alberta*. Edmonton.

Albertans for Quality Education. 1993. Position paper presented to Government of Alberta Education Roundtable.

Alberts, Sheldon, and Anthony Johnson. 1994. Ex-Minister Quits Tories in Protest. *Calgary Herald*, 21 May, A1.

Angus Reid. 1994. *Public Education in Alberta: Assessing Proposed Changes*: Angus Reid Group, Inc.

Apple, Michael. 1986. *Teachers and Texts*. New York: Routledge.

– 1993. *Official Knowledge*. New York: Routledge.

Archer, Keith, and Roger Gibbins. 1997. What Do Albertans Think? The Klein Agenda on the Public Opinion Landscape. In *A Government Reinvented: A Study of Alberta's Deficit Elimination Program*, ed. C. Bruce, R. Kneebone, and K. McKenzie. Toronto: Oxford.

Aronowitz, Stanley. 1997. A Different Perspective on Educational Inequality. In *Education and Cultural Studies*, ed. H. Giroux and P. Shannon. New York: Routledge.

Ball, Stephen. 1987. *The Micro-Politics of the School*. London: Methuen.

– 1990. *Politics and Policy Making in Education*. London: Routledge.

– 1993. Education, Markets, Choice and Social Class: The Market as a Class Strategy in the UK and the US. *British Journal of Sociology* 14 (1): 3–19.

Barlow, Maude, and Heather Jane Robertson. 1994. *Class Warfare*. Toronto: Key Porter.

Bascia, Nina. 1998. Changing Roles for Teachers' Federations. *Orbit* 29 (1): 37–40.

Becker, Gary. 1964. *Human Capital*. New York: National Bureau of Economic Research.

Bell, Daniel. 1973. *The Coming of Post-industrial Society*. New York: Basic Books.

Blackmore, Jill. 1997. The Gendering of Skill and Vocationalism in Twentieth-Century Australian Education. In *Education: Culture, Economy, Society*, ed. A. Halsey, H. Lauder, P. Brown, and A. Wells. Oxford: Oxford University Press.

Bloom, Michael. 1991. Reaching for Success: Business and Education Working Together. In *Conference Report of the Second National Conference on Business-Education Partnership* (Report 77–91–E/F). Ottawa: Conference Board of Canada.

– 1993. *Evaluating Business-Education Collaboration: Value Assessment Process* (Report 104–93). April. Ottawa: Conference Board of Canada.

– 1994. *Enhancing Employability Skills: Innovative Partnerships, Projects and Programs*. Ottawa: Conference Board of Canada.

Bosetti, Lynn. 1990. *Career and Life Management: A Case Study of Curriculum Implementation in Alberta*. Ph.D. diss., University of Alberta.

Bowe, Richard, Stephen Ball, and Anne Gold. 1992. *Reforming Education and Changing Schools*. London: Routledge.

Brown, Phillip. 1990. The 'Third Wave': Education and the Idea of Parentocracy. *British Journal of Sociology of Education* 11 (1): 65–85.

Brown, Phillip, and Hugh Lauder. 1992. Education, Economy and Society: An Introduction to a New Agenda. In *Education for Economic Survival*, ed. P. Brown and H. Lauder. London: Routledge.

Bruce, Christopher, Ronald Kneebone, and Kenneth McKenzie, eds. 1997. *A Government Reinvented: A Study of Alberta's Deficit Elimination Program*. Toronto: Oxford.

Bruce, Christopher, and Arthur Schwartz. 1997. Education: Meeting the Challenge. In *A Government Reinvented: A Study of Alberta's Deficit Elimination Program*, ed. C. Bruce, R. Kneebone and K. McKenzie. Toronto: Oxford.

Calgary Board of Education. 1991. *Partnerships Handbook*. Calgary.

– 1993. Partnerships: How They Make a Difference. *1992/93 Annual Report*. Calgary.

Calgary Chamber of Commerce. 1994. Calgarians among the Nation's Leading Technocrats. *Calgary Commerce* 26 (5): 25–6.

Calgary Human Resources Development Centre. 1993. *What Are the Jobs for the Future?*, May.

Calvert, John, and Larry Kuehn. 1993. *Pandora's Box: Corporate Power, Free Trade and Canadian Education*. Toronto: Our Schools/Our Selves.

Canada. 1991. *Learning Well ... Living Well*, 51, 53. Ottawa: Minister of Supply and Services.

– 1993. *The Prosperity Action Plan: A Progress Report*. Ottawa.

Canada West Foundation (CWF). 1993. *The Red Ink: Alberta's Deficit, Debt and Economic Future*. Calgary: Canada West Foundation.

Canadian Centre for Policy Alternatives (CCPA). 1992. *The Deficit Made Me Do It*. Ottawa.

– 1993. *Bleeding the Patient: The Debt/Deficit Hoax Exposed*. Ottawa.

Canadian Chamber of Commerce. 1990. *Business-Education Partnerships: Your Planning Process Guide*. April. Toronto.

Centre for Contemporary Cultural Studies (CCCS). 1981. *Unpopular Education: Schooling and Social Democracy in Britain since 1944*. London: Hutchinson.

Chambers, Edward. 1998. *Alberta's Labour Force and Employment Structure over the Last Quarter Century: Assessing the Changes*. Edmonton: Western Centre for Economic Research.

Cheal, John. 1963. *Investment in Canadian Youth*. Toronto: Macmillan.

Chitty, Clyde. 1992. *The Education System Reformed*. Manchester: Baseline.

Chubb, John, and Terry Moe. 1990. *Politics, Markets and America's Schools*. Washington: Brookings Institute.

Clement, Wallace, and John Myles. 1994. *Relations of Ruling*. Montreal: McGill-Queen's University Press.

Cockburn, Cynthia. 1985. *Machinery of Dominance: Women, Men and Technical Know-How*. London: Pluto Press.

Collins, Ron. 1994. School Board Tries to Save Jobs. *Calgary Herald*, 9 March.

Commission on Educational Planning. 1972. *The Worth Report: A Choice of Futures*. Edmonton: Queen's Printer for the Province of Alberta.

Connell, R.W., D.J. Ashendon, S. Kessler, and G.W. Dowsett. 1982. *Making the Difference*. North Sydney: Allen & Unwin.

Cooper, David, and Dean Neu. 1995. The Politics of Debt and Deficit in Alberta. In *The Trojan Horse: Ralph Klein's Alberta and the Future of Canada*, ed. G. Laxer and T. Harrison. Toronto: Black Rose.

CUPE 474. 1994. *Privatizing Schools: In The Public Interest?* Edmonton.

Curtis, Bruce., D.W. Livingstone, and Harry Smaller. 1992. *Stacking the Deck: The Streaming of Working Class Kids in Ontario Schools*. Toronto: Our Schools/Our Selves.

Dabbs, Frank. 1995. *Ralph Klein: A Maverick Life*. Vancouver: Greystone Books.

Dacks, Gursten. 1986. From Consensus to Competition: Social Democracy and Political Culture in Alberta. In *Socialism and Democracy in Alberta*, ed. L. Pratt. Edmonton: NeWest.

Dacks, Gursten, Joyce Green, and Linda Trimble. 1995. Roadkill: Women in Alberta's Drive for Deficit Elimination. In *The Trojan Horse: Ralph Klein's Alberta and the Future of Canada*, ed. T. Harrison and G. Laxer. Toronto: Black Rose.

Dale, Roger, and Jenny Ozga. 1993. Two Hemispheres – Both 'New Right'?: 1980s Education Reform in New Zealand and England and Wales. In *Schooling Reform in Hard Times*, ed. B. Lingard, J. Knight, and P. Porter. London: Falmer.

David, Miriam. 1980. *The State, the Family and Education*. London: Routledge and Kegan Paul.

– 1993. *Parents, Gender, and Educational Reform*. Cambridge: Polity Press.

David, Miriam, Anne West, and Jane Ribbens. 1994. *Mother's Intuition? Choosing Secondary Schools*. London: Falmer.

Deaton, Rick. 1973. The Fiscal Crisis of the State. In *The Political Economy of the State*, ed. D. Roussopoulos. Montreal: Black Rose.

Decore, Anne-Marie, and Raj Pannu. 1991. Alberta Political Economy in Crisis: Whither Education? In *Hitting the Books: The Politics of Educational Retrenchment*, ed. T. Wotherspoon. Toronto: Garamond.

Dehli, Kari. 1993. Subject to the New Global Economy: Power and Positioning in Ontario Labour Market Policy Formation. *Studies in Political Economy* (41): 83–110.

– 1996. Travelling Tales: Education Reform and Parental 'Choice' in Postmodern Times. *Journal of Education Policy* 11 (1): 75–88.

– 1998. Shopping for Schools: The Future of Education in Ontario? *Orbit* 29 (1): 29–33.

Dei, George. 1993. Narrative Discourses of Black/African-Canadian Parents and the Canadian Public School System. *Canadian Ethnic Studies* 25 (3): 45–65.

Dempster, Lisa. 1994. Inner Circle Redraws Classroom. *Calgary Herald*, 11 February, A14.

– 1994. Teachers in Tough Spot. *Calgary Herald*, 12 April, B2.

– 1994. Catholics Plan to Battle Tax Plan. *Calgary Herald*, 14 April, B3.

– 1994. Teachers Reject Wage Rollback. *Calgary Herald*, 13 May, A1–2.

– 1994. Parents to Hear Pitch. *Calgary Herald*, 4 October, A8.

– 1995. Education Gets Down to Business. *Calgary Herald*, 14 March.

– 1995. Rainy Day Fund to be Spent. *Calgary Herald*, 11 April, B1.

Dempster, Lisa, and Allyson Jeffs. 1994. Boards to Launch Lawsuit. *Calgary Herald*, 27 May, B3.

Dickerson, Mark, and Greg Flanagan. 1995. The Unique Fiscal Situation in Alberta: Can Alberta's Deficit Reduction Model Be Exported? Paper presented at a meeting of the Economic Association of Canada, Learned Societies Conference. Montreal.

Dobbin, Murray. 1997. Charting a Course to Social Division. *Our Schools / Our Selves* 8 (3): 48–82.

Dougherty, Kevin, and Lizabeth Sostre. 1992. Minerva and the Market: Sources of the Movement for School Choice. In *The Choice Controversy*, ed. P. Cookson. Newbury Park: Corwin.

Douglas, Roger. 1993. *Unfinished Business*. New Zealand: Random House.

Drugge, Sten. 1995. The Alberta Tax Advantage: Myth and Reality. In *The Trojan Horse: Ralph Klein's Alberta and the Future of Canada*, ed. G. Laxer and T. Harrison. Toronto: Black Rose.

Dunning, Paula. 1997. Education in Canada: An Overview. Toronto: Canadian Education Association.

Eagleton, Terry. 1991. *Ideology*. London: Verso.

Economic Council of Canada (ECC). 1991. *Employment in the Service Economy*. Ottawa: Minister of Supply and Services.

– 1992. *A Lot to Learn: Education and Training in Canada*. Ottawa: Minister of Supply and Services.

Ehrenreich, Barbara. 1989. *Fear of Falling*. New York: Harper Collins.

Evans, Judith. 1999. Board Games: The New (But Old) Rules. In *Contested Classrooms*, ed. T. Harrison and J. Kachur. Edmonton: University of Alberta Press and Parkland Institute.

Farrar, Eleanor, and Anthony Cipillone. 1988. After the Signing: The Boston Compact 1982 to 1985. In *American Business and the Public School*, ed. M. Levine and R. Trachtman. New York: Teachers College Press.

Feschuk, Scott, and Miro Cernetig. 1995. Klein Keeps Cutting His Own Budget Trail. *Globe and Mail*, 21 February, A1, A7.

Fine, Michelle. 1993. [Ap]parent Involvement: Reflections on Parents, Power, and Urban Public Schools. *Teachers College Record* 94 (4): 683–710.

Flower, David. 1994. Review of Unfinished Business. *ATA News*, February.

Fraser Institute. 1995. *Alberta Mid-term Report: The Klein Government Critical Issues Bulletin*. www.fraserinstitute.ca/publications/critical-issues/1995/Alberta

Freedman, Joe. 1993. *Failing Grades: Canadian Schooling in a Global Economy*. Text of videotape. Red Deer: Society for Advancing Educational Research.

Froese-Germain, Bernie, and Marita Moll. 1997. Business Partnerships a Troubling Trend. *CCPA Education Monitor*, summer.

Fund, John. 1995. Learning from Canada's Reagan. *Wall Street Journal*, 23 February, A14.

Galvin, Patrick. 1996. School-Business-University Collaboratives: The Economics of Organizational Choice. In *Coordination among Schools, Families and Communities*, ed. J. Cibulka and W. Kritek. New York: SUNY.

Gammage, Philip, and Jennifer Little. 1994. Alberta Must Learn from Britain's Disaster. *ATA News*, 22 March.

Gariepi, Raymond. 1994. When the Centre Will not Hold. *ATA News*, March.

Gaskell, Jane. 1987. Gender and Skill. In *Critical Pedagogy and Cultural Power*, ed. D. Livingstone et al. Toronto: Garamond.

– 1992. *Gender Matters from School to Work*. Toronto: OISE Press.

Gitlin, Andrew. 1983. School Structure and Teachers' Work. In *Ideology and Practice in Schooling*, ed. M. Apple and L. Weis. Philadelphia: Temple University Press.

Gramsci, Antonio. 1971. *Selections from the Prison Notebooks*, ed. Q. Hoare, trans. G. Nowell Smith. New York: International Publishers.

Gregor, Kevin. 1994. The Need to Improve Our Educational System. *Calgary Commerce* 27 (6): 35.

Hall, Stuart. 1988. *The Hard Road to Renewal: Thatcherism and the Crisis of the Left*. London: Verso.

– 1996a. Gramsci's Relevance for the Study of Race and Ethnicity. In *Stuart Hall: Critical Dialogues in Cultural Studies*, ed. D. Morley and K.-H. Chen. London: Routledge.

– 1996b. The Problem of Ideology: Marxism without Guarantees. In *Stuart Hall: Critical Dialogues in Cultural Studies*, ed. D. Morley and K. H. Chen. London: Routledge.

Hargreaves, Andy. 1998. Teachers' Role in Renewal. *Orbit* 29 (1): 10–13.

Harp, John, and Gordon Betcherman. 1980. Contradictory Class Locations and Class Action. *Canadian Journal of Sociology* 5 (2): 145–62.

Harrison, Trevor, and Gordon Laxer. 1995. Introduction. In *The Trojan Horse: Ralph Klein's Alberta and the Future of Canada*, ed. T. Harrison and G. Laxer. Montreal: Black Rose.

Henry, Frances, and Effie Ginzberg. 1988. Racial Discrimination in Employment. In *Social Inequality in Canada: Patterns, Problems, Policies*, ed. J. Curtis, E. Grabb, N. Guppy, and S. Gilbert. Scarborough: Prentice Hall.

Hiebert, Brian, and Garry Tanner. 1995. *Student Employability Skills Portfolio Project Evaluation Report*. Calgary: Faculty of Education, University of Calgary.

Hunter, Floyd. 1963. *Community Power Structures*. New York: Anchor.

Johnson, Anthony. 1990. Public School Head Backs Business Links. *Calgary Herald*, 17 May.

Kach, Nick. 1992. The Emergence of Progressive Education in Alberta. In *Exploring Our Educational Past*, ed. N. Kach and K. Mazurek. Calgary: Detselig.

Kach, Nick, and Kas Mazurek, eds. 1992. *Exploring Our Educational Past*. Calgary: Detselig.

Kachur, Jerrold. 1994. Hegemony and Anonymous Intellectual Practice. Ph.D. diss., University of Alberta.

Kaulback, Camilla, and Keith McKay. 1993. Closing the Deal: Schools and Business Partnerships. In *Partnerships in Education: Trends and Opportunities*, ed. L. Bosetti, C. Webber, and F. Johnson. Calgary: Faculty of Education, University of Calgary.

King, Alan, and M. J. Peart. 1992. *Teachers in Canada: Their Work and Quality of Life: A Study for the Canadian Teachers' Federation.* Ottawa: CTF.

Klein, Ralph. 1993. *Seizing Opportunity: Alberta's New Economic Development Strategy.* Edmonton: Government of Alberta.

Kneebone, Ronald, and Kenneth McKenzie. 1997. The Process behind Institutional Reform in Alberta. In *A Government Reinvented: A Study of Alberta's Deficit Elimination Program,* ed. C. Bruce, R. Kneebone, and K. McKenzie. Toronto: Oxford.

Lafleur, Brenda. 1992. *Dropping Out: The Cost to Canada (Synopsis).* May. Ottawa: Conference Board of Canada.

Laird, Gordon. 1998. *Slumming It at the Rodeo: The Cultural Roots of Canada's Right-Wing Revolution.* Vancouver: Douglas & McIntyre.

Larrain, Jorge. 1996. Stuart Hall and the Marxist Concept of Ideology. In *Stuart Hall: Critical Dialogues in Cultural Studies,* ed. D. Morely and K.H. Chen. London: Routledge.

Leithwood, Kenneth. 1998. Educational Governance and Student Achievement. *Orbit* 29 (1): 34–7.

Levin, Benjamin. 1997. The Lessons of International Education Reform. *Journal of Education Policy* 12 (4): 253–66.

Lies, Valerie, and David Bergholz. 1988. The Public Education Fund. In *American Business and the Public School,* ed. M. Levine and R. Trachtman. New York: Teachers College Press.

Lisac, Mark. 1995. *The Klein Revolution.* Edmonton: NeWest.

Livingstone, D. W. 1983. *Class Ideologies and Educational Futures.* Sussex: Falmer Press.

– 1987. Job Skills and Schooling: A Class Analysis of Entry Requirements and Underemployment. *Canadian Journal of Education* 12 (1): 1–29.

– 1999. *The Education-Jobs Gap.* Toronto: Garamond.

Mackay, Bauni. 1994. Teachers Must Uphold and Defend the Profession. *ATA News.* March/April.

Mackay, Bauni, and David Flower. 1999. *Public Education: The Passion and the Politics.* Edmonton: Authors.

McLaughlin, Mary Ann. 1992. *Employability Skills: What Are Employers Looking For?* (Report 81–92E). April. Ottawa: Conference Board of Canada.

McMillan, Melville. 1996. Leading the Way or Missing the Mark? The Klein Government's Fiscal Plan. Information Bulletin No. 37. Edmonton: Western Centre for Economic Research.

McMillan, Melville, and Allan Warrack. 1993. *Alberta's Fiscal Situation:*

Identifying the Problem, Looking for Solutions. Information Bulletin no. 14. Edmonton: Western Centre for Economic Research.

– 1995. Alberta's Fiscal Update: One-Track (Thinking) towards Deficit Reduction. In *The Trojan Horse: Ralph Klein's Alberta and the Future of Canada,* ed. G. Laxer and T. Harrison. Toronto: Black Rose.

McQuaig, Linda. 1995. *Shooting the Hippo.* Toronto: Penguin.

McRobbie, Angela. 1994. The Tories Bedevilled. *New Left Review* 203: 107–16.

Mansell, Robert. 1997. Fiscal Restructuring in Alberta: An Overview. In *A Government Reinvented: A Study of Alberta's Deficit Elimination Program,* ed. C. Bruce, R. Kneebone, and K. McKenzie. Toronto: Oxford.

Martell, George. 1995. *A New Education Politics: Bob Rae's Legacy and the Response of the Ontario Secondary School Teachers' Federation.* Toronto: Our Schools / Our Selves.

Martin, Don. 1994. Education Revolution Doesn't Add Up. *Calgary Herald,* 19 January, A3.

Mazurek, Kas. 1999. Passing Fancies: Educational Changes in Alberta. In *Contested Classrooms,* ed. T. Harrison and J. Kachur. Edmonton: University of Alberta Press and Parkland Institute.

Meanwell, Richard, and Gail Barrington. 1991. *Senior Executive Views on Education in Alberta.* Prepared by the Alberta Management Group and Gail V. Barrington and Associates for Alberta Education.

Mills, C.W. 1956. *The Power Elite.* New York: Oxford University Press.

Moore, M. Patricia. 1994. *Future Jobs Calgary: Labour Market Development Strategies (summary).* Presented to Calgary Canada Employment Centres by Sobeco, Ernst, and Young.

Morrison, Terrence. 1974. Reform as Social Tracking: The Case of Industrial Education in Ontario 1870–1900. *Journal of Educational Thought* 8 (2): 87–110.

Morrow, Raymond, and Carlos Torres. 1995. *Social Theory and Education.* New York: SUNY.

Neu, Dean. 1999. Re-Investment Fables: Educational Finances in Alberta. In *Contested Classrooms,* ed. T. Harrison and J. Kachur. Edmonton: University of Alberta Press and Parkland Institute.

Newman, Peter C. 1998. *Titans: How the Canadian Establishment Seized Power.* Toronto: Penguin.

Nikiforuk, Andrew. 1993. *School's Out: The Catastrophe in Public Education and What We Can Do about It.* Toronto: Macfarlane Walter & Ross.

Noble, Douglas. 1997. Let Them Eat Skills. In *Education and Cultural Studies,* ed. H. Giroux and P. Shannon. New York: Routledge.

OECD, and the Centre for Educational Research and Innovation. 1992. *Schools and Business: A New Partnership.* Paris: OECD.

OFL. 1990. *Report of the Premier's Council on Education, Training and Adjustment: Comment and Review.* Toronto: Ontario Federation of Labour.

Osborne, David, and Ted Gaebler. 1992. *Reinventing Government.* New York: Plume.

Pal, Leslie. 1997. *Beyond Policy Analysis.* Scarborough, Ont.: International Thomson Publishing.

Palmer, Brian. 1995. Capitalism Comes to Napanee High. *Our Schools/ Our Selves* 6 (3): 14–41.

Pannu, Raj, Daniel Schugurensky, and Donovan Plumb. 1994. From the Autonomous to the Reactive University: Global Restructuring and the Re-Forming of Higher Education. In *Sociology of Education in Canada*, ed. L. Erwin and D. MacLennan. Toronto: Copp Clark.

Pascal, Charles. 1998. Overview. *Orbit* 29 (1): 4–6.

Peters, Frank. 1999. Deep and Brutal: Funding Cuts to Education in Alberta. In *Contested Classrooms*, ed. T. Harrison and J. Kachur. Edmonton: University of Alberta Press and Parkland Institute.

Pommer, Dave. 1994. 'We Are Seen as a Threat Because We Are Questioning,' Says ATA. *Calgary Herald*, 11 February, A15.

Ray, Carol, and Roslyn Mickelson. 1993. Restructuring Students for Restructured Work: The Economy, School Reform, and Non-College-Bound Youths. *Sociology of Education* 66 (1): 1–20.

Robertson, Heather Jane. 1998. *No More Teachers, No More Books.* Toronto: McClelland & Stewart.

Robertson, Heather Jane, and Maude Barlow. 1995. Restructuring from the Right: School Reform in Alberta. In *The Trojan Horse: Ralph Klein's Alberta and the Future of Canada*, ed. G. Laxer and T. Harrison. Toronto: Black Rose.

Seccareccia, Mario. 1995. Keynes and the Debt Questions. *Studies in Political Economy* (46): 43–78.

Seccombe, Wally, and D. W. Livingstone. 1996. 'Down to Earth People': Revisiting a Materialist Understanding of Group Consciousness. In *Recast Dreams: Class and Gender Consciousness in Steeltown*, ed. D. Livingstone and M. Mangan. Toronto: Garamond.

Shaker, Erika. 1998. Corporate Content: Inside and outside the Classroom. In *Education, Limited.* Ottawa: Canadian Centre for Policy Alternatives.

Shapiro, Svi. 1990. *Between Capitalism and Democracy: Educational Policy and the Crisis of the Welfare State.* New York: Bergin & Garvey.

– 1998. Clinton and Education: Policies without Meaning. In *Critical Social Issues in American Education*, ed. S. Shapiro and D. Purpel. Mahwah: Lawrence Erlbaum.

Shor, Ira. 1986. *Culture Wars.* New York: Routledge & Kegan Paul.

Simpson, Don, and Carol Sissons. 1989. Entrepreneurs in Education. Ottawa: International Development Research Centre.

Slaughter, Sheila. 1990. *The Higher Learning and High Technology*. New York: SUNY.

Souque, Jean-Pascal. 1994, April. *Matching Education to the Needs of Society: Canadian Voices on a Vision for Schools*. Working paper. Ottawa: Conference Board of Canada.

Spaull, Andrew. 1996. Slash, Burn and Resistance: Fight and Flight for Teachers in Victoria, Australia. In *Teacher Activism in the 1990s*, ed. S. Robertson and H. Smaller. Toronto: Our Schools/Our Selves.

Steering Group on Prosperity. 1992. *Inventing Our Future: An Action Plan for Canada's Prosperity*. Ottawa.

Steinberg, Ronnie. 1990. Social Construction of Skill: Gender, Power and Comparable Worth. *Work and Occupations* 17(4): 449–82.

Stemmer, Paul, Bill Brown, and Catherine Smith. 1992. The Employability Skills Portfolio. *Educational Leadership* 49 (6): 32–5.

Strinati, Dominic. 1995. *An Introduction to Theories of Popular Culture*. London: Routledge.

Taft, Kevin. 1997. *Shredding the Public Interest*. Edmonton: University of Alberta Press and Parkland Institute.

Taylor, Alison. 1997. Education for Industrial and 'Post-Industrial' Purposes. *Educational Policy* 11 (1): 3–40.

– 1998a. 'Courting Business': The Rhetoric and Practices of School-Business Partnerships. *Journal of Education Policy* 13 (3): 395–422.

– 1998b. Employability Skills: From Corporate 'Wish List' to Government Policy. *Journal of Curriculum Studies* 30 (2): 143–64.

– 2000. 'Spitting in the Wind?': The Demise of a School-Business Partnership. *International Journal of Educational Development* 20 (2): 153–75.

Trebilcock, Michael. 1997. Comments on Chapter Five. In *A Government Reinvented: A Study of Alberta's Deficit Elimination Program*, ed. C. Bruce, R. Kneebone, and K. McKenzie. Toronto: Oxford.

Troyna, Barry, and Bruce Carrington. 1990. *Education, Racism and Reform*. London: Routledge.

Useem, Elizabeth. 1986. *Low Technology Education in a High Tech World*. New York: Free Press.

Useem, Michael. 1980. Corporations and the Corporate Elite. *Annual Review of Sociology* (6): 41–77.

Veltmeyer, Henry. 1987. *Canadian Corporate Power*. Toronto: Garamond.

Vermaeten, Arndt, W. Irwin Gillespie, and Frank Vermaeten. 1995. Who Paid the Taxes in Canada, 1951–1988? *Canadian Public Policy* 21 (3): 317–43.

Vicars, Maryhelen. 1993. New Faces on the Block. *Worksight Magazine.*

Wagner, Michael. 1998. The Progressive Conservative Government and Education Policy in Alberta: Leadership and Continuity. Ph.D. diss., University of Alberta.

Wajcman, Judy. 1991. Patriarchy, Technology and Conceptions of Skill. *Work and Occupations* 18 (1): 29–45.

Watson, Susan. 1999. Equity as a Rationale for the Introduction of School Choice: An Examination of the Dynamics of Class, Race and Gender. Paper presented at the American Educational Research Association.

Watt, David, and Hetty Roessingh. 1994. ESL Drop Out: The Myth of Educational Equity. *Alberta Journal of Educational Research* 40 (3): 283–96.

Whitty, Geoff, Sally Power, and David Halpin. 1998. *Devolution and Choice in Education.* Buckingham: Open University Press.

Williams, Raymond. 1997. *Marxism and Literature.* Oxford: Oxford University Press.

Wilson, L. J. Roy. 1992. Rural Equality. In *Exploring Our Educational Past,* ed. N. Kach and K. Mazurek. Calgary: Detselig.

Winn, Conrad. 1988. The Socio-Economic Attainment of Visible Minorities: Facts and Policy Implications. In *Social Inequality in Canada: Patterns, Problems, Policies,* ed. J. Curtis, E. Grabb, N. Guppy, and S. Gilbert. Scarborough: Prentice Hall.

Winter, James. 1992. *Common Cents.* Montreal: Black Rose.

Wotherspoon, Terry. 1991. Educational Reorganization and Retrenchment. In *Hitting the Books: The Politics of Educational Retrenchment,* ed. T. Wotherspoon. Toronto: Garamond.

Yanitski, Norm, and David Pysyk. 1999. The Principalship at the Crossroads. In *Contested Classrooms,* ed. T. Harrison and J. Kachur. Edmonton: University of Alberta and Parkland Institute.

Young, Beth. In press. 'The Alberta Advantage': DeKleining Career Prospects for Alberta's Women Educators? In *Women and School Leadership: International Perspectives,* ed. C. Reynolds. Albany: SUNY.

– 1999b. Is It Just a Matter of Time? Part-Time Teaching Employment in Alberta. In *Contested Classrooms,* ed. T. Harrison and J. Kachur. Edmonton: University of Alberta Press and Parkland Institute.

Index

A Lot to Learn (ECC), 38–9, 56–7, 83, 92

Academic High School, 142–54, 223–9, 235, 268–9

Alberta Association of Social Workers, 60

Alberta Chamber of Commerce, 98, 121–3, 183–4, 286

Alberta Chamber of Resources (ACR), 28, 32–3, 42, 68, 87, 101–4, 130, 286; Careers: The Next Generation (CNG), 32–3, 104, 130

Alberta Economic Development Authority, 63

Alberta Education, x, 12–14, 26, 28, 64–72, 75, 77–8, 89–92, 97–8, 125–6

Alberta Federation of Labour (AFL), 169, 176, 179, 194

Alberta Federation of Women United for Families, 300

Alberta Home and School Councils' Association (AHSCA), 75–6, 105, 243

Alberta Learning, 51

Alberta School Boards Association (ASBA), 78

Alberta Teachers' Association (ATA), 8, 75–7, 79–80, 84–6, 105–6, 133–4, 168–87, 195, 197, 199–203, 226, 293, 307–8

Alberta Union of Public Employees (AUPE), 141, 169, 176

Albertans for Quality Education (AQE), 14, 22–6, 31–2, 87, 95, 216, 243, 257, 260–3, 273–84, 286, 300–1

Alberts and Johnson, 77

American Institute for Managing Diversity, 49

Angus Reid, 78, 81–2, 92–3

Annual Report on Partnerships, 1992/93, 136

Apple, Michael, 170, 174, 230, 275, 282, 300, 304

Archer and Gibbins, 82, 88

ATA News, 198

Australia, 237

Baldwin, Gary, 100, 102–4, 106–8, 110–13, 116, 120, 235, 288; corporate partnership with public school, 154–7, 159, 161–2, 165

Ball, Stephen, 25–6, 54–5, 204, 236, 261–2, 277–8, 282, 303–4

Banff Centre for Management, 59

Bank of Montreal, 80

Bank of Nova Scotia, 31

Barlow, Maude, 23, 29, 44, 95, 242, 258
Bascia, Nina, 201
Becker, Gary, 26–7
Bell, Daniel, 24
Bergholz, David, 123
Black, Donna, 134–5, 138–41, 185, 205–6
Blackmore, Jill, 236–7
Bloom, Michael, 43, 48
Borger, Tracey, 136–9, 140, 185, 205–6, 213–16, 219, 224, 234
Bowe, Richard, 54–5
Britain, 5, 8–9, 22, 39, 94, 97–8, 193, 204, 236, 243, 262, 277–8, 296–9, 301–4
British Columbia, 24
Brookings Institute, 38
Brown, Phillip, 155, 221
Bruce, Christopher, 83, 92
Bush, George: National Education Strategy, 39
Business Council on National Issues (BCNI), 36, 287
Business-Higher Education Forum (BHEF), 37, 44, 137, 209–10
Business Roundtable on Education, 97

Calgary Board of Education (CBE), 34, 76–81, 134–6, 140, 168, 169, 182, 206–23
Calgary Catholic School District (CCSD), 136–9, 141, 214
Calgary Chamber of Commerce (CCC), 103, 113, 135, 183–4, 214–15
Calgary Civil Liberties Association, 275
Calgary Commerce, 118
Calgary Council of Home and Schools Association (CCHSA), 175, 243, 251–4, 260–1

Calgary District Labour Council (CDLC), 169, 174–5
Calgary Herald, 22, 74–81, 135–6, 139, 181, 286
Calgary Human Resources Development Centre, 118
Calgary Public Teachers, 174–5, 182–4
Calvert, John, 258
Cameron Report, 21
Campbell, Florence, 46–7
Canada: federal government, education policy, 53–8, 132–3; Prosperity Initiative, 11–12, 40, 55, 60, 62, 69, 87
Canada West Foundation (CWF), 17–20, 32, 59, 93, 286–7
Canadian Centre for Policy Alternatives (CCPA), 18–19, 20, 115, 190
Canadian Chamber of Commerce, 47, 97
Canadian Foundation for Economic Education (CFEE), 36
Canadian Labour Force Development Board (CLFDB), 192
Canadian Taxpayers' Federation, 300
Canadian Teachers' Federation (CTF), 44, 169, 172, 195–7, 202
Canadian Union of Public Employees (CUPE), 79, 168–9, 174, 177–8
Carrington, Bruce, 187
Centre for Contemporary Cultural Studies (CCCS), 4–5, 34
Challenging the View (ATA), 84–6
Charter schools, 80–1, 91, 125, 199, 261, 280, 293, 296, 303
Cheal, John, 27
Child Poverty Group, 85
Chitty, Clyde, 298–9, 302
Chubb, John, 38–9, 42, 197–8, 279, 302

Class Warfare (Barlow and Robertson), 23, 95

Collins, Ron, 77–8

Community Power Structures, 128

Conference Board of Canada, ix, 87, 5–6, 11, 28, 33–51, 97, 100–4, 119–20, 209–10, 273, 286–7, 289; relationship with teachers, 185–7, 196–7; Corporate Council on Education (CCE), 34, 36, 41, 43, 45–6; National Business and Education Centre (NBEC), 36; National Council on Education (NCE), 36–9, 41–2, 46, 119–20; 'value assessment process' (VAP), 42–3, 45–6, 49–50

Connell, R.W., 311

Conway, Pam, 168–9, 177–8, 182, 199–200, 222

Corporate-Higher Education Forum (CHEF), 36–7

Coulter, Don, 244, 251–6, 260–2, 270–2

Council of Ministers of Education, Canada (CMEC), 40, 57

Curtis, Bruce, 310

Dabbs, Frank, 70

Dacks, Gursten, 231–2

Dale, Roger, 299

David, Miriam, 220, 243, 251, 304

Day, Stockwell, 96, 300

Deaton, Rick, 19

Decore, Anne-Marie, 180

Dehli, Kari, 251

Dei, George, 267

Dempster, Lisa, 74–5, 78–80

Dickerson, Mark, 63

Dinning, Jim, 37, 66, 71, 76, 88, 96, 124, 126, 286

Discourse on educational restructuring: the dissatisfied employer, 11, 26–32, 40–3, 109–15, 289–90; education for economic prosperity, 256, 265–73, 288–9, 304; fiscal crisis of the state, 11, 16–21, 31–2, 42–3, 88, 109–10, 190, 288–9, 294–5; the unhappy parent, 11, 15, 21–6, 30–2, 42, 256, 260–5, 273, 281–4, 289–90, 294

Dixon, Rhonda, 244, 275

Dougherty, Kevin, 302

Douglas, Roger, 93

Drouin, Marie-Josee, 53–4

Drucker, Peter, 7

Eagleton, 164

Economic Council of Canada (ECC), 38, 41–2, 56–7

Economy, Alberta, 62–4

Edison Schools Inc., 10

Edmonton Raging Grannies, 167, 274

Edmonton School Councils, 283

Education: restructuring of, 8, 73–96; Amended School Act (Bill 19), 78–9, 242–3; business, role of corporations, 5, 7, 12–13, 28, 30–1, 98–166, 208–16, 234–41, 268–73, 286–7; 'business-in-education' network, 98–105, 129–30; effects of, 92–6; government-sponsored roundtables, 82–7, 179, 217; international, 7–11, 295–304; partnership programs, 13, 119–66; women, 232. *See also* Conference Board of Canada

Ellis, Nancy, 169, 174–5, 177, 180–7, 197–8, 200, 205

Elton, David, 17–18

Emily Murphy School, 156, 158–63, 237

England. *See* Britain

ESL, 231–4, 236, 239–40, 252–3, 262, 264, 267

Facts in Alberta, 167–8
Failing Grades (Freedman), 31, 289
Farrell, Joan, 169, 176, 178–9, 190
Fine, Michelle, 208
Flanagan, Greg, 63
Flower, David, 9, 201, 294, 308
Framework for Educational Change in Alberta, A (ATA), 171–2
Framework for Enhancing Business Involvement in Education (CCCS), 34, 69, 103, 125, 130, 133, 163, 230, 294, 310
Fraser Institute, 17, 285, 287
Freedman, Joe, 22–6, 28, 31–2, 37, 42, 50, 80, 87, 95, 104–5, 111, 216, 261, 286, 303
Friedman, Milton, 302
Friends of Public Education, 283
Froese-Germain, Bernie, 202
Future of Choices, a Choice of Futures, A, 64–5

Gaebler, Ted, 7, 20
George, Carl, 206, 225–6, 231, 233–4, 237–8, 240
Getty, Don, 59, 63
Gillespie, W. Irwin, 19
Gitlin, Andrew, 226
Globalization, 16–17, 132–3, 191
Globe and Mail, 3, 22
Gold, Karen, 54–5, 206, 225–7, 231, 233–8
Government Reinvented, A (Bruce, Kneebone, and McKenzie), 87
Gramsci, Antonio, 35
Grant, Lawrence, 45–50, 101–3, 107, 109–10, 114–15, 119–20, 130
Green, Joyce, 231–2

Hall, Justin, 244, 275–6

Hall, Stuart, 5–6, 193, 272, 298, 301–2, 309
Halpin, David, 8–10, 131
Harder Report, 22
Harrison, Trevor, 222
Hennessey, Katherine, 244, 251–6, 258–64, 267–8, 273, 282
Hiebert, Brian, 158
Ho, Cindy, 244–51
Holmes, Mark, 303
Holy Cross, 156
Hudson Institute of Canada, 54
Hunter, Floyd, 128

Information Technology Association of Canada (ITAC), 132–3
International Comparisons in Education (ACR), 28–31, 37–8, 40, 98, 103, 107, 289
International Labour Organization, 191
International Monetary Fund (IMF), 189
Inventing Our Future, 55

Jeffs, Allyson, 78
Jensen, Marcia, 104, 205–6, 208, 210–12, 218, 221–3
Johnson, Anthony, 77
Jones, Stan, 244, 275–6, 279–81
Jonson, Halvar, 66, 80, 85, 87

Kachur, 18, 59
Kao, Lisa, 151–3, 244–51
Kaulback, Camilla, 138
Kennedy, Robert, 38
King, David, 77
Klein, Ralph, 7, 17, 59, 61; educational restructuring, 3–4, 71, 73–96; fiscal crisis, 17–21

Klein Revolution, The (Lisac), 58, 92, 285
Kneebone, Ronald, 73, 95
Kodak, 31
Kowalski, Ken, 124
Kozak, James, 244, 276–7, 290
Kuehn, Larry, 258

Labour, response to government
    restructuring, 13, 141–2; fragmen-
    tation of, 167–203; relationships
    with business, 182–7; relationships
    with government, 179–82. *See also*
    Alberta Teachers' Association
Laird, Andy, 143, 146–50, 206, 229–
    30, 234–5
Lam, Cindy, 151–2
Laval University, 48
Law, Susan, 244, 251–6, 258, 267–8
Laxer, Gordon, 222
Learning Well ... Living Well, 38, 55
Leckie, Ron, 206, 226, 228–9
Leithwood, Kenneth, 228
Levin, Benjamin, 295
Liberal opposition, 21, 89
Lies, Valerie, 123
Lisac, Mark, 3, 7, 58–9, 69, 82–3, 92,
    181, 285
Livingstone, D.W., 5, 28–9, 44, 187,
    309–10
Long, Sally, 142–6, 148
Lougheed, Peter, 63

MacDonald, Chris, 169, 174–6, 179,
    184, 188–92, 194, 221
MacDonald, Sir John A., 155
Mackay, Bauni, 9, 201, 294, 308
McCamus, David, 40, 53–5, 60
McKay, Keith, 138
McKenzie, Kenneth, 83, 95
McQuaig, Linda, 69

Major, John, 94
Manning, Preston, 7
Mansell, Robert, 64, 82
Mar, Gary, 74, 216, 293
Markham, Andrew, 100, 102–7, 110–
    14, 117–18, 120, 149, 220, 288;
    corporate partnership with public
    school, 142–4, 146, 149–50, 165
Martell, George, 308, 311
Martin, Don, 74, 76
Maxwell, Judith, 39
Media, 74–81, 188–9
Meeting the Challenge, 84–5
Moe, Terry, 279, 302
Moll, Marita, 202
Monarch, 100, 102, 120; corporate
    partnership with public school,
    133, 142–54, 164–6, 235, 268–9
Morin, Sandra, 155–6, 159–62, 164
Mulroney, Brian, 54
Murgatroyd, Stephen, 216, 286

National Alliance of Business, 97
Native High School (NHS), 206, 224,
    227–8, 231, 233
New Brunswick, 122
New Zealand, 9, 93, 299–300
Newell, Eric, 28, 51
Newman, Peter C., 7, 300
Nikiforuk, Andrew, 22–5, 31–3, 95,
    261
Nuala Beck and Associates, 118

Ohmae, Kenichi, 7
Oliver, Carol, 206, 225, 231–4, 236–7,
    239–40
Ontario, 24, 94, 163–4, 201, 225, 295–
    6, 308
Ontario College of Teachers (OCT),
    295–6

Ontario Secondary School Teachers' Federation (OSSTF), 296, 308
Organization for Economic Cooperation and Development (OECD), 13, 15, 132
Organization for Quality Education (OQE), 296, 303
Osborne, David, 7, 20
Our Lady of Lourdes, 155
Ozga, Jenny, 299

Pannu, Raj, 180
Panorama, 100, 120, 127; corporate partnership with public school, 133, 154–66, 309–10
Parents, 14, 242–4, 251–6, 259–69, 273–84, 302–4
Parents Advocating for Children and Teachers (PACT), 283
Partners in Education, 174–5, 178
Partnership Handbook (CBE), 135
Pascal, Charles, 225
Pearce, Leslie, 244, 247–9, 251–6, 258–61, 263, 265–6, 273
Peters, Tom, 7
Phillips, Barbara, 143, 146, 148, 150, 206, 232, 235
Pirie, Madsen, 7
Politics, Markets, and America's Schools (Chubb and Moe), 38, 197, 279
Pommer, Dave, 77
Popiel, Mike, 100, 102–4, 108, 110, 113, 116, 126–7, 129, 288
Power, Sally, 8–9, 10, 131
Prosperity Action Plan (Canada), 53
Public Education (Mackay and Flower), 74, 201
Public Education Action Centre (PEAC), 203

Public School Boards Association of Alberta (PSBAA), 77–9
Pysyk, David, 228

Quality Education Coalition (QEC), 169, 176, 178, 292
Queen's University, 47–8

Raging Grannies, The, 274
Ralph Klein: A Maverick Life (Dabbs), 70
Reagan, Ronald, 14
Red Ink: Alberta's Deficit, Debt and Economic Future, The (CWF), 18, 20
Rees, Rebecca, 244, 251–8, 262–5, 268–70
Reform Party, 7, 17, 300
Reid, Bruce, 205–10, 212–20, 221–3
Reinventing Government, 83
Ribbens, Jane, 304
Roberts, Stan, 17
Robertson, Heather Jane, 23, 29, 44, 95, 202, 242, 258
Roessingh, Hetty, 267
Royal Bank, 31, 80

Sanders, Joseph, 100
Save Our Schools (SOS), 283
Save Public Education (SPE), 275, 283
Save Public Education – Act for Kids (SPEAK), 282–3
School boards, 14, 90–2, 122, 181–2, 204–23, 286; relationship with business, 208–16; relationship with labour, 221–3; response to government reforms, 216–21
School's Out: The Catastrophe in Public Education and What We Can Do about It (Nikiforuk), 23

Schools and Business: A New Partnership (OECD), 15–16
Schwartz, Arthur, 92
Seizing Opportunities (Klein), 17, 20–1
Selections from the Prison Notebooks (Gramsci), 35
Senior Executives' Views on Education, 68
Shaker, Erika, 132–3
Shapiro, Svi, 10, 24
Silver, Mark, 169, 172–3, 195–7
Simmons, Marilyn, 205–6, 208, 210–11, 218, 221, 223
Simpson, Don, 59
Slaughter, Sheila, 37, 44, 137, 209–11
Smaller, Harry, 310
Smith, John, 104–5, 123–4
Smith, Wendy, 244–51
Social Credit government, 21; and teachers, 170–1
Society for Advancing Educational Research (SAER), 42, 303
Sostre, Lizabeth, 302
Statistics Canada, 63
Steering Group on Prosperity, 286
Stemmer, Paul, 155
Stentor Canadian Network Management, 46, 50
Stewart, Fred, 124
Stewart, Lillian, 149
Student Achievement Indicators Program (SAIP), 39–40
Students, 243–51; disabled, 66–7; immigrant, 66–8, 231; Native, 66–8, 206, 231, 234, 239. *See also* Native High School
Sylvan Learning Centres, 221
Syncrude, 28, 31, 51, 80
Szabo, Marg, 169, 176, 178–9, 189–94, 213, 292

Taft, Kevin, 19
Tanner, Garry, 158
Teachers, 14, 223–41; and business involvement, 234–8. *See also* Alberta Teachers' Association; Labour
Teachers and Texts (Apple), 170
Thatcher, Margaret, 15
Third International Mathematics and Science Study (TIMSS), 39–40, 43, 57
Thomas, Roosevelt, 49
Thompson, Jennie, 99–100, 108, 116–17, 127–8
Thompson, Mandy, 45–6
Toronto Learning Consortium, 48
Tough Choices, 83–4, 121
Toward 2000 Together, 12, 20, 53, 58–63, 69–71, 87, 219, 278, 299
Trebilcock, Michael, 93–4
Trimble, Linda, 231–2
Troyna, Barry, 187
Trying to Teach (ATA), 171, 308
Trying to Teach: Necessary Conditions (ATA), 171–2

Undereducated, Uncompetitive U.S.A. (Union Carbide), 38
Union Carbide, 38
United Farm Women of Alberta, 21
United States, 9–10, 35–6, 155, 199, 271–2, 296, 302–4
University of Alberta, 86
University of Calgary, 137, 163
Unpopular Education (CCCS), 34
Useem, Elizabeth, 271–2
Useem, Michael, 107

Valcourt, Bernard, 54

Vermaeten, Arndt, 19
Vision for the Nineties, 66–9
Vocational programs, 98, 129–30, 236–7, 239–41, 309–10

Wall Street Journal, 3
Walsh, Murray, 168–9, 177, 182
Watson, Susan, 310
Watt, David, 267
Weis, Janet, 169, 175–6, 179–80, 183–4, 197–9, 232, 279
West, Anne, 303
White, Andrea, 100–1, 103–4, 115–16, 123–5
Whitty, Geoff, 8–9, 10, 131

Williams, Dan, 99, 104–7, 109–11, 115, 120–3, 129, 183–4, 187, 207, 215, 219–20, 253–4, 278, 286–8
Williamson, Dianne, 283
Wilson, Michael, 54–5
Winter, James, 74
Woolhouse, John, 39
World Bank, 189
Worth Report, 21, 64–5
Wyatt, Hal, 59

Xerox Canada, 40, 53–4

Yanitski, Norm, 228
Young, Beth, 232